*Verse by Verse Commentary on*

# JOSHUA

*Enduring Word Commentary Series*
*By David Guzik*

*The grass withers, the flower fades,*
*but the word of our God stands forever.*
Isaiah 40:8

# Contents

# *Joshua 1 – God's Commission to Joshua*

## A. The historical setting of the book of Joshua.

1. God made a covenant with Abraham (Genesis 12:1-3), which was passed on to Isaac, Jacob, and the 12 sons of Jacob (Israel).

    a. The covenant God made with Abraham and his covenant descendants promised them a land, a nation, and a blessing that would extend to all nations.

    b. In the time of Jacob (Israel) and his sons, the family moved to Egypt. They were first received as honored guests but eventually became slaves in Egypt.

2. After approximately 400 years, Israel was delivered from their slavery in Egypt. Led by Moses, the people of Israel left Egypt and came to Mount Sinai, where Israel received God's covenant.

    a. Israel's deliverance from Egypt became the central act of redemption in the Old Testament. God often reminded Israel that He had delivered them from Egypt's bondage, and the feasts of Passover, Unleavened Bread, and Tabernacles were instituted to remind Israel of God's deliverance.

    b. The exodus and everything associated with it were real historical events, but their meaning is greater than mere past events. God spoke through history to give an example of the greater deliverance of His people from the bondage of sin through the new covenant, a better covenant (1 Corinthians 10:6, 11).

    c. The covenant God made with Israel at Sinai included His law, the system of sacrifice, and the choice of blessing or cursing for Israel.

3. After a year at Mount Sinai, God offered Israel the opportunity to enter Canaan by faith, trusting in Him to conquer the people of Canaan.

    a. At Kadesh Barnea, Israel failed to take the opportunity by faith, refusing to enter the land God promised them, and declaring their desire to return to Egypt.

b. Because of their unbelief and rebellion, God decreed that Israel would remain in the wilderness for another 38 years, until the generation of unbelief died, and a new generation was willing to take Canaan by faith.

c. God miraculously sustained Israel in the wilderness until a new generation was ready to trust God's promise for Canaan. The book of Joshua is the story of the generation of faith taking the Promised Land.

d. Therefore, the land of Canaan was a real place that the people of God conquered and possessed under the leadership of Joshua. In a spiritual sense, Canaan also represents the destination God intends for His people, a place of promised rest. This is not a representation of heaven, but a place of rest and security that may be enjoyed by every believer under the new covenant. This is the *promise of rest* of Hebrew 4:1, the rest that remains for the people of God (Hebrews 4:9) that Joshua pointed to but did not completely fulfill (Hebrews 4:8).

> i. Canaan "is a far better emblem of that state and condition of soul in which a man is found when he has become a believer, and by believing has entered into rest, but not into an absolutely perfect deliverance from sin." (Spurgeon)

> ii. In this sense, the book of Joshua relates to the Apostle Paul's letter to the Ephesians in the New Testament. Ephesians describes a spiritual walk of promise, wealth, and security for the believer in Jesus Christ. The book of Joshua is the story of God's material provision in fulfillment of His promise to Israel in the land of Canaan.

> iii. Even as Mount Sinai (the place the law was given) or the wilderness were not the intended destinations for Israel under the old covenant, so the law is not God's intended destination for His people under the new covenant. The abundant life God intends for His people is not found by focusing on the law but on the promise fulfilled in Jesus, whom Joshua points to.

> iv. The Hebrew name Joshua translates as "Jesus" in the Greek language of New Testament times. Joshua is an enduring picture or type of Jesus, leading God's people into the fulfillment of God's promises. Whatever Israel received in the Promised Land, they received through the hand of Joshua; whatever believers receive from God in the new covenant is received through Jesus Christ, our Joshua.

## B. God commissions Joshua's work.

1. (1) After the passing of Moses, God speaks to Joshua.

**After the death of Moses the servant of the LORD, it came to pass that the LORD spoke to Joshua the son of Nun, Moses' assistant, saying:**

a. **After the death of Moses**: Moses was the great **servant of the** LORD and leader of Israel. His death is recorded in Deuteronomy 34. As great as Moses was, he would never lead the people of God into the land of promise.

> i. "No man is indispensable. God's work goes on uninterrupted. The instruments are changed, but the Master-hand is the same, and lays one tool aside and takes another out of the tool-chest as He will." (Maclaren)

> ii. **Moses the servant of the** LORD: The phrase **servant of the** LORD is used of Moses at least 12 times in Joshua; it is used of Joshua himself only once, at the end of the book (Joshua 24:29). Abraham and David also received this honored title.

b. **The** LORD **spoke to Joshua**: Joshua – who was not a young man at this time – had spent his entire career previously as the **assistant** of Moses. Joshua found that now it was his time to lead, but only after God had prepared him.

> i. Joshua was the leader of the group of 12 spies sent to Canaan before Israel's opportunity to enter the Promised Land (Numbers 13:4-16). The Numbers 13 passage explains that Joshua was originally named *Hoshea* (salvation) but Moses changed his name to *Joshua* (Yahweh is salvation). Among those 12 spies, only Caleb and Joshua returned from Canaan with a faith-filled report, confident God would empower Israel to overcome the challenges in the conquest of Canaan. Because of their faithfulness, Joshua and Caleb were the only adult Israelites of the generation that left Egypt to survive the wilderness years and enter Canaan (Numbers 14:30). Some 38 years before the events of Joshua 1, Joshua believed God would work through Israel to give them the land, and he still believed it. Moses was not allowed to lead Israel into the Promised Land because of his disobedience (Numbers 27:12-14).

> ii. "Joshua's name usually is given in the Hebrew Bible as 'Yehoshua,' which means 'Yahweh saves/delivers.' His name is rendered in the Greek traditions (LXX) as *Iesous*, which is the same form as Jesus' name in the New Testament. His original name was 'Hoshea,' which means 'salvation' or 'deliverance' (Num 13:8 and Deut 32:44). Numbers 13:16 explains that Moses himself gave Hoshea his new name 'Joshua.'" (Howard)

> iii. "The Conqueror of Canaan and the Redeemer of the world bear the same name. The Jesus whom we trust was a Joshua." (Maclaren)

c. **Moses' assistant**: At God's command, Moses had already formally recognized Joshua as his successor to lead Israel (Numbers 27:18-23). Though Joshua was not of noble birth or a literal son of Moses, there were many things that qualified him to be the successor of Moses.

- Joshua had led the army of Israel against the Amalekites (Exodus 17:8-16).

- Joshua was an assistant to Moses (Exodus 24:13).

- Joshua helped Moses at the tabernacle after the golden calf disaster (Exodus 33:7-11).

- Joshua was zealous to preserve the authority and leadership of Moses (Numbers 11:28).

- Joshua was one of the two faith-filled spies among the total of twelve who spied out the land of Canaan (Numbers 13:30-14:38).

- Joshua was a "man in whom is the Spirit" (Numbers 27:18), the most important qualification of all. The Holy Spirit would empower and enable him to fulfill the challenging role of leading the nation into Canaan.

  i. God used the consistent, demonstrated faithfulness of Joshua in many small things to prepare him for this essential role of leading Israel into Canaan; land with strong enemies reluctant to leave their land.

  ii. "Joshua was a soldier. He was a brilliant soldier, one of the most extraordinary military commanders of all time. But he was not an exciting person, as far as we can tell. He was probably just a bit of a plugger, a rather straightforward man who was chiefly concerned with carrying out his divine commission to the letter. He had no great sins and made very few mistakes. In short, he was not the kind of person who would make a good hero for a novel. Yet Joshua was eminently God's man." (Boice)

2. (2-3) God's promise of land to Joshua and all Israel.

**"Moses My servant is dead. Now therefore, arise, go over this Jordan, you and all this people, to the land which I am giving to them—the children of Israel. Every place that the sole of your foot will tread upon I have given you, as I said to Moses.**

a. **Moses My servant is dead**: God recognized the transition of leadership from Moses to Joshua. Moses had been appropriately mourned (Deuteronomy 34:8); now it was time to look ahead at the new work God would do through Israel's new leader.

i. God's "instruments are men, and high indeed is the honour of being such. Each will take up a work already begun, and will leave it unfinished. Each is a debtor to those who have gone before, and creditor to those who are to follow. Therefore it behoves us to be filled with humility and restfulness." (Morgan)

ii. "Is it not strange that at the death of Moses utter despair had not overwhelmed the whole camp, as he whom they expected to give them rest had died before any conquest was made in Canaan? We find, however, that they are not discouraged; he who gave them *Moses,* has now given them *Joshua* in his place; and they had now fully learned that if God be for them, none could be successfully against them." (Clarke)

iii. Joshua 1:2-4 gives an outline of the book of Joshua.

- **Go over this Jordan**: the crossing of the Jordan (Joshua 1:5-5:12).

- **The land which I am giving**: the conquest of Canaan (Joshua 5:13-12:24).

- The boundaries of the land in Joshua 1:4 imply the distribution of the land in 13:1-22:34.

b. **To the land which I am giving to them**: God promised this land to Abraham, Isaac, Jacob, and the sons of Jacob (Israel). These promises are prominent in the book of Genesis (12:1-3, 12:7, 13:14-17, 15:7, 15:18-21, 17:8, 24:7, 26:3-4, 28:3-4, 28:13-14, 35:9-13, 48:3-4, 50:24). By title deed, the people of Israel had never possessed any of the land of Canaan except the burial place of the patriarchs in Hebron (Genesis 23:19-20). They had not lived in the land of Canaan for about 400 years. Yet it was the land God had promised to Israel, that He was now **giving to them**.

c. **I have given you**: The whole land was **given** to Joshua and Israel, but they could only possess that which they claimed (**every place that the sole of your foot will tread**). What they possessed must be fought for against determined opposition.

i. Even as the inheritance of Canaan was entrusted to a leader, a representative, so it is true for God's people under the new covenant. All they spiritually possess, they have in Jesus Christ who is both their leader and representative.

ii. Israel could only possess the land as God worked in them and through them; they could never conquer Canaan in their own wisdom and strength. Yet, God would not eliminate their enemies as Israel sat passively by; He called Israel into partnership with Himself to see His will done.

iii. "All the land was given, but every inch of it had to be claimed. Israel had to put her foot down upon the land, whether wilderness or Lebanon, plain or hill, and say, 'This is mine by the gift of God.' And as the right was asserted, God made it good." (Meyer)

iv. Because taking the land took *effort*, the challenge ahead was not for those content with Egypt, but for those who would press ahead for what God had called them to possess.

v. "In the Hebrew text nearly the same wording is found in vv.3–5a as in Deuteronomy 11:24–25a. This is another of the many ties between Joshua and the Pentateuch, especially Deuteronomy. The author has taken pains to demonstrate that the work of Joshua is the fulfillment of the Pentateuch." (Madvig)

3. (4-5) The promise: victory is assured because Joshua is called by God.

**From the wilderness and this Lebanon as far as the great river, the River Euphrates, all the land of the Hittites, and to the Great Sea toward the going down of the sun, shall be your territory. No man shall *be able to* stand before you all the days of your life; as I was with Moses, *so* I will be with you. I will not leave you nor forsake you.**

a. **From the wilderness...as far as the great river**: This describes the precise territory of the land God gave to Israel. The specific geographical boundaries show this was not a spiritual land, but a material land with real wilderness and rivers and earth.

i. "The literal and complete fulfillment of this promise was not experienced by Israel until the reigns of David and Solomon (see 1 Kings 4:21, 24) and then once again in the time of Uzziah and Jeroboam." (Madvig)

ii. **Land of the Hittites**: "Palestine was referred to as 'the Hittite country' by both Egypt and Babylonia even after the Hittites had withdrawn from the area (cf. Judges 1:26)." (Madvig)

iii. Though this refers to a literal land, it has spiritual application. "All that is in Christ is meant for all believers, and therefore all believers may have all that is in Christ, who is all in all. We should not be content with pence when he endows us with pounds." (Spurgeon)

b. **As I was with Moses**: Moses was one of the great men of the Bible, with an important role in God's unfolding plan of the ages. The work of Moses was finished, and now the work of Joshua would begin.

i. Moses, who represented the law, could not lead Israel into the Promised Land. Miriam, who represented the prophets, could not lead God's people into the Promised Land. Aaron, who represented the priesthood, could not lead Israel into the Promised Land. Only Joshua, that is, JESUS, could lead them into the land of God's promise.

c. **I will be with you**: Israel was assured of success, but not because Joshua was a great leader, or because Israel was a great nation. They would triumph because God is a great God, and He promised Joshua, **I will be with you**. This is enough for anyone who seeks to do God's will.

i. **I will not leave you nor forsake you**: This was what God said to all Israel (including Joshua) in Deuteronomy 31:6 and is quoted in Hebrews 13:5, applying it to all believers.

ii. "Therefore the Lord said, 'I will not fail thee, nor forsake thee.' What more was needed? Surely, in the presence of God, Anakim become dwarfs, strongholds become as a lodge in a garden of cucumbers, and chariots of iron are as thistle-down upon the hillside driven before the blast. What is strong against the Most High?" (Spurgeon)

4. (6-9) The conditions of the promise of victory.

**Be strong and of good courage, for to this people you shall divide as an inheritance the land which I swore to their fathers to give them. Only be strong and very courageous, that you may observe to do according to all the law which Moses My servant commanded you; do not turn from it to the right hand or to the left, that you may prosper wherever you go. This Book of the Law shall not depart from your mouth, but you shall meditate in it day and night, that you may observe to do according to all that is written in it. For then you will make your way prosperous, and then you will have good success. Have I not commanded you? Be strong and of good courage; do not be afraid, nor be dismayed, for the LORD your God *is* with you wherever you go."**

a. **Be strong and of good courage**: Joshua was called to be bold in God. The emphasis given to this command (Joshua 1:6, 1:7, 1:9, 1:18) suggests that Joshua needed this strong encouragement. He would need God's strength and courage to conquer Canaan and **divide** the land as an **inheritance** to Israel.

i. The sense is that Joshua would find this strength and courage in Yahweh, not in himself. As Paul would later explain in Ephesians 6:10, Joshua was to be *strong in the LORD and in the power of His might*. This is a pattern for believers, to find their strength in God and not in self.

ii. "Joshua seems to have been afraid of this responsibility. I say this because the most repeated words in the chapter are those commanding him not to be afraid. God tells Joshua to be strong and courageous three times (vv. 6, 7, 9), then adds, 'Do not be terrified; do not be discouraged' (v. 9). At the end of the chapter, the people tell Joshua the same thing: 'Only be strong and courageous!' (v. 18). In spite of what must therefore have been a very acute sense of inadequacy, Joshua did indeed take charge. From the very first, he showed that he was the Lord's man for this hour." (Boice)

b. **That you may observe to do according to all the law**: As a people, Israel was bound to God in covenant (Exodus 24:3-8). A significant part of the covenant was God's promise to bless an obedient Israel (Leviticus 26:1-13, Deuteronomy 28:1-14) and to curse a disobedient Israel (Leviticus 26:14-46, Deuteronomy 28:15-68). When Israel and their leadership did **according to all the law**, they were invincible with God's blessing and strength.

i. This promise to Joshua and Israel repeated a promise God made to Israel at Mount Sinai. There, God promised to defeat the Canaanites and give Israel their land (Exodus 23:22-31), if Israel would obey Him: *if you indeed obey His voice and do all that I speak, then I will be an enemy to your enemies and an adversary to your adversaries* (Exodus 23:22).

ii. **Do not turn from it to the right hand or to the left**: "There is sure to be a right hand, there is sure to be a left hand, and both are probably wrong. There will be extremes on either side. I believe that this is true in ten thousand things in ordinary life, and also true in spiritual things in very many respects." (Spurgeon)

c. **This Book of the Law**: Since obedience to God's law was required for Israel's success, it was important to know and value God's word. Joshua did not only need to read God's word. It had to be on his *lips* (**shall not depart from your mouth**), in his *mind* (**meditate in it day and night**), and he had to *do* it (**observe to do according to all that is written**).

i. "The Hebrew word translated 'meditate' (*hagah*) literally means 'mutter.' When one continually mutters God's Word to himself, he is constantly thinking about it." (Madvig)

ii. "Though there was a copy of the law laid up in the sanctuary, yet this was not sufficient. Joshua must have a copy for himself, and he was to consult it incessantly, that his way might be made prosperous, and that he might have good success." (Clarke)

iii. Joshua was "a book-man as well as a sword-man." (Trapp)

iv. "It is true that in this ancient period before Gutenberg or before scribes were able to make a reasonable number of copies of Moses's text, the people did not have their own Bibles. But this did not mean that the Bible was inaccessible to them or that they had an excuse for not knowing it. Joshua was to read the book. Later on, as at the ceremony conducted on Mount Ebal and Mount Gerizim, the Law was to be read in its entirety in the hearing of all the people (see Deuteronomy 31:11–13)." (Boice)

v. "Joshua's relation to the book teaches us an important lesson about how the canon grew and was accepted. Joshua knew Moses, the writer of the Pentateuch, personally. Joshua knew his strengths and weaknesses as a man; he knew that Moses was a sinner, that Moses made mistakes, that Moses was just a man. Nonetheless, immediately after Moses' death Joshua accepted the Pentateuch as more than the writing of Moses. He accepted it as the writing of God." (Shaeffer)

d. **For then you will make your way prosperous, and then you will have good success**: This promise to prosper and give success to an obedient Israel repeated themes God had previously spoken to Israel.

i. **Prosperous…success**: "Nothing at all is said here about financial success. In fact, of the fifty-nine times that *slh* refers to success, and the ten to eleven times that *slh* does, only *once* are finances even remotely in view. This is in Ezekiel 16:13." (Howard)

ii. Under the new covenant, God's people are not blessed primarily because of their obedience, but because of their relationship of love and trust in Jesus Christ. Yet because God's commands are inherently good and wise, there is a built-in blessing in conforming to this good and wise design. There is a great blessing for the believer in knowing and obeying God's word.

e. **For the LORD your God is with you wherever you go**: The final encouragement, repeated from Joshua 1:5, reminds us that Joshua's success did not depend solely on his ability to keep God's word. The presence of God with him was an even greater factor.

## C. Preparations to cross the Jordan.

1. (10-11) Command to the officers.

**Then Joshua commanded the officers of the people, saying, "Pass through the camp and command the people, saying, 'Prepare provisions for yourselves, for within three days you will cross over this Jordan, to**

**go in to possess the land which the** L**ORD** **your God is giving you to possess.'"**

a. **Prepare provisions for yourselves**: Israel had arrived at this general area on the eastern side of the Jordan River back in Numbers 20. After remaining here through the rest of the book of Numbers and the entire book of Deuteronomy, Israel was about to **cross over this Jordan** and enter Canaan.

i. Joshua's call to the people "was characterized by urgency and dispatch; 'within three days' the hosts were to move forward toward all the conflict and difficulty which had long ago frightened their fathers and turned them back into the wilderness." (Morgan)

ii. The **officers of the people**: "The roles of these 'officers' form a secular counterpart to those of the priests. Joshua will address both, beginning with the *officers*, whose tasks are greater since they involve all the people." (Hess)

iii. The events of verse 10 happened after the spies returned from the mission described in Joshua 2. Like many books of the Bible, the story of the book of Joshua isn't presented in strict chronological order.

b. **To possess the land**: This possession would come by conquest. The wars of conquest against the Canaanites began in Numbers 21, with the victory over Arad the Canaanite.

i. Ahead of Israel were many battles with the Canaanites, to take the land that God promised to Israel, and to carry out a unique war of judgment against the Canaanites. The tribal groups of Canaan were particularly sinful and depraved people, whom God literally gave hundreds of years to repent (Genesis 15:13-16). Just as God sometimes used other nations to bring judgment against Israel, in this period the LORD used His people to bring judgment against the Canaanites.

ii. "Alas! many of God's people are still in this unsatisfactory condition: they have come out of Egypt, the depths have swallowed up their adversaries, and they are on the way to the promised heritage; but they have not yet entered into rest. They will, we trust, ultimately reach the peace of God which passeth all understanding, for they have faith sufficient to prove them to be God's people, and, therefore, the Lord will surely bring them in; but, assuredly, they make a great deal of marching for very small progress. For lack of faith they go about, when, with a step, they might possess the promised Canaan." (Spurgeon)

2. (12-15) Reminder to the eastern tribes.

**And to the Reubenites, the Gadites, and half the tribe of Manasseh Joshua spoke, saying, "Remember the word which Moses the servant of the LORD commanded you, saying, 'The LORD your God is giving you rest and is giving you this land.' Your wives, your little ones, and your livestock shall remain in the land which Moses gave you on this side of the Jordan. But you shall pass before your brethren armed, all your mighty men of valor, and help them, until the LORD has given your brethren rest, as He *gave* you, and they also have taken possession of the land which the LORD your God is giving them. Then you shall return to the land of your possession and enjoy it, which Moses the LORD's servant gave you on this side of the Jordan toward the sunrise."**

    a. **And to the Reubenites, the Gadites, and half the tribe of Manasseh Joshua spoke**: These were the tribes which chose to settle on the east side of the Jordan, land that Israel had already conquered. These two and a half tribes had promised to cross over and help the rest of the nation take the land on the west side of the Jordan River (Numbers 32:16-32).

    b. **But you shall pass before your brethren armed, all your mighty men of valor, and help them**: This was the fulfillment of the promise these two and a half tribes had made in Numbers 32. Though these tribes already occupied their land, they were to **help** their brothers who had yet to conquer their lands.

        i. This same principle operates in the body of Christ. When one member has a need, it is the common need of the body (1 Corinthians 12:25-26). Believers should never refuse to help a brother in need because their own state is settled.

3. (16-18) The eastern tribes promise their allegiance to Joshua.

**So they answered Joshua, saying, "All that you command us we will do, and wherever you send us we will go. Just as we heeded Moses in all things, so we will heed you. Only the LORD your God be with you, as He was with Moses. Whoever rebels against your command and does not heed your words, in all that you command him, shall be put to death. Only be strong and of good courage."**

    a. **All that you command us we will do, and wherever you send us we will go**: This was a display of unity in Israel that was essential to fulfill God's calling and promise for them. They overcame the temptation to see the eastern tribes as separate from the rest of Israel.

b. **Just as we heeded Moses in all things, so we will heed you**: The willingness of the people to receive Joshua as their leader, replacing Moses, was a confirmation of the LORD's words to Joshua previously in the chapter.

c. **Only be strong and of good courage**: The representatives from the tribes of Reuben, Gad, and Manasseh spoke the same thing to Joshua that he previously heard from the LORD (Joshua 1:6, 7, 9). This is an example of God's people encouraging one another with God's word.

# Joshua 2 – The Rescue of Rahab

**A. Spies are sent to the city of Jericho.**

1. (1a) Joshua sends spies to Jericho.

**Now Joshua the son of Nun sent out two men from Acacia Grove to spy secretly, saying, "Go, view the land, especially Jericho."**

a. **Joshua the son of Nun sent out two men**: Joshua's careful preparation was evidence of faithfulness, not a lack of faith. God promised success to Joshua (Joshua 1:3-6), but those promises were not meant to encourage passivity or inaction on Joshua's part. They were meant to encourage his faith-filled activity.

i. The passage doesn't say who these two spies were, but some Jewish traditions speculate that they were faithful Caleb and the high priest Eliezer. Those legends don't have any biblical foundation.

ii. This happened during the three days Joshua commanded Israel to wait on the banks of the Jordan (Joshua 1:11). God had a special work to accomplish in those three days.

b. **To spy secretly**: It was wise for Joshua to send these spies **secretly**. A generation earlier, the public sending of spies into Canaan ended in disaster when most of the spies returned with a discouraging report of the land and its people (Numbers 13).

i. In the Numbers 13 sending of the spies, only two of the twelve sent returned with a faith-filled, God-honoring report (Caleb and Joshua, Numbers 14:6-9). A generation later, Joshua sent only two spies instead of twelve.

ii. The secrecy of their mission may have been to conceal it from Israel, as well as the rulers of Jericho. Given the results of the mission of the spies in Numbers 13-14, it is reasonable to think Joshua didn't want Israel to know in advance of these spies and their mission.

c. **Go, view the land, especially Jericho**: The city of Jericho was relatively close to Israel's planned crossing point of the Jordan River and it was one of the most secure and fortified cities in Canaan.

> i. "The account of the conquest of Jericho makes no use of any information which might have been gained from this expedition." (Hess)

> ii. "Whatever the report of the spies might be, he would go forward, but it was important for him as a military leader to know the condition of affairs." (Morgan)

2. (1b) The spies at Rahab's house.

**So they went, and came to the house of a harlot named Rahab, and lodged there.**

a. **A harlot named Rahab**: Throughout the history of Christianity, it has embarrassed some Bible interpreters that these two spies went to the house of a prostitute. Some have tried to say that Rahab was merely an "innkeeper," but the description of her as a *harlot* in Hebrews 11:31 confirms that she was a prostitute.

> i. Some early Christians saw a likeness in the sending of these forerunners before Joshua that was fulfilled in men like John the Baptist, the forerunner before Jesus the Messiah. In the second century Origen wrote: "As the first Jesus sent his spies before him and they were received into the harlot's house, so the second Jesus sent His forerunners, whom the publicans and harlots gladly received." (Cited in Lias)

b. **And lodged there**: The harlot's house was a good place to stay if one wanted to stay anonymous and remain hidden despite the strict guard set over the city of Jericho. There's no indication that the two spies engaged Rahab's services as a harlot.

> i. "The text carefully avoids implying a sexual liaison between the spies and their hostess. There is a common expression for going into buildings of all sorts (cf. Judg. 9:5; 2 Sam. 12:20; 2 Kgs 19:1). It does not imply sexual relations with a prostitute." (Hess)

3. (2-3) The king of Jericho seeks the Israelite spies.

**And it was told the king of Jericho, saying, "Behold, men have come here tonight from the children of Israel to search out the country." So the king of Jericho sent to Rahab, saying, "Bring out the men who**

**have come to you, who have entered your house, for they have come to search out all the country."**

a. **Men have come here tonight**: Somehow, the leader of the city-state of Jericho learned that two Israelite men had come to the city as spies (**to search out the country**). This was of great concern, because the city was already on alert (Joshua 2:9), fearful of the Israelite invasion.

b. **Bring out the men**: Using either informers or logic, the king of Jericho believed the spies were with Rahab and demanded they be turned over.

4. (4-7) Rahab hides and protects the spies.

**Then the woman took the two men and hid them. So she said, "Yes, the men came to me, but I did not know where they *were* from. And it happened as the gate was being shut, when it was dark, that the men went out. Where the men went I do not know; pursue them quickly, for you may overtake them." (But she had brought them up to the roof and hidden them with the stalks of flax, which she had laid in order on the roof.) Then the men pursued them by the road to the Jordan, to the fords. And as soon as those who pursued them had gone out, they shut the gate.**

a. **Then the woman took the two men and hid them**: The culture of the ancient near east had a strong tradition of protecting guests. Even considering this, Rahab went much further than these cultural traditions regarding hospitality. She put her own life at risk for the Israelite spies.

i. "When Rahab hid the spies, she sided with Israel against her own people. It was an act of treason!" (Madvig)

ii. "This was an act of her praiseworthy faith. See Hebrews 11:31, where it is honourably mentioned, but nothing is said of the lie she told. God layeth the finger of mercy on the scars of our sins." (Trapp)

b. **Yes, the men came to me, but I did not know where they were from**: The Bible simply reports Rahab's lie; it does not praise it or excuse it. Rahab faced an ethical challenge: either option was bad. She decided that it was worse for her to betray the spies than to lie about their presence.

c. **The men went out**: Rahab's protection of the spies was courageous. Despite her pagan upbringing, culture, and morally compromised profession, she allied herself with Israel and the God of Israel.

**B. Salvation for Rahab.**

1. (8-11) Rahab's confession of faith.

Now before they lay down, she came up to them on the roof, and said to the men: "I know that the LORD has given you the land, that the terror of you has fallen on us, and that all the inhabitants of the land are fainthearted because of you. For we have heard how the LORD dried up the water of the Red Sea for you when you came out of Egypt, and what you did to the two kings of the Amorites who *were* on the other side of the Jordan, Sihon and Og, whom you utterly destroyed. And as soon as we heard *these things,* our hearts melted; neither did there remain any more courage in anyone because of you, for the LORD your God, He *is* God in heaven above and on earth beneath.

a. **I know that the LORD has given you the land**: This surprising outburst of faith shows that God had a plan in bringing Rahab and the spies together. God had already been speaking to Rahab in some way, and she had begun to believe in the superiority of Yahweh (**the LORD**), the God of Israel.

i. God continues to speak in remarkable and unusual ways to unlikely people who are seemingly distant from the gospel. The phenomenon of dreams leading many in the Islamic world to Jesus Christ and His gospel is one modern example of this.

ii. "She was pressured by a powerful city and an ancient culture continuing on in its normal life—eating, drinking, marrying, and so forth. At that moment she could see nothing with her eyes that indicated it would fall." (Schaeffer)

b. **Has given you the land**: Rahab's confession of faith included recognition that God had promised the **land** of Canaan to Israel and that He would fulfill that promise. She saw God's supernatural work of causing **terror** among the Canaanites, leading them to be **fainthearted**.

c. **For we have heard**: In her confession of faith Rahab reported that the people of Jericho had heard of and believed the mighty works God did for Israel in freeing them from Egypt (**dried up the water of the Red Sea**) and defeating their enemies along the way (**what you did to the two kings**).

i. "If we ask, 'From whom had Rahab heard these tales of the God of Israel?' the answer is probably from the men who frequented her establishment. Her home would have been a place of great gossip as strangers from near and far reported their tales of foreign wonders." (Boice)

d. **He is God in heaven above and on earth beneath**: Rahab's confession of faith declared the greatness and superiority of Yahweh, the God of Israel. This phrase is used in declarations of faith for the people of Israel (Exodus 20:4, Deuteronomy 4:39, 5:8).

i. "This confession of the true God is amazingly full, and argues considerable light and information. As if she had said, 'I know your God to be omnipotent and omnipresent:' and in consequence of this faith she hid the spies, and risked her own life in doing it." (Clarke)

e. **Our hearts melted**: The combination of these truths was overwhelming. Many among the Canaanites believed that the God of Israel:

- Was greater than their Canaanite gods.
- Did miracles for His people, bringing them out of Egypt.
- Had recently enabled Israel to defeat kings.
- Had promised Israel the land of Canaan.

  i. Believing these things made many among the Canaanites lose all **courage**; yet few of them acted in faith as Rahab the harlot did. Rahab showed admirable faith (Hebrews 11:31, James 2:25).

  ii. "As an oath of fealty, this covenant would bring Rahab's family into Israelite society. As would happen with the Gibeonites, so Rahab and her family here ceased to be Canaanite and became part of Israel's family." (Hess)

2. (12-13) Rahab's plea for rescue and salvation.

**Now therefore, I beg you, swear to me by the LORD, since I have shown you kindness, that you also will show kindness to my father's house, and give me a true token, and spare my father, my mother, my brothers, my sisters, and all that they have, and deliver our lives from death."**

a. **That you also will show kindness to my father's house**: Rahab's desire to see her family saved, and the effort she made to save their lives, shows that her love should be noticed, as well as her faith.

  i. "The family members would demonstrate their personal faith by gathering in Rahab's house and remaining there." (Madvig)

b. **Swear to me by the LORD**: This shows that Rahab wanted assurance of her rescue by asking for an oath. She wanted to leave her sinful life and culture and live with God's people.

  i. Putting herself at risk, Rahab rejected her past identity as a Canaanite and wanted to be identified with the people of God, with Israel. She married a man from the tribe of Judah named Salmon. They had a son named Boaz, who married a Moabite woman named Ruth. They had a son named Obed, who had a son named Jesse, who had a son named David (Matthew 1:5-6). Rahab was a direct ancestor of David, the great king of Israel, and assuming no generations are left out of the record, she was his great-great-grandmother (the grandmother of David's grandfather Obed).

3. (14) The response of the Israelite spies.

**So the men answered her, "Our lives for yours, if none of you tell this business of ours. And it shall be, when the LORD has given us the land, that we will deal kindly and truly with you."**

a. **Our lives for yours**: This was a solemn oath, made on their **lives**. Rahab and her family would be spared the coming judgment. Joshua is a book of harsh judgment on the Canaanites, but the first story dealing with someone other than Joshua is about God's mercy to an unlikely yet believing Canaanite.

i. "The inhabitants of Jericho presumably had the same opportunity to embrace Israel's God that Rahab did, but only she seized the opportunity, and consequently only she and her family were spared destruction." (Howard)

b. **We will deal kindly and truly with you**: The promise was to rescue Rahab and her family from the coming judgment against Jericho.

i. In one sense, Jesus didn't have to go through Samaria on His way to Galilee; there were other roads available. But Jesus did have to go through Samaria (John 4:4), to reach one Samaritan woman. In one sense, Joshua didn't have to send the two spies; they didn't bring back specific intelligence that would prove helpful in the conquest of Jericho. But Joshua did need to send them, to rescue Rahab and her household.

4. (15-21) The means of Rahab's salvation: the scarlet cord.

**Then she let them down by a rope through the window, for her house *was* on the city wall; she dwelt on the wall. And she said to them, "Get to the mountain, lest the pursuers meet you. Hide there three days, until the pursuers have returned. Afterward you may go your way."**

**So the men said to her: "We *will be* blameless of this oath of yours which you have made us swear, unless, *when* we come into the land, you bind this line of scarlet cord in the window through which you let us down, and unless you bring your father, your mother, your brothers, and all your father's household to your own home. So it shall be *that* whoever goes outside the doors of your house into the street, his blood *shall be* on his own head, and we *will be* guiltless. And whoever is with you in the house, his blood *shall be* on our head if a hand is laid on him. And if you tell this business of ours, then we will be free from your oath which you made us swear."**

**Then she said, "According to your words, so *be* it." And she sent them away, and they departed. And she bound the scarlet cord in the window.**

a. **She let them down by a rope**: Rahab's belief in the God of Israel was confirmed by her actions. She protected and assisted the Israelite spies because she really believed in the greatness of Yahweh and the reliability of His promise to Israel. In this sense, she was justified by her faith-filled works (James 2:25).

i. "As the city gates were now shut there was no way for the spies to escape but through this window; and in order to [do] this she let them down through the window in a basket suspended by a cord, till they reached the ground on the outside of the wall." (Clarke)

b. **Bind this scarlet cord in the window**: This was the signal to the army of Israel that the people in this home were to be spared. Despite Rahab's desire, despite her faith, despite the promises of these spies, she would have perished unless she put her trust in a blood-red cord cast down from her window. Without the scarlet cord, she could not have been saved.

i. "The spies, who were unaware of the mighty miracle that God would perform, were anticipating a house-to-house battle in which the Israelites would have been instructed to spare the house so marked." (Madvig)

ii. As early as the first century, commentators such as Clement of Rome, Justin Martyr, Irenaeus, Origen and others saw **this scarlet cord** as a symbol of the blood of Jesus.

iii. "There is a tradition in the church, going all the way back to Clement of Rome and possibly earlier, that the scarlet cord represents the blood of Jesus Christ, and teachers have talked about the cord running all through the Bible, from Abel's sacrifice to Calvary." (Boice)

c. **And she bound the scarlet cord in the window**: Though known only to Rahab and the Israelites, this was a declaration of her allegiance with Israel and the God of Israel. In binding the scarlet cord in the window, Rahab *immediately* displayed her identity and trust in the security offered by the scarlet cord. She also trusted in the ones who made the promise connected with the scarlet cord (**according to your words, so be it**).

i. In a sense, Joshua would be a savior for Rahab, but he would be a judge of the rest of Jericho. In the same way, Jesus is a savior for those who trust Him, but a judge for those who reject Him.

ii. "We can imagine Rahab rushing out and gathering all her family into her house upon the city wall. We can imagine her going through the city and calling out, 'Hurry! Hurry! Hurry! Come under the mark of the scarlet cord!' Lot did the same thing in Sodom, you remember, but without success." (Schaeffer)

d. **According to your words, so be it**: Rahab's destiny was to marry one of the princes of Judah and be found in the lineage of King David and Jesus Himself.

i. "Rahab tied the scarlet line, not in some secret part of the house, but in the window. It was her public declaration of faith.... Let it be a scarlet line that you tie in the window, however, namely, an avowal of true faith in his precious blood, a declaration of confidence, in atonement by blood; for there are some who profess a sort of faith, but it is not faith in the substitution of Christ." (Spurgeon)

ii. The law of judgment against the Canaanites condemned Rahab to death. Yet there were many aspects of God's work in Rahab related to her triumph over the law that condemned her and Rahab's becoming part of God's story of redemption:

• Rahab's understanding of Yahweh, the God of Israel.

• Rahab's faith in Yahweh.

• Rahab's rejection of her Canaanite identity and embrace of her Israelite identity.

• Rahab's willingness to publish an emblem of her trust in God's promise of rescue.

5. (22-24) Mission accomplished.

**They departed and went to the mountain, and stayed there three days until the pursuers returned. The pursuers sought *them* all along the way, but did not find *them*. So the two men returned, descended from the mountain, and crossed over; and they came to Joshua the son of Nun, and told him all that had befallen them. And they said to Joshua, "Truly the LORD has delivered all the land into our hands, for indeed all the inhabitants of the country are fainthearted because of us."**

a. **The pursuers sought them all along the way**: God supernaturally protected the Israelite spies. God's help came to them through Rahab and by the confusion of their enemies.

b. **Told him all that had befallen them**: The two spies made a full report to Joshua, but there is no record of anything they told him that was essential to the conquest of Jericho. It was encouraging to hear the Canaanites were **fainthearted** and hear of the faith of Rahab, but this did not give Israel a strategy of attack against Jericho. That strategy would come from God, not the intelligence gained by the spies.

i. **Truly the LORD has delivered all the land into our hands**: "As with the two spies and Rahab, what Gideon heard (Judges 7:13-15) gave encouragement through the words of an enemy. This conversation convinced him of the final outcome, thus enabling him to say with courage, 'There is no question that we are going to be victorious. From the mouth of somebody on 'the other side' came a verbalization that completely settled the situation." (Schaeffer)

ii. The greater purpose in sending the two spies was to arrange and assure the salvation of Rahab and her family. She was one that some might consider "impossible" to save, but God did what seemed impossible. God continues to save those who seem impossible to save.

iii. "The salvation of Rahab is an example of what God would have done for others also. The king and the other citizens of Jericho knew all that she knew, but they did not turn to Israel's God for mercy. The fear that drove her to beg for mercy drove them in their stubborn rebellion. Accordingly, the others are called 'the disobedient' in Hebrews 11:31." (Madvig)

# *Joshua 3 – Crossing the Jordan*

**A. Instructions for crossing the Jordan River.**

1. (1) Israel at the Jordan River.

**Then Joshua rose early in the morning; and they set out from Acacia Grove and came to the Jordan, he and all the children of Israel, and lodged there before they crossed over.**

a. **They set out from Acacia Grove and came to the Jordan**: This was the last step in Israel's journey from Egypt to Canaan. They now camped on the banks of the Jordan, the last obstacle between Israel and the Promised Land.

i. Israel had been waiting for the moment to enter the Promised Land and take possession of it for some 500 years, since God promised the land to Abraham and his covenant descendants (Genesis 15:18-21). Joshua and Caleb were more than 80 years old and waited for this moment. All Israel had been waiting for the generation of unbelief to die in the wilderness and a new generation of faith to take the land as they trusted God.

b. **Lodged there before they crossed over**: God told Israel to prepare themselves for **three days** at the shore of the Jordan River (Joshua 1:11). All that time, the people of Israel **lodged** in view of a rushing river, swollen with the spring rains. They were faced with the impossibility of the crossing.

i. The two spies had made their way across the Jordan River and back when they spied out Jericho (Joshua 2:1, 2:23). One could swim across the Jordan during flood season, but it was a heroic act (1 Chronicles 12:14-15). The whole nation with its women, children, and elderly, with all their livestock and possessions, could never be expected to cross the river that way. God gave Israel three days to consider the problem.

ii. "These events in Israel's history describe a time of preparation for this new generation who would be called upon to occupy the land. Although Christians are not called to carry out the same physical acts, preparation is necessary for any life of ministry and service. As with Israel's preparation, it involves hearing and believing God's Word and the discipline of obedience to that word." (Hess)

2. (2-5) The ark of God will lead the way.

**So it was, after three days, that the officers went through the camp; and they commanded the people, saying, "When you see the ark of the covenant of the LORD your God, and the priests, the Levites, bearing it, then you shall set out from your place and go after it. Yet there shall be a space between you and it, about two thousand cubits by measure. Do not come near it, that you may know the way by which you must go, for you have not passed *this* way before." And Joshua said to the people, "Sanctify yourselves, for tomorrow the LORD will do wonders among you."**

a. **When you see the ark of the covenant of the LORD your God…set out from your place and go after it**: Joshua didn't first send the engineers and builders of Israel's army. Instead, he sent the priests who carried the ark of the covenant, which was the visible representation of God's presence with Israel. Joshua knew this was primarily a *spiritual* challenge, more than a test of man's ability to plan and build.

i. The ark of the covenant had not yet been built when Israel crossed the Red Sea; there, God used other ways to manifest His presence to them. Here, God's presence was mainly evident through the presence and the prominence of the ark of the covenant.

ii. On this occasion, God wanted the priests to carry the ark, when usually it was the responsibility of another family of the tribe of Levi, the sons of Kohath (Numbers 4:15, 7:9). The priests were of the family of Aaron, who descended from Kohath (1 Chronicles 6:1-3), yet there was normally a distinction between the duties of the priests and the sons of Kohath. Priests carried the ark on other special occasions (Joshua 6:3, 2 Samuel 15:25).

b. **Yet there shall be a space between you and it, about two thousand cubits by measure**: God required that His people keep some 1,000 yards (1km) behind the ark. This was for at least two reasons. First, to respect the holy nature of the ark of the covenant. Second, to make it possible for all Israel to see the ark. The ark of the covenant would show **the way** they **must go**, leading the way. Israel would accomplish this impossible task as they set their eyes upon God's presence and followed the representation of His presence.

c. **Sanctify yourselves**: Because this would be a spiritual battle, Joshua required Israel to make spiritual preparations. **Sanctify yourselves** means they were to separate themselves from common things to focus on the LORD, and to see that **the LORD** would **do wonders among** them.

> i. "What was implied in this command we are not informed; but it is likely that it was the same as that given by Moses, Exod. 19:10–14. They were to wash themselves and their garments, and abstain from every thing that might indispose their minds from a profitable attention to the miracle about to be wrought in their behalf." (Clarke)

> ii. "While the act was wholly God's, it was performed on the fulfilment of certain conditions by the people. Charged so to do by Joshua, they sanctified themselves and thus made possible the action of God. Moreover, they moved in obedience to His command, setting themselves in array, with the priests leading before the parting of the waters." (Morgan)

3. (6) Joshua's step of faith: he sends the priests to walk across a swollen Jordan River.

**Then Joshua spoke to the priests, saying, "Take up the ark of the covenant and cross over before the people." So they took up the ark of the covenant and went before the people.**

a. **Take up the ark of the covenant and cross over before the people**: God *told* Joshua to command this radical step of faith (Joshua 3:7-8). Joshua didn't do this because of foolish presumption. Joshua acted as a man led by the LORD, and who remembered the similar work in the crossing of the Red Sea (Exodus 14).

> i. Joshua's success depended on and grew out of the promise of God to him: *This Book of the Law shall not depart from your mouth, but you shall meditate in it day and night, that you may observe to do according to all that is written in it. For then you will make your way prosperous, and then you will have good success* (Joshua 1:8). Joshua had the word of God on his lips, on his mind, and it guided his actions.

> ii. "You may very properly join the dividing of the Red Sea to that of the Jordan, for so the Holy Spirit has done in the one hundred and fourteenth Psalm: 'The sea saw it, and fled: Jordan was driven back.'" (Spurgeon)

b. **So they took up the ark of the covenant and went before the people**: Even considering God's guidance, this was still an impressive step of faith for Joshua and the **priests**. This was the bold faith that would ideally mark the people of Israel in the Promised Land.

4. (7-8) God's encouragement to Joshua.

**And the LORD said to Joshua, "This day I will begin to exalt you in the sight of all Israel, that they may know that, as I was with Moses, *so* I will be with you. You shall command the priests who bear the ark of the covenant, saying, 'When you have come to the edge of the water of the Jordan, you shall stand in the Jordan.'"**

a. **This day I will begin to exalt you in the sight of all Israel**: The step of faith commanded by God and observed by Joshua was encouraged by the LORD Himself. This is the graciousness of God toward His people, giving them constant encouragement in the things which He commands them to do.

b. **That they may know that as I was with Moses, so I will be with you**: God promised to make Joshua a leader like Moses in the eyes of the people. The LORD would do this by using Joshua to miraculously lead the people across an impassable body of water, as He did with Moses at the Red Sea (Exodus 14).

c. **When you have come to the edge of the water...you shall stand in the Jordan**: Once in the water at the bank of the Jordan River, the priests of Israel were commanded to stop and **stand**, holding the ark of the covenant.

5. (9-13) Joshua encourages and instructs Israel.

**So Joshua said to the children of Israel, "Come here, and hear the words of the LORD your God." And Joshua said, "By this you shall know that the living God *is* among you, and *that* He will without fail drive out from before you the Canaanites and the Hittites and the Hivites and the Perizzites and the Girgashites and the Amorites and the Jebusites: Behold, the ark of the covenant of the Lord of all the earth is crossing over before you into the Jordan. Now therefore, take for yourselves twelve men from the tribes of Israel, one man from every tribe. And it shall come to pass, as soon as the soles of the feet of the priests who bear the ark of the LORD, the Lord of all the earth, shall rest in the waters of the Jordan, *that* the waters of the Jordan shall be cut off, the waters that come down from upstream, and they shall stand as a heap."**

a. **Come here, and hear the words of the LORD your God**: Joshua rightly put the emphasis on God's word. He was only the messenger of the **words of the LORD**.

i. It was necessary for them to **hear the words of the LORD**, not to only see the things God would do. "For miracles do but excite men; they do but as the bells that call us to the sermon, they cannot work faith in us: but faith cometh by hearing." (Trapp)

b. **By this you shall know that the living God is among you**: Joshua understood that God's work here at Jordan would give Israel confirmation that God was with them and **among** them in the future conquest of Canaan.

> i. "Seven peoples are listed in v. 10. Twenty-three times in the Old Testament we find such lists, including five times in Joshua (3:10; 9:1; 11:3; 12:8; 24:11). The number and order of the names vary in each list, but seven is used often, probably as a number symbolic of completeness. Twelve peoples occur in all, but a core of seven—the seven mentioned here—comprises the 'standard' list." (Howard)

c. **Behold, the ark of the covenant of the Lord of all the earth is crossing over before you into the Jordan**: God commanded that the visible emblem of God's presence – the **ark of the covenant** – would lead the way. By leading with priests carrying the ark instead of soldiers, God declared the key to Israel's victory in the Promised Land would be fundamentally spiritual, not military.

> i. "What was the ark? It was a representation of the character of God. The people had no image to worship; in fact, they were commanded not to make an image. One cannot make an image of God, for God is spirit. But God has a character, and the ark was a statement of that character." (Schaeffer)

d. **The waters of the Jordan shall be cut off, the waters that come down from upstream, and they shall stand as a heap**: God had apparently revealed to Joshua how the Jordan would become a dry bed and passable by Israel. The waters would not be divided, as they were at the Red Sea (Exodus 14:21-22). Instead, the waters of the Jordan would be **cut off** upstream, leaving a dry riverbed before Israel.

> i. God's work at the Jordan of dividing the waters so Israel could pass was similar to what God did at the Red Sea (Exodus 14:21-22), but *not the same*. From generation to generation, God's work is in some ways the same and in other ways brand new.

> ii. "From a geological perspective, the Jordan River Valley lies at the juncture of tectonic plates that create an unstable region. Earthquakes can occur and have been known to block the flow of the river. No mention of an earthquake appears in the account in Joshua. Whatever secondary causes there were, the primary purpose was the exaltation of Israel's God and his people." (Hess)

**B. Crossing the Jordan River.**

1. (14-15) The faith of the priests and of Joshua.

**So it was, when the people set out from their camp to cross over the Jordan, with the priests bearing the ark of the covenant before the people, and as those who bore the ark came to the Jordan, and the feet of the priests who bore the ark dipped in the edge of the water (for the Jordan overflows all its banks during the whole time of harvest),**

a. **The feet of the priests who bore the ark dipped in the edge of the water**: The priests began the procession, with the ark of the covenant some 1,000 yards or meters (Joshua 3:4) in front of the people. When the priests stepped into the river and stood there, the waters were still flowing as at flood season.

i. The text doesn't tell how long the priests stood in the river. It might have been a moment, but it also may have been a long time. In a situation like that, even a moment *seems* like a long time.

b. **Dipped in the edge of the water**: It is human nature to want the riverbed to be dry before making a step. God called the priests of Israel to step out in faith.

i. "When the priest's foot touches them, they shrink away. Jesus has stepped down into these floods as our High Priest. In Gethsemane their overflowing tide washed around Him. At Calvary the water-spouts went over his head. In the grave He seemed momentarily to have succumbed. But since then they have been cut off. Through the ages He has stood, bearing the ark of propitiation, and arresting the tumultuous floods. 'Thus far, and no further.'" (Schaeffer)

c. **For the Jordan overflows all its banks during the whole time of harvest**: This was not the time of year when the Jordan was reduced to a trickle. Because of the spring rains, the time of early harvest, the river was swollen and overflowing its banks.

i. "The Jordan, as we have already seen, has its origin at the foot of Mount Lebanon, which mountain is always *covered with snow* during the winter months; in those months therefore the river is low: but when the summer's sun has melted these snows, there is consequently a prodigious increase of waters, so that the old channel is not capable of containing them." (Clarke)

2. (16-17) The Jordan is stopped, and the people cross over on dry ground.

**That the waters which came down from upstream stood *still, and* rose in a heap very far away at Adam, the city that *is* beside Zaretan. So the**

**waters that went down into the Sea of the Arabah, the Salt Sea, failed,
*and* were cut off; and the people crossed over opposite Jericho. Then
the priests who bore the ark of the covenant of the LORD stood firm on
dry ground in the midst of the Jordan; and all Israel crossed over on
dry ground, until all the people had crossed completely over the Jordan.**

a. **The waters which came down from upstream stood still**: In some
miraculous manner, God stopped the flow of the Jordan River. He may
have used a natural occurrence such as an earthquake or a landslide. Even if
the stoppage had an outwardly natural cause, the *timing* of it was a miracle
of God.

i. "Adam is a site in the Jordan Valley, identified with Tell ed-Damiye,
18 miles north of Jericho." (Hess)

ii. "It is possible that a landslide caused by an earthquake stopped the
flow of the Jordan River. Landslides are common in the soft clay banks
of the Jordan. At least two such landslides, each of which resulted in a
damming of the river, are recorded in history: in A.D. 1267 and again
in 1927. In the latter instance the slide occurred near the town of
Adam (cf. 3:16), and the flow of the river was interrupted for about
twenty-one hours." (Madvig)

iii. "In some respects the *passage* of the *Jordan* was more strikingly
miraculous than that even of the *Red Sea*. In the latter God was pleased
to employ an *agent; the sea went* back *by a strong east wind all that
night, and made the sea dry* land, Exod. 14:21. Nothing of this kind
appeared in the passage of the Jordan; a very *rapid* river (for so all
travellers allow it to be) went back to its source without any kind of
agency but the invisible hand of the invisible God." (Clarke)

iv. Later Jewish teachers couldn't resist embellishing this remarkable
miracle, claiming that "the waters of the river were piled up to a height
of three hundred miles" and "all the peoples of the earth were witnesses
of the wonder." Some rabbis made the fanciful claim that "when the
people arrived on the further shore, the holy Ark, which had all the
while been standing in the bed of the river, set forward of itself, and,
dragging the priests after it, overtook the people." (Ginzberg)

b. **On dry ground in the midst of the Jordan**: As well, even with the flow
of the river stopped, it was miraculous that the people could cross over on
**dry ground**. God miraculously dried the riverbed so that they didn't slog
through marshy mud.

i. "The Hebrew term for 'dry ground' (*harabah*) does not require that
the riverbed be powdery dry but simply means that it was no longer

covered with water. This indicates terra firma as contrasted to the flooding river." (Madvig)

ii. This miracle obviously connects with the miracle the nation experienced some 40 years earlier: the passing through the Red Sea (Exodus 14). God brought Israel *out* of Egypt's bondage with a miracle, and He brought them *into* the Promised Land with a miracle.

iii. In some sense, it took greater faith for Israel to cross the Jordan River than it took for them to cross the Red Sea. At the Red Sea, Israel was pursued by the Egyptian army (Exodus 14:8-28). Crossing the Red Sea was to travel away from danger, and to put a barrier between Israel and the danger pursuing them. In crossing the Jordan River, Israel travelled towards potential danger, the many Canaanites who would war against them. When Israel crossed the Jordan River, they cut off their path of retreat and could be "trapped" and slaughtered in Canaan. Crossing the Jordan River mean that Israel was completely committed to the task of conquering the land of Canaan; they were left with no other option. This was a demonstration of great faith.

iv. Clarke suggests why the Canaanites did not fight Israel as they crossed the Jordan: "It was not merely because they were *panic-struck* that they did not dispute this passage, but because they must have supposed it *impossible;* and when they found the attempt was made, the passage was effected before they could prepare to prevent it."

c. **The priests who bore the ark of the covenant of the LORD stood firm on dry ground in the midst of the Jordan**: In the record of this remarkable miracle, the **ark of the covenant** was central. The ark is referred to 14 times in these 17 verses. This was all about the trust Joshua, the priests, and Israel had in the God they knew was present with them. That representation of God's presence remained in the middle of the riverbed until all Israel crossed over.

i. Present-day believers understand that Jesus Christ is the fulfillment of the ark of the covenant. He is *Immanuel, which is translated, "God with us"* (Matthew 1:23). Jesus Christ was Himself greater evidence of the presence of God than the ark of the covenant.

ii. Even as the ark led Israel across the Jordan, so Jesus has cleared the way for the victory of His people: *Having disarmed principalities and powers, He made a public spectacle of them, triumphing over them in it* [the cross] (Colossians 2:15).

iii. "It was easier to believe that the torrent would not rush down on them when they could look at the priests standing there motionless, with the visible symbol of God's presence on their shoulders. The ark was no more the cause of the miracle than were its carriers; but, just as Jesus helped one blind man by laying moistened earth on his eyes, and another by sending him to Siloam to wash, so God did here. Children learn best when they have something to look at. Sight is sometimes the servant of faith." (Maclaren)

iv. As believers observe the word of God, obey the commands of God, follow after Jesus, and keep Jesus and His victory central, God will open miraculous paths for the progress of His kingdom.

# Joshua 4 – Memorial Stones

**A. The completion of the crossing of the Jordan River.**

1. (1-3) The command to select twelve men and twelve stones.

**And it came to pass, when all the people had completely crossed over the Jordan, that the LORD spoke to Joshua, saying: "Take for yourselves twelve men from the people, one man from every tribe, and command them, saying, 'Take for yourselves twelve stones from here, out of the midst of the Jordan, from the place where the priests' feet stood firm. You shall carry them over with you and leave them in the lodging place where you lodge tonight.'"**

a. **When all the people had completely crossed over the Jordan**: The people of Israel waited some 40 years for this moment. Having come out of Egypt 40 years before, they now had **crossed** the final geographical barrier to the land of Canaan. They had come this far by faith and were now called to even greater faith to possess and live in the Promised Land.

i. Israel had camped on the eastern side of the Jordan River for many months, since Numbers 22:1. Now they were on the plains of Jericho, near to the city (Joshua 4:13). Yet there was not an immediate rush to attack Jericho. By God's direction, Israel dealt with important spiritual matters before beginning the conquest of Canaan.

b. **Take for yourselves twelve stones from here, out of the midst of the Jordan, from the place where the priests' feet stood firm** Each tribe was to send a representative to take a stone – undoubtedly a large stone – from the dry riverbed where Israel had crossed over and specifically where the priests held the ark of the covenant. These stones would be used for a memorial.

i. "The raising of stones as a memorial is common in the OT (cf. 7:26; 24:26–27; Genesis 28:18–22; 31:45–47; 1 Samuel 7:12). These memorials were intended to provoke questioning so that the story of God's miraculous interventions might be told over and over." (Madvig)

c. **In the lodging place**: This was the place later named Gilgal (Joshua 4:19).

2. (4-7) The purpose of the twelve stones.

**Then Joshua called the twelve men whom he had appointed from the children of Israel, one man from every tribe; and Joshua said to them: "Cross over before the ark of the LORD your God into the midst of the Jordan, and each one of you take up a stone on his shoulder, according to the number of the tribes of the children of Israel, that this may be a sign among you when your children ask in time to come, saying, 'What do these stones *mean* to you?' Then you shall answer them that the waters of the Jordan were cut off before the ark of the covenant of the LORD; when it crossed over the Jordan, the waters of the Jordan were cut off. And these stones shall be for a memorial to the children of Israel forever."**

a. **Joshua called the twelve men**: The twelve men and twelve stones were obvious representations of the twelve tribes of Israel. Joshua wanted all Israel to take part in this ceremony and the memorial that would remain afterwards.

b. **That this may be a sign**: The stones would be a **sign** and a **memorial** for Israel, reminding them of the remarkable miracle of the dry riverbed crossing of the Jordan River. This was the final miracle of the exodus journey. Israel left Egypt through miraculously parted waters (Exodus 14), and they entered Canaan through miraculously parted waters. This was worth remembering.

i. It was a **sign** because of where the stones came from: the dry riverbed of the Jordan, making them unique markers of a work that could no longer be seen. It was a **memorial**, establishing a lasting testimony remembering God's great work.

c. **When your children ask in time to come**: This memorial looked forward to future generations that did not personally experience the miracle of the Jordan crossing. God did not want His work to be forgotten among the generations.

i. God's people often fail in their trust in God because they forget the great things He has done. The faith of future generations is often weak because they have never been told how great and real God is.

• Memorials are necessary because God's people forget what they should remember.

- Memorials are necessary because the truth of what God has done does not diminish with time.

- Memorials are helpful in teaching the children of believers.

- Memorials may be visible or unseen.

- Memorials are especially helpful in times of crisis.

ii. "This crossing of the Jordan by all the Israelites is not just an experience of the present generation. Future generations of Israelites will also acknowledge it. They will 'participate' in it through observing the sign and through hearing the explanation." (Hess)

3. (8-9) The building of the memorial.

**And the children of Israel did so, just as Joshua commanded, and took up twelve stones from the midst of the Jordan, as the LORD had spoken to Joshua, according to the number of the tribes of the children of Israel, and carried them over with them to the place where they lodged, and laid them down there. Then Joshua set up twelve stones in the midst of the Jordan, in the place where the feet of the priests who bore the ark of the covenant stood; and they are there to this day.**

a. **The children of Israel did so**: Israel had received Joshua as their leader, replacing Moses. Directed by God, Joshua **commanded** Israel to build the memorial, and they did. This respect for God's appointed leaders would be an important part of their success in conquering Canaan.

b. **Then Joshua set up twelve stones in the midst of the Jordan**: In addition to the memorial on the western bank of the Jordan, Joshua also set up a memorial on the riverbed of the Jordan, where **the priests** stood holding the ark of the covenant. These stones would be visible in drought seasons when the level of the Jordan was low.

i. "Occasionally, the Jordan gets very low, and the Israelites were able from time to time to see these twelve stones and to recall the great things God had done for them." (Schaeffer)

c. **They are there to this day**: At the time the book of Joshua was written, these stones in the midst of the Jordan remained. They were an enduring testimony to the faithfulness of God, visible in times of drought.

4. (10-14) A summary of Israel's crossing of the Jordan.

**So the priests who bore the ark stood in the midst of the Jordan until everything was finished that the LORD had commanded Joshua to speak to the people, according to all that Moses had commanded Joshua; and the people hurried and crossed over. Then it came to pass, when all the people had completely crossed over, that the ark of the LORD**

and the priests crossed over in the presence of the people. And the men
of Reuben, the men of Gad, and half the tribe of Manasseh crossed
over armed before the children of Israel, as Moses had spoken to them.
About forty thousand prepared for war crossed over before the LORD
for battle, to the plains of Jericho. On that day the LORD exalted Joshua
in the sight of all Israel; and they feared him, as they had feared Moses,
all the days of his life.

a. **So the priests who bore the ark stood in the midst of the Jordan until
everything was finished**: The priests stood with the ark of the covenant
for the entire time it took the nation to cross over. The ark, as the visible
representation of the presence of God, remained in the river as Israel
**hurried** across the Jordan.

i. **The people hurried and crossed over**: Israel was excited to come
into the land promised to them and their ancestors some 500 years
before, finally finishing the journey from Egypt. They may also have
been in a hurry, wondering when the waters of the Jordan would
resume their flow. "The circumstance itself thus marked is a proof that
the relater was an eyewitness of this miraculous passage." (Clarke)

b. **And the men of Reuben, the men of Gad, and half the tribe of
Manasseh crossed over armed before the children of Israel**: The people
content to settle on the east side of the Jordan stayed on their side of the
Jordan but sent their armies over to fight on behalf of the rest of the nation,
just as they had promised (Joshua 1:12-16).

c. **On that day the LORD exalted Joshua in the sight of all Israel**: God
fulfilled His promise to Joshua (Joshua 3:7), raising him up as a great leader
for Israel, even as the LORD had done for Moses.

i. "Joshua is now, in effect, the 'new Moses.' After the great crossing of
the Red Sea, "the people feared the LORD and put their trust in him
and in Moses his servant" (Exodus 14:31b). Here, now, Joshua found
himself in a remarkably similar position after a remarkably similar
miracle. He was growing into Moses' job as Israel's leader." (Howard)

5. (15-18) The Jordan River returns to its normal flow.

**Then the LORD spoke to Joshua, saying, "Command the priests who
bear the ark of the Testimony to come up from the Jordan." Joshua
therefore commanded the priests, saying, "Come up from the Jordan."
And it came to pass, when the priests who bore the ark of the covenant
of the LORD had come from the midst of the Jordan, *and* the soles of
the priests' feet touched the dry land, that the waters of the Jordan
returned to their place and overflowed all its banks as before.**

a. **Command the priests who bear the ark of the Testimony to come up**: The priests carrying the ark of the covenant had a long, difficult day. They entered the waters of the Jordan first, stood in the middle through the entire crossing, and only came up out of the riverbed when Joshua commanded. Their great privilege of bearing the ark was matched by the great responsibility.

b. **The waters of the Jordan returned to their place and overflowed all its banks as before**: As soon as the priests came out of the riverbed, the Jordan resumed its normal flood-stage flow. The manner and timing with which the Jordan returned to its natural flow show that this event was supernaturally arranged by God.

i. "Retreat was impossible now. A new page in their history was turned. The desert was as unreachable as Egypt." (Maclaren)

## B. The first work at Gilgal: memorial stones set up.

1. (19-20) The stones are set up as a memorial in Gilgal.

**Now the people came up from the Jordan on the tenth *day* of the first month, and they camped in Gilgal on the east border of Jericho. And those twelve stones which they took out of the Jordan, Joshua set up in Gilgal.**

a. **On the tenth day of the first month**: According to Exodus 12:2-3, Israel was to begin their celebration of Passover on this day. This was the day lambs were selected for sacrifice and kept with the household until the fourteenth day of the first month (Exodus 12:3-6). Passover celebrated Israel's exit from Egypt, and they entered Canaan on the anniversary of that event.

b. **They camped in Gilgal**: **Gilgal** would become Israel's base of operations for the conquest of Canaan. Therefore, it was appropriate that the first work at Gilgal was to set up a memorial to God's great works.

2. (21-24) The purpose of the memorial stones.

**Then he spoke to the children of Israel, saying: "When your children ask their fathers in time to come, saying, 'What *are* these stones?' then you shall let your children know, saying, 'Israel crossed over this Jordan on dry land'; "for the LORD your God dried up the waters of the Jordan before you until you had crossed over, as the LORD your God did to the Red Sea, which He dried up before us until we had crossed over, that all the peoples of the earth may know the hand of the LORD, that it *is* mighty, that you may fear the LORD your God forever."**

a. **What are these stones?** It's easy to imagine the scene suggested by this passage. A future generation of Israelite **children** see the curious pile of stones near Gilgal, on the western bank of the Jordan River. The children ask their **fathers** what the stones mean or signify.

i. The purpose of remembering God's great works is not so that God's people can live in a dreamland of the past, thinking that the best days of one's life with God are in the past. God's great works should be memorialized and remembered to provide a point of faith, so believers can trust God for greater and greater works in the future. This trust is based on what has been seen, experienced, and memorialized of God's past power and faithfulness.

ii. We tend to remember our pains more than our joys, our losses more than our victories. Great athletes will often think more about the championships they lost than the ones they won. This is why it is good to make deliberate memorials for the great things God has done.

b. **Then you shall let your children know**: The memorial had an important purpose for their **children**, giving them a point of contact with God's work in the past. They would understand that God's work did not begin with them and their time.

i. "None of the lessons of the present must be lost. They must be perpetuated in memory throughout the coming days. In order that this may be so, Jehovah deliberately arranged for such things as would appeal to the natural curiosity of a child." (Morgan)

c. **That all the peoples of the earth may know the hand of the LORD**: The memorial also had a purpose beyond Israel. It was so that **all the peoples of the earth** would know that there was a God in heaven who could work miracles, a God they should seek with all their heart.

i. "This is an ancient and commendable practice, by lasting monuments to propagate and perpetuate the memory of special mercies and signal deliverances; to set up some marks and mementoes upon them, that they grow not stale or moth-eaten." (Trapp)

# Joshua 5 – Circumcision and Passover at Gilgal

**A. The second work at Gilgal: Israel's radical obedience.**

1. (1) The fear of Israel's enemies at the faith and obedience of Israel.

**So it was, when all the kings of the Amorites who *were* on the west side of the Jordan, and all the kings of the Canaanites who *were* by the sea, heard that the LORD had dried up the waters of the Jordan from before the children of Israel until we had crossed over, that their heart melted; and there was no spirit in them any longer because of the children of Israel.**

> a. **Their heart melted; and there was no spirit in them any longer because of the children of Israel**: The idea of a **melted** heart is a complete loss of strength and resistance. The Canaanites were stunned and terrified by the Israelites and the God who was with them.

> > i. "For the Canaanites, the events of the preceding days were a horror story. They had been terrified enough by seeing the Israelite hordes— some two million strong—spread out along the eastern bank of the Jordan. It was obvious that the Jews intended to invade the western lands. But the water was at flood stage. The people could not cross. There seemed to be time to get ready. Suddenly the waters ceased flowing, the people crossed over, and a battle was imminent. The suddenness of the crossing terrified everyone." (Boice)

> > ii. "Worldly wisdom would have called for an immediate attack while the people of the land were disheartened and before they could make last-minute preparations. Instead, God called for a three-day delay while Israel observed the two sacraments." (Boice)

> > iii. "'Amorites' and 'Canaanites' are terms used to describe the same peoples. Their locations refer to peoples living between the Jordan and the Mediterranean. The descriptions, two parallel lines, identify all the areas of the land and emphasize the total number of the rulers in Canaan." (Hess)

b. **Heard that the LORD had dried up the waters of the Jordan from before the children of Israel**: The miraculous passage through the Jordan was not only a testimony to Israel, but also to the Canaanites. It was an additional warning to them that God's judgment was on the way, coming through the armies of Israel.

i. Rahab had already reported to the Israelite spies that the Canaanites knew of, and were terrified by, the great things God had done for Israel (Joshua 2:9-11). The miraculous crossing of the Jordan added to their dread that judgment was coming from the LORD, Yahweh, the covenant God of Israel.

2. (2-3) The circumcision of Israel at Gilgal.

**At that time the LORD said to Joshua, "Make flint knives for yourself, and circumcise the sons of Israel again the second time." So Joshua made flint knives for himself, and circumcised the sons of Israel at the hill of the foreskins.**

a. **Make flint knives for yourself, and circumcise the sons of Israel again the second time**: Apparently, none of the sons born during the forty years of waiting in the wilderness had been circumcised. There is no biblical record of circumcision being practiced during the Exodus, and Exodus 4:24-26 suggests it was a neglected practice among the Jewish people. This was put right at Gilgal.

i. "In front of them lies Jericho and hundreds of other places like it that have to be captured. War is about to begin, for blessings and battles always go together in the Christian life. The greater the blessing, the greater the battle with the powers of darkness, and only the Christian who presses right in to God will secure His best. But before they engage in war, before they rush in to attack Jericho, the Israelites have to learn some vital lessons while they wait at Gilgal. To wait to receive instructions from God is what every Christian finds to be the hardest thing in life to do." (Redpath)

ii. Here, **flint knives** were used even though the Israelites had use of metals. This may have been because of a tradition, connected to symbolic significance. "And as God commanded the people to make him an altar of unhewn stone, on which no tool of iron had been lifted up, because this would *pollute* it, (see Exodus 20:25, and Deuteronomy 27:5,) he might require that no instrument of iron should be used in a rite by which the body and soul of the person were in the most solemn and sacred manner dedicated to him to be his house and temple." (Clarke)

iii. "The *flint knives* are best understood as obsidian.... The smooth and sharp surface of this sort of knife enjoyed popularity for ritual and non-ritual purposes long after the development of metal knives." (Hess)

b. **The hill of the foreskins**: With an entire generation left uncircumcised in the wilderness years, virtually all the men of Israel needed to have their foreskins surgically removed with **flint knives**. They didn't make a hill out of the foreskins; the place where the surgeries were performed came to be known as **the hill of the foreskins**.

i. "When God reaffirmed his covenant with Abraham, promising him the land of Canaan, he warned him that anyone who was not circumcised would be violating the covenant (Gen 17:7–14). Consequently, Israel could not claim the covenant land until the sign of the covenant had been restored." (Madvig)

3. (4-7) The reason why so many men of Israel were uncircumcised.

**And this *is* the reason why Joshua circumcised them: All the people who came out of Egypt *who were* males, all the men of war, had died in the wilderness on the way, after they had come out of Egypt. For all the people who came out had been circumcised, but all the people born in the wilderness, on the way as they came out of Egypt, had not been circumcised. For the children of Israel walked forty years in the wilderness, till all the people *who were* men of war, who came out of Egypt, were consumed, because they did not obey the voice of the Lord; to whom the Lord swore that He would not show them the land which the Lord had sworn to their fathers that He would give us, "a land flowing with milk and honey." Then Joshua circumcised their sons *whom* He raised up in their place; for they were uncircumcised, because they had not been circumcised on the way.**

a. **For all the people who came out had been circumcised**: The men of the generation that left Egypt had been circumcised, but that generation **did not obey the voice of the Lord** and they failed to take by faith the promise of **a land flowing with milk and honey**. Because of this failure to trust God, they **died in the wilderness on the way**.

i. It's hard to explain why none of the male children born to the Israelites during the 40 years in the wilderness were circumcised. Circumcision was an important part of the covenant God made with Abraham and his descendants (Genesis 17:9-14). It was affirmed by the law of God given at Mount Sinai (Leviticus 12:3). Yet there were apparently no circumcisions carried out on the males of Israel during the 40-year exodus.

ii. After the first Passover held when leaving Egypt (Exodus 12:1-28), Israel commemorated a second Passover at Mount Sinai one year later (Numbers 9:1-2). They probably circumcised all who had been born in the previous year before the celebration of Passover at Sinai. There is no record of Passover observance in the 38 years in the wilderness, and it is likely that no children were circumcised after the Sinai Passover until Israel crossed the Jordan and came into the Promised Land.

iii. "The generation of Joshua 5 took upon itself all the responsibilities of the covenant through the covenantal sign of circumcision. Through circumcision, it could lay claim to the promises of the land that God had given to Abraham and to his descendants." (Hess)

b. **Then Joshua circumcised their sons**: In obedience to God under both the covenants God made with Abraham (Genesis 17:9-14) and the nation of Israel (Leviticus 12:3), the **sons** of the new generation were circumcised at Gilgal.

i. Circumcision was not unknown in the ancient world. It was a ritual practice among various peoples. Yet for the Israelite, "Circumcision was to every man a *constant, evident* sign of the covenant into which he had entered with God, and of the moral obligations under which he was thereby laid." (Clarke)

ii. There were undoubtedly hygienic reasons for circumcision, especially making sense in the ancient world. But more importantly, circumcision is a cutting away of the flesh and an appropriate sign of the covenant for those who should put no trust in the flesh. Also, because circumcision deals with the organ of procreation, it was a reminder of the special seed of Abraham, which would ultimately bring the Messiah.

iii. In Colossians 2:11-12, the Apostle Paul connected the ideas of circumcision and Christian baptism. His idea was that in Jesus we are *spiritually* circumcised, and we are also buried with Jesus in baptism. Paul did not say that baptism is the sign of the covenant Christians receive and live under, the new covenant. Even if that connection is made, it is important to note that one was genetically born into the covenant described here and in Genesis 17. One is not genetically born into the new covenant; one is born again into it by God's grace through faith. It is wrong and harmful to make the analogy, "babies were circumcised, so babies should be baptized."

4. (8) The faith demonstrated by Israel's obedience to the command to circumcise.

**So it was, when they had finished circumcising all the people, that they stayed in their places in the camp till they were healed.**

a. **They stayed in their places in the camp till they were healed**: The surgical procedure carried at this time and place made all the men of fighting age completely vulnerable and unable to defend the nation for a period of several days, **till they were healed**.

i. Genesis 34:24-25 describes how Simeon and Levi killed all the men in a city after tricking them into becoming circumcised. While the men of Shechem were unable to fight and defend themselves properly, they were slaughtered in retaliation for the rape of Dinah, the sister of Simeon and Levi. This could have been the fate of Israel here in Joshua 5.

ii. "This circumcising was a strange thing for Joshua, a keen military commander, to do. He was incapacitating his whole fighting force, an absolutely unmilitary act. It is silly to march your men right into the teeth of the enemy and then disable your own people. Joshua did it, nevertheless, because God told him to." (Schaeffer)

b. **Till they were healed**: Israel had camped for many months in the plains on the eastern side of the Jordan River, across from Jericho (Numbers 22:1). God could have commanded this mass circumcision then, when they were protected from the Canaanites by the barrier of the Jordan. Instead, God waited until they had crossed the Jordan, and were more vulnerable to the Canaanites, to make their army defenseless. In faith, Israel obeyed. They trusted God to protect them when their fighting men couldn't. This faith would lead to the conquest of Canaan.

i. God only required this great trust from Israel after He showed His greatness by the Jordan River crossing (Joshua 3:14-17). God requires radical acts of trusting obedience from His people, but He also gives them many and great reasons to trust Him.

5. (9) God rolls away Israel's disgrace.

**Then the LORD said to Joshua, "This day I have rolled away the reproach of Egypt from you." Therefore the name of the place is called Gilgal to this day.**

a. **This day I have rolled away the reproach of Egypt from you**: This disgrace or **reproach** was the disgrace Israel carried from **Egypt**, the shame of their degrading slavery.

i. The reproach was rolled away by their radical trust and obedience to God, by taking the specific action He told them to.

ii. It could be said of the generation that died in the wilderness, "they remind us of Egypt." The new generation was to have no such connection; by their faith and obedience they were a Promised Land people, not a slave people.

iii. The people of God suited for His Promised Land:

- Have been set free from Egypt.
- Have left Egypt.
- Know God is real and put Him first.
- Observe God's commands and His rules. They accept His Lordship.
- Make a true assessment of their present condition.
- Bring order and organization into their lives.
- Receive and practice God's ordinances.
- Trust in God's provision.
- Trust God's provision through their hard work.
- Make memorials of the great things God has done.
- Live their lives on the principle of faith.
- See God work in their day as in previous days, but not in exactly the same way.
- Take risks for God.
- Don't expect lives of ease and comfort.
- Deal with sin in their midst.
- Conquer as they follow their Joshua.
- Are in a process that takes patience.

b. **Therefore the name of the place is called Gilgal**: The name **Gilgal** means "rolling." When Israel came into Canaan through the miracle of the dry riverbed of the Jordan and by the radical obedience at Gilgal, these marked the final steps in their transition from being a slave people in Egypt to being a free people suited for God's Promised Land. This completed a dramatic shift in their national identity.

i. By analogy, God does a similar work among His people today. God takes away the dishonor and shame of previous sin and rebellion and lifts His people into freedom and high standing in Jesus Christ. Faith and obedience on the part of God's people play a significant role in this work.

**B. The third work at Gilgal: Israel remembers God's work of redemption.**

1. (10-11) The Passover is celebrated: looking back to their redemption from Egypt.

**Now the children of Israel camped in Gilgal, and kept the Passover on the fourteenth day of the month at twilight on the plains of Jericho. And they ate of the produce of the land on the day after the Passover, unleavened bread and parched grain, on the very same day.**

a. **And kept the Passover**: God brought Israel through the Jordan and into Canaan on the day when Passover preparations were to begin (Joshua 4:19, Exodus 12:2-3). Now as the **fourteenth day of the month** began at **twilight** (Exodus 12:6) they celebrated their first Passover in the Promised Land.

b. **After the Passover**: The feast of Passover commemorated the great work of redemption God did for Israel in freeing them from their slavery in Egypt. There was a sense of completion in this Passover, they were no longer in the wilderness but in the Promised Land.

2. (12) A new source of provision: God stops the manna.

**Then the manna ceased on the day after they had eaten the produce of the land; and the children of Israel no longer had manna, but they ate the food of the land of Canaan that year.**

a. **Then the manna ceased on the day after they had eaten the produce of the land**: When Israel was able to provide for themselves from the rich produce of Canaan, God stopped the manna. He didn't want Israel to get lazy but to live in a new partnership of trust with Him.

i. Israel had to trust God to bring the manna every day, but they also had to trust Him to provide through other means. This fulfilled what God had said in Exodus 16:35: *And the children of Israel ate manna forty years, until they came to an inhabited land; they ate manna until they came to the border of the land of Canaan.*

b. **They ate the food of the land of Canaan that year**: God always provides, but He is perfectly free to change the source of His provision as it pleases Him. God's people should trust in Him, not in His manner of provision.

i. "They were now fed with the corn of the land, and their future supply would depend on their own labour. They would be as surely fed by God in the land as they had been in the wilderness; but they would now be responsible for co-operation with Him in the labour of their own hands. This is ever so. For the needs of His people God always provides.... When it is possible for them to act and to work,

He provides for them through that activity. God never employs supernatural methods of supplying needs which can be met by natural means." (Morgan)

ii. Gilgal was marked by three important things.

- A memorial of the miraculous crossing of the Jordan (Joshua 4:19-24).
- The radical, faith-filled obedience of Israel in carrying out circumcision when vulnerable to their enemies (Joshua 5:1-9).
- The remembrance of God's work of redemption in Passover (Joshua 5:10-11).

Gilgal became a beachhead and camp for Israel in their conquest of Canaan. They returned to Gilgal after battle and remembered, finding strength in the remembrance of the memorial, of their obedience, and of their redemption.

iv. By analogy, it is good for the believer to have the things Gilgal represented to Israel. God's people need memorials of His great works, events of radical, faith-filled obedience, and remembrance of their redemption.

3. (13-15) Joshua meets the **Commander of the army of the Lord.**

**And it came to pass, when Joshua was by Jericho, that he lifted his eyes and looked, and behold, a Man stood opposite him with His sword drawn in His hand. And Joshua went to Him and said to Him, *"Are* You for us or for our adversaries?"**

**So He said, "No, but *as* Commander of the army of the Lord I have now come."**

**And Joshua fell on his face to the earth and worshiped, and said to Him, "What does my Lord say to His servant?"**

**Then the Commander of the Lord's army said to Joshua, "Take your sandal off your foot, for the place where you stand *is* holy." And Joshua did so.**

a. **Behold, a Man stood opposite him with His sword drawn in His hand**: Joshua boldly approached this mysterious **Man** with a drawn sword. As a shepherd over God's people, Joshua had a responsibility to see if this armed **Man** was a friend or a foe.

i. **His sword drawn in His hand**: "This expression appears in two other places in the Bible, with reference to the angel who stops Balaam and his donkey (Numbers 22:23) and to the angel who stands ready to execute punishment for David's census (1 Chronicles 21:16). A figure *with a drawn sword* is one not to be toyed with. He is one who threatens divine judgment." (Hess)

ii. "It is in His Hand, not in the minister's hand, not even in an angel's hand, but the sword drawn is in His hand. Oh, what power there is in the gospel when Jesus holds the hilt, and what gashes it makes into hearts that were hard as adamant, when Jesus cuts right and left at the hearts and consciences of men!" (Spurgeon)

b. **Are you for us or for our adversaries?** This was a logical question asked of this impressive **Man**. The response of the **Man** was curious, almost vague. **No** was not a proper answer to Joshua's question.

i. In a sense, the **Man** refused to answer Joshua's question because it was not the right question, and it was not the most important question to be asked at the time. The question really wasn't if the LORD was on Joshua's side. The proper question was if Joshua and the people of Israel that he led were on the LORD's side.

c. **Commander of the army of the LORD**: Joshua was a great military leader, having led Israel to victory over Amalek (Exodus 17:9-13). Yet here was a Man of clearly higher rank, the **Commander** in Chief of God's armies. Joshua **worshiped** this remarkable **Man**, falling **on his face to the earth** before Him and submissively awaiting His command.

i. The **Man** standing before Joshua was God.

- He held the title **Commander of the army of the LORD**, commanding angelic armies. Jesus said that God the Father has "fighting angels" at His command, more than twelve legions of them (Matthew 26:53). A Roman legion was normally 5,000 soldiers. This **Man** was the commander of those large, mighty, angelic armies, an unstoppable force.

- Joshua **worshiped** Him, and He received the worship. Mere angels refuse such worship (Revelation 22:8-9). Mere men are to refuse this kind of worship (Acts 14:8-20).

- Joshua submitted himself to this Man.

- The **Man** asked for the same submission and respect that Moses had shown to God on Mount Sinai (Exodus 3:4-6), shown by the removing of sandals.

ii. This was an appearance of God the Son, the Second Person of the Trinity, appearing as a **Man** to His people before the incarnation recorded by the New Testament Gospels. Jesus the Messiah *existed* before His human conception in Nazareth or birth in Bethlehem (Micah 5:2). The Old Testament records several significant occasions where God appears in a human form (Genesis 18:16-33, 32:24-30, Judges 13:1-23).

iii. "Commander-in-chief of all creatures, and captain also of his people's salvation (Hebrews 2:10)." (Trapp)

iv. "The children of Israel may be likened to yonder gallant vessel, prepared for a long voyage. All the cargo is on board that is needed, all the stores are there, and every man in his place. In all respects, the good ship is fully equipped, but why does she linger? Why do not the sailors weigh the anchor? If you ask the man at the helm, he will tell you, 'We are waiting for the captain.' A good and sufficient reason indeed, for till the captain has come on board, it is idle for the vessel to put out to sea. So here Israel had been circumcised, and the blessed feast of the paschal lamb had been celebrated, but still they must not go to the conflict until the captain himself had arrived; and here, to Joshua's joy, the angel of the presence of the Most High appeared to claim the presidency of the war, and lead forth the hosts of God to certain victory." (Spurgeon)

v. "I feel it no small relief to my own mind to feel that though I have been at your head these fourteen years, leading you on in God's name to Christian service, yet I am not your captain, but there is a greater one, the presence angel of the Most High, the Lord Jesus—He is in our midst as Commander-in-chief. Though my responsibilities are heavy, yet the leadership is not with me. He is a leader and commander for the people. Brethren, wherever Christ is, we must recollect that He is Commander-in-chief to us all. We must never tolerate in the church any great man to domineer over us; we must have no one to be Lord and Master save Jesus." (Spurgeon)

d. **And Joshua did so**: Joshua's total submission to the **Commander** – to Jesus Christ – shows that he knew this **Man** was of infinitely greater rank. This was also a virtual guarantee of victory for Israel. If Israel obediently carried out the orders of the **Commander of the army of the Lord**, they could not lose.

i. "The point of the exchange seems to be that it was not for Joshua to claim the allegiance of God for his cause, however right it was, but rather for God to claim Joshua. The two would fight together, but Joshua would be following the commander of the armies of the Lord in his cause and battles rather than it being the other way around." (Boice)

ii. "Though he does not reappear in the story of the Conquest, the stranger was a heavenly being who fought behind the scenes in the spiritual realm. His presence was a sign that the Lord was the real military leader of the Conquest." (Madvig)

iii. Jesus came to Israel at this strategic time for at least two reasons.

- Jesus came to instruct Joshua in the plan to capture Jericho. In the following chapter, Joshua will carry out a plan so improbable it could *only* have been initiated at the direct command of God.

- Jesus came to assert His authority over Israel. Before Israel could conquer anything else in Canaan, they had to be conquered by God. Joshua's complete submission was a demonstration that at this time, Israel truly accepted God's rule. This is a missing element in a life of victory for many believers; they have not been, and are not continually being, conquered by God. They fail to accept His authoritative rule over every aspect of life.

# *Joshua 6 – The Fall of Jericho*

**A. God's commands and Israel's obedience before the fall of Jericho.**

1. (1-2) God's promise of victory against Jericho.

**Now Jericho was securely shut up because of the children of Israel; none went out, and none came in. And the LORD said to Joshua: "See! I have given Jericho into your hand, its king, *and* the mighty men of valor.**

a. **Now Jericho was securely shut up because of the children of Israel**: Jericho was already regarded as the best-defended city of Canaan, the most difficult to conquer. Now, the city was on the highest alert because tens of thousands of Israelites were camped nearby. The Canaanites were terrified of the Israelites (Joshua 2:9-11), they knew Israelite spies had visited the city (Joshua 2:15-16, 22), and therefore the city was **securely shut up**.

i. Almost 40 years before this, Israelite spies surveyed the land of Canaan and were afraid of the fortified walls of Canaan's cities (Numbers 13:28). Jericho was one of the most fortified and strongly defended cities of the region.

ii. "Jericho was not a big city; it was only about seven acres in its entirety. It was really more of a fortress—a very strong fortress prepared to resist siege." (Schaeffer)

b. **The LORD said to Joshua**: The person who spoke in verse 2 was the same one who met Joshua at the end of Joshua 5. This was the commander of the armies of the LORD giving Joshua military direction.

c. **I have given Jericho into your hand**: Despite all the defensive measures taken by Jericho, God boldly told Joshua that the battle was as good as over. Speaking in the past tense, God said that Jericho already belonged to Israel.

i. Regarding the conquest of Canaan, everything to this point had been preliminary and preparatory. Now the real task before Israel must be faced and accomplished. The Canaanites must be dispossessed if Israel was to occupy what God had promised them.

ii. Jericho was not a large city, but it was an important and formidable fortress city. If Israel could defeat Jericho, they could defeat any other enemy facing them in Canaan. In God's wisdom, He gave Israel their greatest single military challenge first.

2. (3-5) Instructions for the action against Jericho.

**You shall march around the city, all *you* men of war; you shall go all around the city once. This you shall do six days. And seven priests shall bear seven trumpets of rams' horns before the ark. But the seventh day you shall march around the city seven times, and the priests shall blow the trumpets. It shall come to pass, when they make a long *blast* with the ram's horn, *and* when you hear the sound of the trumpet, that all the people shall shout with a great shout; then the wall of the city will fall down flat. And the people shall go up every man straight before him."**

a. **You shall march around the city**: God's commanded plan against Jericho made no military sense. It depended on God, not brilliant strategy, or military might. Soldiers and priests of Israel would **march around** Jericho, making the approximately half-mile (1 km) walk around the 7-acre city.

i. There were two basic strategies for defeating a strongly defended walled city. One was to attack by digging under, punching through, or climbing over the walls. The other was to circle the city, launch a siege, and wait for the city to surrender because of starvation and lack of re-supply. Neither strategy was used at Jericho; the commander of the LORD's armies gave a different way to conquer this city.

ii. Israel was to march around Jericho once a day for six days, with the priests carrying the ark and trumpets made of ram's horns. Each day the priests were to sound their horns while marching, and the people were to remain silent. On the seventh day, after marching around the city seven times, the priests were to make a long blast with a trumpet made with a ram's horn. At that signal, all the people of Israel were to loudly shout. God promised that then, the formidable walls of Jericho would collapse, and Israel could rush in to conquer the city no longer defended by walls.

iii. This plan required great faith from Israel and her soldiers. It required great faith from Joshua because he had to explain and lead the nation according to this plan. It required great faith from the elders and the people of Israel because they had to follow Joshua in this plan.

iv. The number seven is used 14 times in this chapter. "'Seven' is the number of totality, completion, and perfection in the Scriptures; and its predominance in this chapter emphasizes the completeness of Yahweh's victory on Israel's behalf." (Howard)

v. "Here were many sevens, as also in the Revelation. Many mysteries throughout the Scriptures are set forth by this number: the Hebrew word signifieth fulness." (Trapp)

b. **All you men of war**: It is unlikely that the entire army of Israel participated in this, rather these were representative soldiers from every tribe. The fighting men of Israel numbered more than 600,000 (Numbers 26:51), and Jericho was only about 7 acres in size (about 3 hectares).

i. The procession had soldiers in the front, priests with trumpets and the ark in the middle, and soldiers in the back (Joshua 6:9).

c. **The wall of the city will fall down flat. And the people shall go up every man straight before him**: If Israel conquered Jericho by this plan, it would clearly be the work of the LORD. Yet, God did not send an angelic army or fire from heaven against Jericho, working while Israel stood aside and did nothing. God's plan required the active participation of His people.

i. God could have conquered Jericho and defeated the city for Israel without any participation on the part of His people. Sometimes God works this way, but not on this occasion. He wanted Israel to be a part of His work. God often works today after this same pattern, choosing to wait for the active participation of His people before He decisively acts.

3. (6-7) Joshua tells the priests and the people what to do.

**Then Joshua the son of Nun called the priests and said to them, "Take up the ark of the covenant, and let seven priests bear seven trumpets of rams' horns before the ark of the LORD." And he said to the people, "Proceed, and march around the city, and let him who is armed advance before the ark of the LORD."**

a. **Then Joshua the son of Nun called the priests**: Joshua communicated this unusual plan to the priests of Israel. It wasn't normal practice to carry the ark of the covenant in battle. Yet in some sense, this wasn't a battle; it was a declaration of God's authority over Jericho and the coming triumph.

i. Circling the city walls of Jericho over seven days as God commanded would speak to Israel: "Trust in God, even when it doesn't seem to make sense. Put Him first, exalt Him, and trust that the LORD will do His work." Spurgeon noted how this might have challenged the faith of Israel: "'Why,' the fool might have said, 'you are doing nothing, you are not loosening a single stone,' and at the end of the fifth or sixth day, I suppose it was suggested by many, 'What is the good of it all?'"

ii. Circling the city walls of Jericho over seven days as God commanded would speak to the priests: "This isn't a normal battle; here, the ark will be prominent, and you will carry it. You will need to trust the LORD, even as you did in the crossing of the Jordan River."

iii. Circling the city walls of Jericho over seven days as God commanded would speak to Jericho: "Israel, the covenant people of Yahweh, are not afraid of you. They run circles around you, proclaiming the greatness of their God. Your judgment is coming soon."

iv. Trapp noticed Joshua's prompt response: "He yielded prompt and present obedience, ready and speedy, without shucking or hucking, without delays and consults; leaving us herein an excellent precedent."

b. **Take up the ark of the covenant**: The ark would be prominent in this victory, even as it was in the crossing of the Jordan River. Israel had to keep their hearts and minds on the LORD who was present with them, instead of putting their hearts and minds on the difficulty of the task in front of them.

c. **And he said to the people**: Joshua had to tell the people because what they were asked to do was unusual. This wasn't the customary way to conquer a walled, fortified city. There would not be a long, drawn-out siege of Jericho.

i. The **people** who marched around Jericho may have been only soldiers and priests (Joshua 6:9). There may have been other Israelites among the **people** who were to walk around the city, but since these were the same ones who later attacked and took the city, it is likely that that the majority were soldiers (Joshua 6:20).

3. (8-14) The march of the first six days.

**So it was, when Joshua had spoken to the people, that the seven priests bearing the seven trumpets of rams' horns before the LORD advanced and blew the trumpets, and the ark of the covenant of the LORD followed them. The armed men went before the priests who blew the trumpets, and the rear guard came after the ark, while *the priests* continued blowing the trumpets. Now Joshua had commanded the people, saying, "You shall not shout or make any noise with your voice, nor shall a word proceed out of your mouth, until the day I say to you, 'Shout!' Then you shall shout." So he had the ark of the LORD circle the city, going around *it* once. Then they came into the camp and lodged in the camp. And Joshua rose early in the morning, and the priests took up the**

**ark of the LORD. Then seven priests bearing seven trumpets of rams' horns before the ark of the LORD went on continually and blew with the trumpets. And the armed men went before them. But the rear guard came after the ark of the LORD, while *the priests* continued blowing the trumpets. And the second day they marched around the city once and returned to the camp. So they did six days.**

a. **When Joshua had spoken to the people**: Joshua did not hesitate to do what the LORD told him to do. Delayed obedience is often caused by lack of faith.

b. **Advanced and blew the trumpets**: God told Joshua to have the seven priests carry the trumpets made of **ram's horns** (Joshua 6:4). Here we learn that they sounded the horns as the procession walked around the city.

c. **So he had the ark of the LORD circle the city, going around it once**: Jericho was not a large city; they could easily march around the walls of the city in a day. As the people of Jericho saw the Israelites silently marching around their city, they should have understood the judgment they dreaded (Joshua 2:9-11) would soon come upon them.

   i. "Notice that the central feature of the procession was the Ark of the Covenant—it is mentioned eleven times in this chapter." (Redpath)

   ii. "We must not overlook the possibility that the march around the city was another expression of God's grace giving the people one last opportunity to repent." (Madvig)

d. **So they did six days**: It took *courage* for Israel to do this. The procession was vulnerable to attack from the city walls during those days. When their obedience to God made them seem vulnerable, Israel trusted God to protect them. This also took *endurance*. Israel did the same thing daily, for **six days**, with no immediate result.

   i. During the six days, Israel was silent except for the sound of the trumpets. "I can well imagine that the silence of the army was often broken by the taunts of the people who watched behind the walls." (Redpath)

e. **So they did six days**: Walking around Jericho, silent except for the sound of the trumpets, God gave Israel a close look at Jericho's impressive walls. They saw how difficult it would be to conquer the city through direct attack or siege. This sense of helplessness increased their sense of dependence on God.

   i. "They had the difficulty, I say, always before them, yet they kept on in simple faith, going round the city. Sometimes we get into the habit of shutting our eyes to difficulty; that will not do: faith is not a fool, faith does not shut her eyes to difficulty, and then run head — foremost against a brick wall — never. Faith sees the difficulty, surveys it all, and then she says, 'By my God will I leap over a wall;' and over the wall she goes." (Spurgeon)

4. (15-16) The march of the seventh day.

**But it came to pass on the seventh day that they rose early, about the dawning of the day, and marched around the city seven times in the same manner. On that day only they marched around the city seven times. And the seventh time it happened, when the priests blew the trumpets, that Joshua said to the people: "Shout, for the LORD has given you the city!**

a. **On the seventh day**: God commanded that the processions around Jericho take place every day over seven days. This means that they marched around the city on a Sabbath, breaking normal Sabbath-keeping customs.

i. This is a reversing of God's order at creation. When God created the earth and all that is in it (Genesis 1), He worked over six days, moving the universe from chaos to order and resting on the seventh day. At Jericho, God commanded His people to do their most strenuous work on the seventh day, as He completed His work of judgment.

b. **Shout, for the LORD has given you the city!** The command was given for the people to **shout**. After the days of silence, this was a recognition that God would now give Israel what He promised: conquest of **the city**.

i. The **shout** had a double meaning. It was a war cry or shout of alarm (Judges 7:20-21, 1 Samuel 17:52, Isaiah 42:13, 2 Chronicles 13:15), but it was also an exclamation of enthusiastic praise to God (Ezra 3:11-13, Psalm 95:1-2, 98:4-6, 100:1). "By raising such a shout, the people would at the same time have been sounding a war cry, which would frighten the inhabitants of Jericho, and also praising God for the victory he was giving them." (Howard)

5. (17-19) The command to destroy the city and to save Rahab.

**Now the city shall be doomed by the LORD to destruction, it and all who *are* in it. Only Rahab the harlot shall live, she and all who *are* with her in the house, because she hid the messengers that we sent. And you, by all means abstain from the accursed things, lest you become accursed when you take of the accursed things, and make the camp of Israel a curse, and trouble it. But all the silver and gold, and vessels of bronze and iron, *are* consecrated to the LORD; they shall come into the treasury of the LORD."**

a. **Only Rahab the harlot shall live**: Joshua was careful to protect Rahab according to the promise made to her (Joshua 2:12-14). God's people would honor Rahab's faith in the living God.

b. **By all means abstain from the accursed things**: Joshua had to command the people of Israel to stay away from the **accursed things**. This was a broad category that included the idols and things associated with the demonic and depraved worship of the people of Canaan.

i. The severe judgment that was brought against Jericho, and all of Canaan didn't come because they were an obstacle or inconvenience for Israel. Judgment came because the Canaanites were a people in total rebellion against God and in league with the occult, as the artifacts recovered from this period demonstrate. God held back His judgment against the Canaanites a long time (Genesis 15:16), giving them time to repent. Because they did not repent, judgment came through the armies of Israel.

ii. The importance of this warning will be seen in the consequences of Achan's sin in the following chapter. "This was a fair warning to that foul sinner Achan; but…covetousness is deadly, daring, and desperate." (Trapp)

c. **But all the silver and gold, and vessels of bronze and iron,** *are* **consecrated to the L**ORD: All the valuables belonged to God. Jericho was the first city to fall in Israel's conquest of Canaan, and so the valuables of Jericho were set apart for **the treasury of the L**ORD, being **consecrated** as a first-fruits offering.

i. "Metals are not destroyed by fire. They must be removed from common use by being placed in the treasury of the sanctuary where they would provide for the necessities of the sanctuary and the priests." (Madvig)

## B. The fall of Jericho.

1. (20-21) The walls come down and the city is destroyed.

**So the people shouted when** *the priests* **blew the trumpets. And it happened when the people heard the sound of the trumpet, and the people shouted with a great shout, that the wall fell down flat. Then the people went up into the city, every man straight before him, and they took the city. And they utterly destroyed all that** *was* **in the city, both man and woman, young and old, ox and sheep and donkey, with the edge of the sword.**

a. **The people shouted with a great shout**: This was the first time the voice of the people was heard over the seven days of circling Jericho. The ram's horn **trumpets** had sounded every day, but the people were silent until this moment on the seventh day. It was a glorious shout of praise and victory from the people of God.

b. **The wall fell down flat**: This clear miracle (Hebrews 11:30) must have been shocking to all involved; a glorious wonder to the people of Israel and a terrifying event to the people of Jericho.

i. "There has been much learned labour spent to prove that the shouting of the people might be the natural cause that the wall fell down! To wait here, either to detail or refute any such arguments, would be lost time." (Clarke)

c. **They utterly destroyed all that was in the city**: God commanded such complete destruction of Jericho because these were unique wars of judgment against the Canaanites. Deuteronomy 18:9-14 (among other passages) explains that the spiritual corruption of the Canaanites was significant.

i. Such judgment seems harsh to the modern reader because it *is* harsh. Modern readers must recognize, that at unique times, God has commanded such judgments. They may happen either through an army that He has used (as here), or through judgment that He directly brings, as in the destruction of Sodom and Gomorrah (Genesis 19:24-25).

ii. "Some have dared to speak of it as a hideous massacre; but being commanded of the great Judge, who has the power of life and death, it is to be solemnly regarded as a terrible execution for which there was a stern necessity." (Spurgeon)

d. **They took the city**: Israel **took** after God had *given* (Joshua 6:2). It was clear that God gave, but it was also true that Israel had to *take* by obedient, persistent faith. The same principle is true regarding the blessings that believers have in Jesus Christ; God has given them in Christ, and believers take them by faith.

2. (22-25) The rescue of Rahab.

**But Joshua had said to the two men who had spied out the country, "Go into the harlot's house, and from there bring out the woman and all that she has, as you swore to her." And the young men who had been spies went in and brought out Rahab, her father, her mother, her brothers, and all that she had. So they brought out all her relatives and left them outside the camp of Israel. But they burned the city and all that *was***

in it with fire. Only the silver and gold, and the vessels of bronze and iron, they put into the treasury of the house of the LORD. And Joshua spared Rahab the harlot, her father's household, and all that she had. So she dwells in Israel to this day, because she hid the messengers whom Joshua sent to spy out Jericho.

a. **Bring out the woman and all that she has, as you swore to her**: Rahab and her household were rescued. Rahab and her family coupled their faith in the God of Israel with a willingness to follow through on what God's messengers told them to do: stay at the house with the scarlet cord hanging from the window (Joshua 2:17-19).

b. **They burned the city and all that was in it with fire.... Joshua spared Rahab the harlot**: This is a contrast between judgment and salvation. All Jericho heard about the God of Israel (Joshua 2:8-11), but only Rahab responded positively in faith towards God with that knowledge. The rest of the city was destroyed, with only certain treasures brought to the **house of the LORD**.

i. The rescue of Rahab and her family was not a contradiction to the command that everything in Jericho must be devoted to the LORD. "Those who ceased to be Canaanites and 'devoted' themselves to the God of Israel were already 'devoted'. Therefore they escaped the terrible destruction of the ban." (Hess)

ii. "Rahab and her family were put in 'a place outside the camp' as a kind of ritual quarantine. The camp of Israel was holy, and nothing unclean could be allowed to enter (cf. Leviticus 13:46; Numbers 5:3; 31:19; Deuteronomy 23:3, 14). After the passage of time and the observance of appropriate rituals, they were received into the congregation (see v.25)." (Madvig)

iii. Hebrews 11:31 notes Rahab's faith and sets her in contrast to the unbelieving of Jericho and Canaan: *By faith the harlot Rahab did not perish with those who did not believe, when she had received the spies with peace.*

iv. Rahab demonstrated her faith in many ways.

- By believing the reports of what God had done for and through Israel.

- By declaring the truth about God.

- By seeing the greatness of the God of Israel and choosing Him over the gods of the Canaanites.

- By forsaking the gods and values of her culture.

- By receiving the Israelite spies with peace.
- By hiding the Israelite spies and refusing to turn them over to the Canaanites.
- By asking for the salvation of her family.
- By persuading her family to also trust the God of Israel.
- By marking her home as a place of faith as instructed.
- By leaving Jericho behind and becoming part of the people of God.

c. **So she dwells in Israel to this day**: This shows that the book of Joshua was written at the time of Joshua; this was not the fanciful re-construction of an imaginative writer working centuries after the fact.

i. "She is not distinguished from, but is part of, Israel. She has ceased to be a Canaanite or non-Israelite and has now become an Israelite.... The text stresses that Rahab rejected her past associations with the Canaanites and transferred her loyalty to Israel. By so doing, it demonstrates how Israel could receive others with kindness." (Hess)

ii. "For the Christian, the story of Rahab is the story of the shepherd's search for the one lost sheep (Matthew 18:12–14; Luke 15:4–7). It is the concern of Jesus for the despised of the world (Matthew 15:21–28; John 8:1–11). It is the transformation of values to which Christianity calls disciples. Those rejected by the world are precious to God (1 Corinthians 1:18–31; James 2:5)." (Hess)

3. (26-27) Joshua curses the man who would re-fortify Jericho.

**Then Joshua charged *them* at that time, saying, "Cursed *be* the man before the LORD who rises up and builds this city Jericho; he shall lay its foundation with his firstborn, and with his youngest he shall set up its gates." So the LORD was with Joshua, and his fame spread throughout all the country.**

a. **Cursed be the man before the LORD who rises up and builds this city Jericho**: As the most formidable city of Canaan and the first city to fall under the judgment of God through Israel, there was a special curse set on **the man** who dared to build Jericho again.

i. Later, a man named Hiel built Jericho again. His firstborn son and his youngest son did not survive the building, in fulfillment of this curse (1 Kings 16:34).

ii. "The city was soon resettled (Joshua 18:21; Judges 3:13–14; 2 Samuel 10:5); but the curse was not fulfilled until the time of King

Ahab, when Hiel, a resident of Bethel, rebuilt the wall around Jericho to make it a fortress once again (1 Kings 16:34)." (Madvig)

b. **So the LORD was with Joshua**: This completes the story of Israel's victory at Jericho. There is much to learn from the things that marked their victory.

- *Faith*: Joshua and Israel believed the battle plan given by God, as unusual as it was.
- *Obedience*: Joshua and Israel followed God's battle plan exactly.
- *Courage*: Israel followed God's battle plan despite the danger it posed.
- *Endurance*: Israel followed God's battle plan over a period, even when it seemed that nothing was happening.
- *Trust*: Israel *did not* rely on their own wisdom or familiar methods; their trust was in the *LORD*, not in human ingenuity.

c. **His fame spread throughout all the country**: Joshua's leadership in the conquest of Jericho was a further warning to all the people of Canaan that the judgment of God was coming. They knew this and had the opportunity to be spared judgment by leaving the land or by forsaking their Canaanite gods and practices, coming under the God of Israel as Rahab did. They knew judgment was coming, but few prepared for it.

i. "The outcome of a leader's first 'campaign' was considered important in the Ancient Near East.... The success of the first battle was considered essential in establishing leadership. Such a victory on the part of Joshua would secure him respect, not only among the Israelites (who already had ample evidence) but also among the Canaanites." (Hess)

# Joshua 7 – Defeat at Ai and Achan's Sin

**A. Defeat at Ai.**

1. (1) Not all of Israel obeyed the law of the devoted things.

**But the children of Israel committed a trespass regarding the accursed things, for Achan the son of Carmi, the son of Zabdi, the son of Zerah, of the tribe of Judah, took of the accursed things; so the anger of the LORD burned against the children of Israel.**

a. **The children of Israel committed a trespass regarding the accursed things**: Joshua commanded the nation in Joshua 6:18-19 that they should not take of any of the accursed things. These included objects associated with the demonic and debasing worship and practices of the Canaanites, and treasures that were only for the house of the LORD.

i. The chapter begins with the word **but** connecting it to the last verse of Joshua 6, which spoke of Joshua's spreading fame. "There is an intentional contrast. Although Joshua's fame spread because of Jericho, Israel's unfaithfulness provoked God's anger." (Hess) A leader of God's work may enjoy great fame and attention, while sin works its deadly rot among the people of God.

ii. "We must learn from this that God takes sin seriously, even if we do not, and that sin is the real cause of defeat for God's people." (Boice)

iii. **Committed a trespass**: "More generally, the sin was that Israel 'acted unfaithfully' with regard to the things devoted to destruction. The term in question here *(ml)* is used to describe a wife's adultery (see Numbers 5:12–13): it was a betrayal of a trust that existed between two parties." (Howard)

b. **The accursed things**: The wars fought by Israel in Canaan were not fought as plundering wars of personal gain; they were an unusual, sacred instrument in God's hand, used for judgment against a society over-ripe for judgment. Therefore, the spoil or plunder of Jericho was either regarded as **accursed** or as specially devoted to the LORD.

> i. "God owned the *devoted things* (Ⓧ*erem*) in the capture of Jericho (Joshua 6:18–19, 24). To take God's property is theft. The denial of the theft is deceit…. Either Israel must destroy the devoted things that it possesses or it will be destroyed as devoted things." (Hess)

c. **So the anger of the LORD burned against**: Israel's disobedience brought the **anger** of God against them. Israel could not be defeated by the Canaanites, but they could defeat themselves by their disobedience, inviting the corrective judgment of God.

> i. "It is certain that *one* only was guilty; and yet the trespass is imputed here to the whole congregation; and the whole congregation soon suffered shame and disgrace on the account." (Clarke)

2. (2-3) Spies report from the city of Ai.

**Now Joshua sent men from Jericho to Ai, which *is* beside Beth Aven, on the east side of Bethel, and spoke to them, saying, "Go up and spy out the country." So the men went up and spied out Ai. And they returned to Joshua and said to him, "Do not let all the people go up, but let about two or three thousand men go up and attack Ai. Do not weary all the people there, for *the people of Ai are* few."**

a. **So the men went up and spied out Ai**: When the returning spies recommended sending only **two or three thousand men**, it could have been a response of faith or of self-confidence. In the end, it did not matter which it was. In their state of disobedience, Israel could have sent 100,000 troops against Ai and it would have made no difference.

> i. "This was the first time in the Conquest that Joshua did anything on his own initiative, and it was doomed to failure. It is ominous that nothing is said about Joshua seeking guidance from the Lord. The great victory at Jericho made him overly confident of God's help." (Madvig)

> ii. **To Ai**: "This is the place called *Hai,* Genesis 12:8. It was in the east of Beth-el, north of Jericho, from which it was distant about ten or twelve miles." (Clarke)

b. **Do not weary all the people there, for the people of Ai are few**: Israel's success in the conquest of Canaan depended on their own surrender to God. Achan's rebellion showed that in that respect, they were not surrendered to the LORD – and therefore powerless before even relatively small and weak enemies.

3. (4-5) Israel is defeated at Ai.

**So about three thousand men went up there from the people, but they fled before the men of Ai. And the men of Ai struck down about thirty-six men, for they chased them *from* before the gate as far as Shebarim, and struck them down on the descent; therefore the hearts of the people melted and became like water.**

a. **About three thousand men went up**: Joshua, a wise military leader, commanded the larger number recommended by his military intelligence (Joshua 7:3). But the number of men made no difference. Israel was defeated at Ai, and **they fled before the men of Ai**.

i. "When God is with us, Jericho is not too strong to be captured; when He is driven from us by our own sin, Ai is not too weak to defeat us." (Maclaren)

b. **And the men of Ai struck down about thirty-six men**: The thirty-six men killed were thirty-six more than were killed at Jericho, which was thought to be a much more difficult city to conquer. Though this number was small from a military standpoint, the meaning of these losses was a disaster for Israel. It meant that Israel *could* be defeated in the Promised Land.

i. **As far as Shebarim**: "*Shebarim* signifies *breaches* or *broken places,* and may here apply to the *ranks* of the Israelites, which were *broken* by the men of *Ai;* for the people were totally routed, though there were but few slain. They were panic-struck, and fled in the utmost confusion." (Clarke)

ii. The defeat at Ai showed that what mattered was not the strength of the opponent, but the help of God. Without God's help, all would be lost.

c. **Therefore the hearts of the people melted and became like water**: The people of Israel had good reason to be afraid. Their panic was completely logical, because if God did not fight for them, they could expect only defeat.

i. "The very same words that Rahab used to describe the demoralized population of Jericho (2:9, 11; cf. 5:1) are here applied to Israel." (Madvig)

**B. In a time of crisis, Joshua goes before the LORD.**

1. (6-9) Joshua's fear: God's unfaithfulness was the cause of defeat at Ai.

**Then Joshua tore his clothes, and fell to the earth on his face before the ark of the LORD until evening, he and the elders of Israel; and they**

put dust on their heads. And Joshua said, "Alas, Lord GOD, why have
You brought this people over the Jordan at all—to deliver us into the
hand of the Amorites, to destroy us? Oh, that we had been content, and
dwelt on the other side of the Jordan! O Lord, what shall I say when
Israel turns its back before its enemies? For the Canaanites and all the
inhabitants of the land will hear *it,* and surround us, and cut off our
name from the earth. Then what will You do for Your great name?"

a. **Then Joshua tore his clothes**: Joshua followed his culture's customs
in times of mourning for the dead. He and the **elders of Israel** tore their
clothes and **put dust on their heads**. They mourned not only the death
of thirty-six men, but more so, they mourned the loss of God's blessing,
guidance, and protection.

b. **Alas, Lord GOD, why have You brought this people over the Jordan at
all**: For Joshua and the elders of Israel, this defeat was a national calamity.
They understood that every battle mattered, and that there is always a
*reason* for defeat.

i. "Though Joshua could not be expected to know about Achan's sin,
confidence in God's faithfulness should have made him look elsewhere
for the reason for Israel's defeat." (Madvig)

c. **Oh, that we had been content, and dwelt on the other side of the
Jordan!** Joshua knew that if God's blessing, guidance, and protection were
not with them, it would have been better if they had not come to Canaan
at all. If God did not deliver them, all would be lost.

i. Israel relied on God so greatly that the loss of His constant support
or the lessening of His hand of blessing meant certain disaster. Sadly,
many churches and ministries are so reliant on the programs and power
of men that if God withdrew His blessing and guidance, it wouldn't be
noticed for a long time.

d. **Then what will You do for Your great name?** Joshua's greatest concern
was for the glory of God. When God's people stumble or fail, their greatest
disappointment should be that they may have caused some great shame to
the **great name** of God.

2. (10-11) The real reason for defeat: Israel has sinned.

So the LORD said to Joshua: "Get up! Why do you lie thus on your face?
Israel has sinned, and they have also transgressed My covenant which
I commanded them. For they have even taken some of the accursed
things, and have both stolen and deceived; and they have also put *it*
among their own stuff.

a. **Israel has sinned**: God spoke to Joshua and Israel directly, explaining that He had not failed Israel. The defeat was caused by the sin of Israel. The problem was not with God but with the people of God.

    i. This was why God told Joshua to **get up**. Joshua didn't need to ask God to change His heart towards Israel. Joshua had to change Israel's heart before God. Schaeffer paraphrased God's response to Joshua: "Don't you remember that, Joshua? You should not be here on your face. You should be out dealing with sin among the people, for sin has made the difference."

    ii. God provides the believer with the resources for victory over sin, but God will never, on this side of resurrected glory, make defeat impossible, taking away the ability of His people to choose sin or obedience at a particular moment.

b. **Israel has sinned...they.... they...they also**: God explained that **Israel** had sinned, not only one man. The whole nation was declared guilty, and thirty-six men were dead, all for the sin of one man and his family.

    i. Hundreds of years later, the same principle was at work among the Corinthian believers. Regarding sin among the Corinthian church, Paul wrote: *Do you not know that a little leaven leavens the whole lump?* (1 Corinthians 5:6) A small amount of sin accepted and tolerated among God's people can invite God's response against the whole group.

    ii. "This passage shows that God was not open to the charge of a double standard with reference to his treatment of Israel and the Canaanites. He had ordered Israel to exterminate the Canaanites because of their sin, but here he allowed all Israel to be affected by the sin of one man." (Howard)

c. **For they have even taken some of the accursed things, and have both stolen and deceived**: This was the sin of taking things that were devoted to God alone. These objects were devoted either by their donation to His tabernacle or by their complete destruction. When this man took **some of the accursed things**, he was stealing from God and deceiving the people of Israel.

    i. The failure to honor God through giving was regarded as robbing God (Malachi 3:8-11). Under the law of Israel, if one wanted to keep something that belonged to God, they had to give to God the value of the object plus a 20% (one-fifth) penalty (Leviticus 22:14, 27:15, 27:19, 27:31). This was the same amount required for restitution in theft (Leviticus 6:4-5).

ii. The New Testament teaches us that giving should be regular and proportional (1 Corinthians 16:1-2), and that it should be generous, purposeful, and cheerful (2 Corinthians 9:6-8). When we don't give as God directs us, we must regard it as sin and repent of it.

3. (12-13) The effect of the sin: Israel had no power against their enemies.

**Therefore the children of Israel could not stand before their enemies,** *but* **turned** *their* **backs before their enemies, because they have become doomed to destruction. Neither will I be with you anymore, unless you destroy the accursed from among you. Get up, sanctify the people, and say, 'Sanctify yourselves for tomorrow, because thus says the LORD God of Israel:** *"There is* **an accursed thing in your midst, O Israel; you cannot stand before your enemies until you take away the accursed thing from among you."**

a. **Therefore the children of Israel could not stand before their enemies**: Israel could not fight in God's power and with His presence unless they walked in obedience to Him. Israel was under a covenant with God that promised blessing for their obedience and promised curses on their disobedience (Leviticus 26, Deuteronomy 28).

i. Believers today are not under the same covenant. The believer's standing with God is established by the work of Jesus on our behalf, not the works of the believer. Nevertheless, if the people of God desire the power and presence of God in their daily battles to live righteously, they must walk in fellowship with Him, and this fellowship is hindered by the believer's sin and rebellion.

ii. The believer's position before God is secure in Jesus, but their fellowship with Him may be hindered by their sin (1 John 1:6). This fellowship with God is the source of power for life in the Spirit.

b. **They have become doomed to destruction**: This was the tragic destiny for a disobedient Israel under the Law of Moses. The curses of Leviticus 26 and Deuteronomy 28 would surely find them and bring great **destruction**.

c. **You cannot stand before your enemies until you take away the accursed thing from among you**: Israel could not successfully continue their conquest of Canaan without dealing with the **accursed thing** that should have been devoted to God but was taken for the benefit of man.

i. "When either life in the church or doctrine is not cared for, the blessing stops as much as when an individual sins. Sin among the people of God either diminishes the blessing or brings the blessing to a halt until that sin is confessed, judged, and removed." (Schaeffer)

ii. "No individual Christian can sin without affecting the whole Church. No child of God can grow cold in his spiritual life without lowering the temperature of everybody else around him. The victory of the whole community depends on the victorious life of every individual church member." (Redpath)

4. (14-15) Instructions for judgment of the sin.

**In the morning therefore you shall be brought according to your tribes. And it shall be *that* the tribe which the LORD takes shall come according to families; and the family which the LORD takes shall come by households; and the household which the LORD takes shall come man by man. Then it shall be *that* he who is taken with the accursed thing shall be burned with fire, he and all that he has, because he has transgressed the covenant of the LORD, and because he has done a disgraceful thing in Israel.'"**

a. **The tribe which the LORD takes**: Though the identity of the sinning family was unknown to Joshua, it was known to God. Sin may be kept secret among men but is never hidden before God. Living with this recognition can help the believer walk in obedience

i. "Yet all this while Achan repenteth not, confesseth not his fault. The devil had gagged him, and his heart was hardened by the deceitfulness of that cursed sin of covetousness, the property whereof is first to turn men's hearts into earth and mud, and afterwards to freeze and congeal them into steel and adamant." (Trapp)

b. **Then it shall be that he who is taken with the accursed thing shall be burned with fire**: The judgment against the sinning individual would be strong and complete. Once this was dealt with, blessing could come again on all Israel.

## C. The public judgment of Achan's sin.

1. (16-18) God reveals the identity of the head of the family that had sinned.

**So Joshua rose early in the morning and brought Israel by their tribes, and the tribe of Judah was taken. He brought the clan of Judah, and he took the family of the Zarhites; and he brought the family of the Zarhites man by man, and Zabdi was taken. Then he brought his household man by man, and Achan the son of Carmi, the son of Zabdi, the son of Zerah, of the tribe of Judah, was taken.**

a. **Achan the son of Carmi, the son of Zabdi, the son of Zerah, of the tribe of Judah, was taken**: The text does not explain *how* the tribe, family, and individual was chosen or **taken**. It's possible that Joshua or the high priest used the Urim and Thummim (Exodus 28:30).

i. The use of the discerning tools of the Urim and Thummim is described on a few occasions (Numbers 27:21, 1 Samuel 28:6, Ezra 2:63, Nehemiah 7:65) and their use may be implied in other passages (Judges 1:1, 20:18, 20:23). It is commonly thought that the Urim and Thummim were stones drawn from a pouch, one indicating "yes" and the other "no." By asking, "Is this the tribe/clan/family/household?" and receiving a yes or no answer, an individual from all Israel could be identified.

b. **Achan the son of Carmi**: Achan knew he was the guilty one, and it must have been agonizing for him to see his tribe, clan, family, and household chosen – until he was revealed as the guilty man. Achan was filled with regret, but it was too late.

i. In some way, taking some of the accursed things from Jericho pleased Achan. He was pleased to have them. He was pleased by the thrill of transgression. He was pleased to have his wealth increased. He was pleased that he was not immediately found out. He was pleased he was able to hide them. Those pleasures were real, but they were also fleeting, temporary. The penalty of his sin would outweigh any pleasure it gave, and the penalty would last much longer than the pleasure of the sin.

ii. "I have often wondered that only Achan did it, but that one Achan brought defeat upon Israel at the gates of Ai. I wonder how many Achans there are here this morning. I should feel myself very much at ease if I thought there were only one, but I am afraid that there are many who have the accursed thing hidden within them, the love of money, or wrong ways of doing business, or unforgiving tempers, or an envious spirit towards their fellow Christians." (Spurgeon)

2. (19-21) Joshua confronts Achan, and he confesses.

**Now Joshua said to Achan, "My son, I beg you, give glory to the LORD God of Israel, and make confession to Him, and tell me now what you have done; do not hide *it* from me."**

**And Achan answered Joshua and said, "Indeed I have sinned against the LORD God of Israel, and this is what I have done: When I saw among the spoils a beautiful Babylonian garment, two hundred shekels of silver, and a wedge of gold weighing fifty shekels, I coveted them and took them. And there they are, hidden in the earth in the midst of my tent, with the silver under it."**

a. **My son, I beg you, give glory to the LORD God of Israel, and make confession to Him**: Even when sin is committed and covered up, it is still possible to **give glory to the LORD** by openly and honestly confessing the sin. Hidden sin always has a special power over the one who practices it.

i. Confession of sin is an important way that people may give glory to God. Often, we would rather glorify God in any other way, but Joshua's words still stand. He called on Achan to make an open confession of his sin and in so doing to **give glory to the LORD God of Israel**.

ii. This is not the only place in the Scriptures where the idea of giving glory to God and confessing sin are linked together. 1 Samuel 6:5, Malachi 2:2, and John 9:24 carry the same idea.

iii. The confession of sin brings glory to God in several ways.

- Confession of sin recognizes God's omniscience.
- Confession of sin recognizes God's righteousness.
- Confession of sin recognizes God's authority.
- Confession of sin recognizes God's judgments.
- Confession of sin demonstrates a desire to be in a right relationship and fellowship with God.

iv. "Confession of sins is a neglected doctrine. It only comes into its rightful place in times of revival, when the Holy Spirit comes in doubly-convicting power and makes it impossible for the erring believer to have any peace of mind until the wrong is confessed whenever necessary." (J. Edwin Orr)

b. **A beautiful Babylonian garment, two hundred shekels of silver, and a wedge of gold weighing fifty shekels**: This was enough to make Achan and his family rich, yet measured against the lives of the thirty-six men who died at Ai and the welfare of the entire nation, what Achan gained was insignificant. Truly, *the love of money is a root of all kinds of evil* (1 Timothy 6:10).

i. **A beautiful Babylonian garment**: "It is very probable that this was the robe of the king of Jericho, for the same word is used, Jonah 3:6, to express the royal robe, of the king of Nineveh, which he laid aside in order to humble himself before God." (Clarke)

c. **I coveted them and took them**: Achan's honesty was welcome. There were many excuses he could have made, but he honestly revealed his covetousness and his theft. Achan's guilt was plainly seen because he carefully *hid* the stolen articles to begin with.

i. "This verse gives us a notable instance of the progress of sin. It 1. *enters* by the *eye;* 2. *sinks* into the *heart;* 3. *actuates* the *hand;* and, 4. leads to *secrecy* and *dissimulation.* I *saw,* &c. I *coveted,* &c. I *took* and *hid* them in the earth." (Clarke)

ii. "The same three verbs 'I saw,' 'I coveted,' 'I took' are found in the story of the Fall (Gen 3:6)." (Madvig)

iii. Achan could have rationalized his sin in many ways.

- "No one will know."
- "These things won't be missed."
- "Think of how I'll be admired in this beautiful Babylonian garment."
- "The people I am taking this from are bad people, deserving of judgment."
- "I'm not hurting anyone."
- "I deserve this."

None of these excuses or rationalizations justify what Achan did. Believers must avoid making excuses for their sin and should confess as honestly as Achan did. Maclaren noted this about Achan's covetousness: "Did anybody ever hear of church discipline being exercised on men who committed Achan's sin? He was stoned to death, but we set our Achans in high places in the Church."

iv. There is a sense in which Achan was honest, but too late with his honesty. "His silence during the long process of casting lots is evidence of the hardness of his heart. As the selection came closer and closer to him—first his tribe, then his clan, then his family—he obviously hoped to avoid detection. His confession is not indicative of repentance because he would not have confessed if he had not been caught." (Madvig)

v. "The confession he made was complete, but it was worthless. The reason of its worthlessness lay in the fact that it was never made until there was no escape." (Morgan)

2. (22-26) The confession confirmed, and judgment executed.

**So Joshua sent messengers, and they ran to the tent; and there it was, hidden in his tent, with the silver under it. And they took them from the midst of the tent, brought them to Joshua and to all the children of Israel, and laid them out before the LORD. Then Joshua, and all Israel with him, took Achan the son of Zerah, the silver, the garment, the**

wedge of gold, his sons, his daughters, his oxen, his donkeys, his sheep, his tent, and all that he had, and they brought them to the Valley of Achor. And Joshua said, "Why have you troubled us? The LORD will trouble you this day." So all Israel stoned him with stones; and they burned them with fire after they had stoned them with stones.

Then they raised over him a great heap of stones, still there to this day. So the LORD turned from the fierceness of His anger. Therefore the name of that place has been called the Valley of Achor to this day.

a. **His sons, his daughters**: Achan's sons and daughters had specific knowledge of the sin because it is unlikely that he could bury so much under their tent without their knowledge. At the same time, they were not necessarily stoned with Achan. Instead of being killed with their father, Achan's children were probably brought forward to witness the judgment against their father.

i. There is notable usage of the singular in Joshua 7:25 and 7:26 (**you.... you.... him.... him**), in reference to a person being stoned. The use of the plural in Joshua 7:24 and 7:25 (**them.... them...them**) probably has reference to Achan's possessions, not his children.

ii. "With great deference to the judgment of others, I ask, Can it be fairly proved from the text that the *sons* and *daughters* of Achan were stoned to death and burnt as well as their father? The text certainly leaves it *doubtful*, but seems rather to intimate that *Achan* alone was stoned, and that his *substance* was burnt with fire." (Clarke)

iii. **And laid them out before the LORD**: "The return of the goods and their display *before the LORD*.... symbolizes the return by Israel of these items to God's possession. The act called upon God to bear witness that Israel held back nothing that belonged to him." (Hess)

iv. "Because he had violated God's command concerning the booty from Jericho, Achan found himself in the position of the inhabitants of Jericho: he himself was devoted to destruction. He in effect had become a Canaanite by his actions." (Howard)

b. **The name of that place has been called the Valley of Achor to this day**: The Israelites aptly named this place *Valley of Trouble* (or, *disaster*, as it is in the NIV). It was trouble for Israel, because of the defeat at Ai and what it could mean for the continued conquest of Canaan. It was trouble for Achan and his family because they were severely judged for their sin.

i. Adam Clarke gave an appropriate warning: "Reader, is the face of God turned against *thee*, because of some private transgression? Are not thy circumstances and family suffering in consequence of something in thy private life? O search and try thy ways, return to God, and humble thyself before him, lest thy iniquity instantly *find thee out!*"

c. **So the LORD turned from the fierceness of His anger**: Even sin as great as Achan's can be forgiven, and the occasion can contribute to future victory and success. Having dealt with Achan's sin, Israel was once again in a position to walk in the power, protection, and guidance of God.

i. This kind of victory came only after a *death*. The believer today must die to such besetting sins and know that *those who are Christ's have crucified the flesh with its passions and desires* (Galatians 5:24). The power and victory of Jesus' resurrection are active for believers as they crucify their flesh with Him every day.

# *Joshua 8 – Victory over Ai, Israel at Gerizim and Ebal*

## A. Plans for victory.

1. (1-2) God encourages Joshua and gives him instructions.

**Now the LORD said to Joshua: "Do not be afraid, nor be dismayed; take all the people of war with you, and arise, go up to Ai. See, I have given into your hand the king of Ai, his people, his city, and his land. And you shall do to Ai and its king as you did to Jericho and its king. Only its spoil and its cattle you shall take as booty for yourselves. Lay an ambush for the city behind it."**

a. **Do not be afraid, nor be dismayed**: Israel was defeated at Ai (Joshua 7:4-5), losing 36 men in battle. But worse than their defeat was that it exposed the truth that God was *not* with Israel in the battle at Ai. Without God's continued blessing, presence, and protection, Israel could never hope to conquer Canaan and they would be destroyed in the land. After having exposed and dealt with the sin that led to the loss at Ai (Joshua 7:10-26), Israel could once again receive encouragement from God. Sin practiced and unconfessed made them weak, and deservedly **afraid** and **dismayed**. With sin dealt with, they could trust in God's restoration and put away fear and dismay.

i. The failure of obedience at Jericho (Joshua 7:11, 7:20-21) and the defeat at Ai (Joshua 7:4-5) could, in some way, be put to good use. Properly dealt with, they could serve as a starting place for future victory.

b. **Take all the people of war with you, and arise, go up to Ai**: It was time for Israel to go back to the place where they were previously defeated. Once again in God's favor, they could in faith expect a different result.

c. **Only its spoil and its cattle you shall take as booty for yourselves**: Graciously, God would allow Israel to keep **spoil** from the city of Ai. This makes the sin of Achan seem even more foolish and tragic. Had he obeyed God at Jericho, he could have received spoil from the battle at Ai.

i. God did not allow Israel to take **spoil** or **booty** from Jericho. Yet this was allowed in most of the battles after that. "Although this was the custom for most battles, its specification signifies a break with the practice regarding the plunder of Jericho. There everything became devoted. This divine instruction signifies a flexibility on the meaning of the ban, which could be interpreted by God according to the particular needs of the people. Since everything captured belonged to God, he could also choose to give some of it back to Israel." (Hess)

d. **Lay an ambush for the city behind it**: God gave Joshua a plan for conquering the city of Ai. It was up to Joshua and the armies of Israel to follow God's plan.

2. (3-8) Plans made for an ambush upon Ai.

**So Joshua arose, and all the people of war, to go up against Ai; and Joshua chose thirty thousand mighty men of valor and sent them away by night. And he commanded them, saying: "Behold, you shall lie in ambush against the city, behind the city. Do not go very far from the city, but all of you be ready. Then I and all the people who *are* with me will approach the city; and it will come about, when they come out against us as at the first, that we shall flee before them. For they will come out after us till we have drawn them from the city, for they will say, '*They are* fleeing before us as at the first.' Therefore we will flee before them. Then you shall rise from the ambush and seize the city, for the LORD your God will deliver it into your hand. And it will be, when you have taken the city, *that* you shall set the city on fire. According to the commandment of the LORD you shall do. See, I have commanded you."**

a. **Joshua chose thirty thousand mighty men of valor**: In the first battle against Ai, Joshua sent only 3,000 soldiers (Joshua 7:4). For the second battle, he sent 30,000 **mighty men of valor**. Joshua obviously trusted in God but was also willing to use every resource and the best resources available to him.

i. **All the people of war** means all the 30,000 who would take part in this battle. "As Ai was but a small city, containing only twelve thousand inhabitants, it would have been absurd to have employed an army of several hundred thousand men against them." (Clarke)

b. **Behold, you shall lie in ambush against the city, behind the city**: Though God gave Joshua the general plan for battle (Joshua 8:2), He left it up to Joshua's experience and sanctified common sense to lay out the specific ways the plan would be carried out.

> i. "God also hath his stratagems; he seemeth sometimes to retire, that he may come upon his enemies with the greater advantage. At the end of all the present troubles will be the ruin of the Antichristian faction, and we shall see the Church in her more perfect beauty." (Trapp)

3. (9-10) Joshua stays with the people.

**Joshua therefore sent them out; and they went to lie in ambush, and stayed between Bethel and Ai, on the west side of Ai; but Joshua lodged that night among the people. Then Joshua rose up early in the morning and mustered the people, and went up, he and the elders of Israel, before the people to Ai.**

> a. **Joshua lodged that night among the people**: Joshua was especially near his people during this crucial time of trying to regain victory. The people needed to know he was near, and they needed to follow his leadership.

> > i. As an anticipation of Jesus Christ, Joshua was with his people even as Jesus promised to be with His people to the end of the age (Matthew 28:20).

> b. **Joshua rose up early in the morning and mustered the people**: The second battle of Ai would be fought with initiative and energy. There was no attempt to delay the battle for any reason.

> > i. "He is much noted for his early rising: his vigilancy being equal to his valour." (Trapp)

> > ii. "It would appear that Joshua spent the night with the people, across the valley from Ai (vv. 9, 11), but late in the night he got up and went into the valley in preparation for the day's events (v. 13)." (Howard)

**B. Victory at the second battle of Ai.**

1. (11-13) Preparations for the second battle of Ai.

**And all the people of war who *were* with him went up and drew near; and they came before the city and camped on the north side of Ai. Now a valley *lay* between them and Ai. So he took about five thousand men and set them in ambush between Bethel and Ai, on the west side of the city. And when they had set the people, all the army that *was* on the north of the city, and its rear guard on the west of the city, Joshua went that night into the midst of the valley.**

a. **All the people of war who *were* with him went up and drew near**: In the second battle of Ai, Israel took the initiative. They didn't wait for Ai to bring the battle to them; they brought the battle to Ai.

b. **Joshua went that night into the midst**: Joshua took active, personal responsibility in the second battle of Ai. At Jericho, there was no special role Joshua played, except to make sure that the people of God obedient to God's commands. At the first battle of Ai, Joshua sent men to the battle, not going himself (Joshua 7:3-5). After the defeat at the first battle of Ai, Joshua would not make the same mistake again. He was in the **midst** of this military action.

2. (14-17) The ambush works; the fighting men of Ai leave the city.

**Now it happened, when the king of Ai saw *it*, that the men of the city hurried and rose early and went out against Israel to battle, he and all his people, at an appointed place before the plain. But he did not know that *there was* an ambush against him behind the city. And Joshua and all Israel made as if they were beaten before them, and fled by the way of the wilderness. So all the people who *were* in Ai were called together to pursue them. And they pursued Joshua and were drawn away from the city. There was not a man left in Ai or Bethel who did not go out after Israel. So they left the city open and pursued Israel.**

a. **When the king of Ai saw it, that the men of the city hurried and rose early and went out against Israel to battle**: The men of Ai used the same strategy against Israel as worked in the first battle of Ai (Joshua 7:4-5).

i. Believers sometimes observe that Satan, the enemy of God's people (Ephesians 6:12, 1 Peter 5:8) will continue with a strategy against God's people until it doesn't work anymore. This is why it is always important to resist the devil, his agents, and his strategies.

ii. "Careful preparations for war, such as those described here, were used as an illustration of discipleship by Jesus. He reminded his disciples of the need to count the cost of following him (Luke 14:31–33)." (Hess)

b. **And Joshua and all Israel made as if they were beaten before them**: God directed Joshua to use a completely different strategy against Ai. This feigned defeat would lead to victory for Israel.

i. **Not a man left in Ai or Bethel**: "The proximity of Ai to Bethel may have encouraged the army of Bethel to come to the aid of Ai. The Israelite ambush had to be hidden from the main road to keep the troops coming from Bethel from discovering them." (Madvig)

3. (18-20) The trap is carried out against Ai.

**Then the LORD said to Joshua, "Stretch out the spear that** *is* **in your hand toward Ai, for I will give it into your hand." And Joshua stretched out the spear that** *was* **in his hand toward the city. So** *those in* **ambush arose quickly out of their place; they ran as soon as he had stretched out his hand, and they entered the city and took it, and hurried to set the city on fire. And when the men of Ai looked behind them, they saw, and behold, the smoke of the city ascended to heaven. So they had no power to flee this way or that way, and the people who had fled to the wilderness turned back on the pursuers.**

a. **Stretch out the spear that is in your hand**: Moses, the predecessor to Joshua, often exerted God's victorious power with a hand or rod stretched out (Exodus 9:22-23, 10:12-13, 10:21-22, 14:21). Here, God told Joshua to do the same thing. The spear extended **toward Ai** was an illustration of the power God had over the Canaanite city. The Bible often uses the figure of God's outstretched hand or arm as a demonstration of His power (Exodus 15:12, Deuteronomy 4:34, 5:15, 7:19, 9:29, Psalm 136:12, 138:7).

b. **They entered the city and took it, and hurried to set the city on fire**: The plan worked perfectly. With the fighting men of Ai out chasing the Israelite army, the city was exposed.

i. **Set the city on fire**: "Probably this means no more than that they should kindle a fire in the city, the smoke of which should be an indication that they had taken it." (Clarke)

4. (21-29) The complete defeat of Ai.

**Now when Joshua and all Israel saw that the ambush had taken the city and that the smoke of the city ascended, they turned back and struck down the men of Ai. Then the others came out of the city against them; so they were** *caught* **in the midst of Israel, some on this side and some on that side. And they struck them down, so that they let none of them remain or escape. But the king of Ai they took alive, and brought him to Joshua.**

**And it came to pass when Israel had made an end of slaying all the inhabitants of Ai in the field, in the wilderness where they pursued them, and when they all had fallen by the edge of the sword until they were consumed, that all the Israelites returned to Ai and struck it with the edge of the sword. So it was** *that* **all who fell that day, both men and women,** *were* **twelve thousand; all the people of Ai. For Joshua did not draw back his hand, with which he stretched out the spear, until he had**

utterly destroyed all the inhabitants of Ai. Only the livestock and the spoil of that city Israel took as booty for themselves, according to the word of the LORD which He had commanded Joshua. So Joshua burned Ai and made it a heap forever, a desolation to this day. And the king of Ai he hanged on a tree until evening. And as soon as the sun was down, Joshua commanded that they should take his corpse down from the tree, cast it at the entrance of the gate of the city, and raise over it a great heap of stones *that remains* to this day.

a. **They struck them down, so that they let none of them remain or escape**: The victory and God's judgment was complete at the second battle of Ai. Because of God's faithfulness to Israel and Israel's obedient response to God, this was not a partial victory.

i. "The tables are turned. The same expressions that earlier described Ai's success and Israel's defeat are now used to enhance Joshua's leadership in reversing the apparent defeat." (Clarke)

ii. "The story of the taking of Ai is one of brilliant military strategy. Thus again the fact was brought into prominence that in prosecuting the work of Jehovah there must ever be a recognition of the value and use of the best in human reason." (Morgan)

b. **Joshua did not draw back his hand, with which he stretched out the spear**: In Exodus 17:8-16, Joshua was the general leading the army of Israel that benefited from the outstretched arms of Moses in prayer in the battle against the Amalekites. Here, Joshua is the one who inspires Israel to victory with his outstretched arm.

i. "Joshua maintained his arm outstretched, with his sword in his hand, until the defeat of Ai was complete. This shows that the outstretched sword was more than a signal to start the battle (see on v. 18): it was also a symbol of God's presence and help in the battle." (Howard)

c. **Until he had utterly destroyed all the inhabitants of Ai**: According to God's command, Israel showed no mercy to the people of Ai. This was part of Israel's unique role as God's instrument of long-deserved judgment of the Canaanites, and as just repayment for Ai's victory in the first battle (Joshua 7:5).

i. By spiritual analogy, God's people must remain unsparing in the battle against the flesh and against the devil and all his agents.

ii. **The king of Ai he hanged on a tree**: "He had gone out at the head of his men, and had been taken prisoner, ver. 23; and the battle being over, he was ordered to be hanged." (Clarke)

iii. "The king's body was taken down at sundown, in accordance with the injunction in Deuteronomy that a body could not remain exposed overnight (Deuteronomy 21:22-23). Here again, Joshua was observing the law as closely as possible." (Howard)

d. **According to the word of the LORD which He had commanded Joshua**: So far, Israel's experience was an illustration of their future story, and the spiritual history of many Christians. This cycle will be especially prominent in the book of Judges.

- Obedience followed by victory.
- Victory followed by blessing.
- Blessing followed by pride and disobedience.
- Disobedience followed by defeat.
- Defeat followed by judgment.
- Judgment followed by repentance.
- Repentance followed by obedience.
- Obedience followed by victory, and the cycle continues.

## C. Blessings proclaimed from Mount Gerizim, curses from Mount Ebal.

1. (30-31) An altar built at Mount Ebal.

**Now Joshua built an altar to the LORD God of Israel in Mount Ebal, as Moses the servant of the LORD had commanded the children of Israel, as it is written in the Book of the Law of Moses: "an altar of whole stones over which no man has wielded an iron *tool*." And they offered on it burnt offerings to the LORD, and sacrificed peace offerings.**

a. **Now Joshua built an altar to the LORD God of Israel**: This was in fulfillment of what God commanded in Deuteronomy 11:29-32 and Deuteronomy 27-28, especially 27:1-8. The LORD told Israel to come to **Mount Ebal** and Mount Gerizim. At Ebal, they were to build an altar, sacrifice to the LORD, and read the law.

i. The blessings and curses of Deuteronomy 27-28 were not only announced by Moses to Israel on the plains of Moab. According to God's command, they were also ceremonially read to all Israel at Gerizim and Ebal, the hills of blessing and curses. Six tribes stood at each mountain.

- At Gerizim (blessing): Simeon, Levi, Judah, Issachar, Joseph, and Benjamin.

- At Ebal (curses): Reuben, Gad, Asher, Zebulun, Dan, and Naphtali.

- In between them: the ark of the covenant.

ii. "Ebal and Gerizim are about a mile and a half apart at the top but only about 500 yards apart at the bottom. Gerizim reaches to approximately 2,895 feet above sea level, Ebal to 3,077 feet. This means that Gerizim stands about 800 feet above the valley and Ebal about 1,000 feet." (Schaeffer)

iii. The **altar to the LORD God of Israel** and the sacrifices on it were at **Mount Ebal**, the hill associated with curses. That was where it was needed, and that was where God provided for the failure of His people: through the sacrificial system.

b. **And they offered on it burnt offerings to the LORD, and sacrificed peace offerings**: This was an appropriate act of worship and consecration to God, following a great victory. Israel was careful to give God the thanks and the glory for their triumph at the second battle of Ai.

i. Even the altar built at Ebal would not display the glory of man, because it was not made with an **iron tool** used to engrave the stones. They were **whole stones**, not beautified by man. The altar displayed what God made, not what man made.

ii. "It is interesting that a thousand years later the Samaritans built their altar on Gerizim, not Ebal. So when the woman of Samaria told Jesus, 'Our fathers worshiped on this mountain, but you Jews claim that the place where we must worship is in Jerusalem,' she was pointing to Gerizim (John 4:20). Jesus responded by turning her away from that mountain (as well as from Mount Zion) to himself and his coming sacrifice." (Boice)

2. (32-35) Blessings read from Mount Gerizim, curses from Mount Ebal.

**And there, in the presence of the children of Israel, he wrote on the stones a copy of the law of Moses, which he had written. Then all Israel, with their elders and officers and judges, stood on either side of the ark before the priests, the Levites, who bore the ark of the covenant of the LORD, the stranger as well as he who was born among them. Half of them *were* in front of Mount Gerizim and half of them in front of Mount Ebal, as Moses the servant of the LORD had commanded before, that they should bless the people of Israel. And afterward he read all the words of the law, the blessings and the cursings, according to all that is written in the Book of the Law. There was not a word of all that Moses had commanded which Joshua did not read before all the assembly**

**of Israel, with the women, the little ones, and the strangers who were living among them.**

a. **He wrote on the stones a copy of the law of Moses, which he had written**: In this act of obedience, we see Joshua as a *man of the Book*, obeying the command of Joshua 1:8. We also see Israel as a *people of the Book* ordering their lives after God's word.

> i. "The word 'stones' has an article in Hebrew and refers to special stones covered with plaster that Moses had commanded to be prepared for this purpose (Deuteronomy 27:4)." (Madvig)

> ii. "The Israelites just picked up field stones and piled them together. Then somebody covered these big stones with a coating that could be easily etched or painted quickly with a brush as was done on the shards. Someone carefully wrote the Ten Commandments in this coating." (Schaeffer)

> iii. They obeyed God and gave attention to His word at a cost or inconvenience. The distance from Ai to Ebal and Gerizim was a long way to move all the tribes of Israel, from 20 to 25 miles (32 to 40 km).

> iv. "Surveys and excavations on Mount Ebal have revealed a site there, on the third highest peak, that the excavator suggests could be identified with Joshua's altar." (Hess) There was evidence of burnt animal offerings at this altar, but no religious figurines (idols).

b. **The stranger as well as he who was born among them**: This means that among the group considered the nation of Israel were those who were born as Gentiles yet had come under the law and covenant of the God of Israel. These were **strangers** by birth but **living among** the covenant people.

> i. In between Ebal and Gerizim was Shechem, a significant city that is not mentioned in this part of Joshua. Shechem has a long history with the covenant people of God, tracing back to the time of Abraham.

> ii. The lack of mention of any battle with the people of Shechem suggests the possibility that they surrendered to Israel, denied their Canaanite gods, and submitted to the God of Israel as Rahab had done (Joshua 2:8-14, 6:25). This is also suggested by the mention of the **stranger** (8:33) and the **strangers** (8:35) in this immediate context.

> iii. "'Aliens and citizens alike' were included in Israel and participated in the covenant renewal. The religion of Israel at its best has always been a missionary religion. From the time of the Exodus, aliens who chose to live with Israel and worship her God were assimilated into the nation as, for example, Rahab and her family (cf. 1 Kings 8:41–43)." (Madvig)

iv. "In this sense, these aliens were true 'converts' to faith in Israel's God. Indeed, the Old Greek translates the Hebrew term here with the Greek word *proselutos*, which forms the basis of the English word 'proselyte' (i.e., one who converts). This shows—as does the story of Rahab—that Israel's faith was not a closed system: it was open to outsiders." (Howard)

c. **Half of them were in front of Mount Gerizim and half of them in front of Mount Ebal**: This was an appropriate place to do this, and the whole nation could hear this reading of the law. The area has a natural amphitheater effect because of the contour of the hills.

i. This event was suggestive of many enduring spiritual principles.

- There is a choice between blessing and cursing for humanity, especially for the people of God.
- Often the curses seem more significant than the blessings.
- Atonement is needed on the ground of curses, and God has made provision for this atonement, rooted in the sacrifice of an innocent victim.

ii. This event, at this place, showed that Israel controlled the middle of the land of Canaan and the highlands. This set them in a good strategic position to conquer the rest of the land of Canaan.

iii. "The strategic aspect of the battle moves Israel from the 'edge' of Canaan on the plains of Jericho to the centre of the hill country. From the strategic region of Bethel and Ai, Israel would be poised for the forthcoming events to the north (Joshua 8:30–35; 11) and to the south (Joshua 9–10)." (Clarke)

c. **There was not a word of all that Moses had commanded which Joshua did not read before all the assembly of Israel**: This focus on God's revealed word was the foundation for Israel's future security and blessing. When they stayed attentive and generally obedient to God's word, they were blessed.

i. "He caused them [all the words of the law] to be read by the Levites (Deuteronomy 27:14), and haply the sense to be given, as Nehemiah 8:8." (Trapp)

ii. The time and attention given to the blessings and curses of the law at Gerizim and Ebal reflect the heart of Moses in his plea to Israel, calling them to obey God and be blessed instead of inheriting the curses promised to disobedient Israel: *I call heaven and earth as witnesses today against you, that I have set before you life and death, blessing and cursing; therefore choose life, that both you and your descendants may live; that you may love the LORD your God, that you may obey His voice, and that you may cling to Him, for He is your life and the length of your days; and that you may dwell in the land which the LORD swore to your fathers, to Abraham, Isaac, and Jacob, to give them.* (Deuteronomy 30:19-20)

iii. "We see in the reading of the blessings and curses not only a continuity of the authority of the written, propositional Scriptures, but also an emphasis on the fact that bare knowledge is not enough. It was not that the Pentateuch gave these people knowledge, and that was the end of it. This knowledge demanded action." (Schaeffer)

iv. "Thus every precaution is taken to ensure obedience to the Divine precepts, and consequently to promote the happiness of the people; for this every ordinance of God is remarkable, as he ever causes the *interest* and *duty* of his followers to go hand in hand." (Clarke)

# Joshua 9 – The Gibeonite Deception

### A. Two different strategies of attack against Israel.

1. (1-2) Canaanite kings gather against Israel.

**And it came to pass when all the kings who** *were* **on this side of the Jordan, in the hills and in the lowland and in all the coasts of the Great Sea toward Lebanon; the Hittite, the Amorite, the Canaanite, the Perizzite, the Hivite, and the Jebusite; heard** *about it,* **that they gathered together to fight with Joshua and Israel with one accord.**

a. **When all the kings who were on this side of the Jordan...heard about it**: When the Canaanite kings heard how the LORD had delivered Jericho to Israel, they had reason to be troubled. When they heard how the LORD gave them victory in the second battle of Ai, they had more reason to be concerned.

b. **They gathered together to fight with Joshua and Israel with one accord**: Their plan was a classic, frontal attack, with armies battling one another. These kings hoped to unite and defeat Israel on the field of battle, in head-to-head confrontation.

i. The confederation of the Canaanite tribes was prompted by at least two factors. The first was desperation; they banded together for survival. The second was hearing the news of Israel's defeat at the first battle of Ai. They knew it was at least possible for Israel to lose a battle. This was another part of the terrible effect of Achan's sin.

2. (3-6) The Gibeonites approach Joshua and Israel in another way.

**But when the inhabitants of Gibeon heard what Joshua had done to Jericho and Ai, they worked craftily, and went and pretended to be ambassadors. And they took old sacks on their donkeys, old wineskins torn and mended, old and patched sandals on their feet, and old garments on themselves; and all the bread of their provision was dry** *and* **moldy. And they went to Joshua, to the camp at Gilgal, and said to**

him and to the men of Israel, "We have come from a far country; now therefore, make a covenant with us."

a. **When the inhabitants of Gibeon heard**: The Gibeonites **heard** what Yahweh, the covenant God of Israel, had done through Joshua and Israel, just as all the Canaanites had heard (9:1-2). The other Canaanites gathered for war, but the Gibeonites used a different strategy.

i. "The rest of the Canaanites had heard as much, but made not so good a use of it. Some hear and fear; others hear and are hardened." (Trapp)

b. **They worked craftily, and went and pretended to be ambassadors**: The Gibeonites did not try open warfare against the armies of Israel. They hoped to deceive Israel into making a peace treaty with them, though Israel was forbidden to make peace with any of the tribes of Canaan (Exodus 23:31-33).

i. "The Gibeonites came from the region north of Jerusalem, the Palestinian town of el-Jib. The identification seems assured, based on later Israelite wine-jar handles found there with the name Gibeon stamped on them." (Hess)

c. **They worked craftily**: The Gibeonites carefully planned their trick. They were clever (working **craftily**), they misrepresented themselves (**pretended**), and they even gave false evidence as part of their deception (**old sacks…old wineskins…old and patched sandals…dry and moldy bread**).

i. This is an example of the principle that old things (or things that appear old) are not inherently better or worthy of trust. Appeals to age without the support of truth are unreliable.

d. **From a far country**: Beyond their deceptive appearance, the Gibeonites simply *lied*. They claimed to have **come from a far country** when they had not. All their other tricks were in support of this lie.

## B. How Joshua and the leaders of Israel were deceived.

1. (7-13) The Gibeonites explain their story to Joshua and the leaders of Israel.

**Then the men of Israel said to the Hivites, "Perhaps you dwell among us; so how can we make a covenant with you?"**

**But they said to Joshua, "We *are* your servants."**

**And Joshua said to them, "Who *are* you, and where do you come from?"**

**So they said to him: "From a very far country your servants have come, because of the name of the LORD your God; for we have heard of His**

fame, and all that He did in Egypt, and all that He did to the two kings of the Amorites who *were* beyond the Jordan—to Sihon king of Heshbon, and Og king of Bashan, who was at Ashtaroth. Therefore our elders and all the inhabitants of our country spoke to us, saying, 'Take provisions with you for the journey, and go to meet them, and say to them, "We *are* your servants; now therefore, make a covenant with us."' This bread of ours we took hot *for* our provision from our houses on the day we departed to come to you. But now look, it is dry and moldy. And these wineskins which we filled *were* new, and see, they are torn; and these our garments and our sandals have become old because of the very long journey."

a. **Perhaps you dwell among us**: The **men of Israel** understood they could not make a **covenant** of peace with the people of Canaan. They understood the possibility of being deceived by those who lived **among** them. Yet, they didn't take their skepticism far enough, and they didn't seek the LORD about the matter.

i. **We are your servants**: "When the Gibeonites said, 'We are your servants,' they were offering to become Israel's vassals. In return they expected Israel, the stronger party, to protect them from their enemies (cf. 10:6)." (Madvig)

b. **From a very far country your servants have come**: Plainly, the Gibeonites lied to Israel. But despite their lies, they had a proper admiration and honor for the God of Israel. They had **heard of His fame**, and they knew they would be conquered just as Jericho and Ai were. In some ways, their deception was a kind of tribute to Israel and to Israel's God.

2. (14-15) Joshua and the leaders of Israel accept the deception of the Gibeonites.

Then the men of Israel took some of their provisions; but they did not ask counsel of the LORD. So Joshua made peace with them, and made a covenant with them to let them live; and the rulers of the congregation swore to them.

a. **The men of Israel took some of their provisions**: They looked at the torn wineskins and moldy bread and were convinced. The Gibeonites were good liars, but the men of Israel were too easily convinced and didn't think this through. They trusted their senses instead of the LORD. "Look at this bread. Feel and taste how stale it is. Surely, they must have come a long way." They walked by sight, not by faith. They didn't consider that there are many possible explanations for stale bread.

b. **They did not ask counsel of the LORD**: The Gibeonite deception was clever and therefore powerful. But the real problem was that Joshua and the leaders of Israel never sought the Lord. God's people will often find trouble when they fail to **ask counsel of the Lord**, who has revealed His wisdom in His word.

i. The great error of Joshua and Israel with the Gibeonites was that they relied only on what they could see, hear, and touch from the Gibeonites. The material evidence said, "they come from a long distance." Convinced by the material, they didn't seek God. Relying only on the material and neglecting the spiritual led Israel to deception.

ii. "The mistake on Israel's and Joshua's part was not that they were deceived per se, but that they did not ask for the Lord's counsel. This is certainly a warning to all who read this passage: God is there to be consulted, and we ignore him at our peril." (Howard)

iii. Meyer warned about how believers today are often deceived: "So the children of God are imposed upon still! Women get married to unconverted husbands, supposing all the while that they are converted. Ministers of churches admit ravening wolves into their midst, deceived by the device of the sheepskin. Young converts get seduced from the simplicity and purity of the faith by lying spirits, that seem as lovely as God's angels. This is due to their relying on their own judgment, and not asking counsel of God. We must try the spirits, whether they be of God, for many false spirits are gone out into the world."

c. **So Joshua made peace with them**: Because they believed that the Gibeonites were from a distant land, they made the treaty with them. God permitted Israel to make treaties with distant nations, but not with the Canaanites.

### C. The deception of the Gibeonites uncovered and dealt with.

1. (16-20) Joshua and the leaders of Israel discover they have been deceived, yet they abide by their sworn oath to the Gibeonites.

**And it happened at the end of three days, after they had made a covenant with them, that they heard that they *were* their neighbors who dwelt near them. Then the children of Israel journeyed and came to their cities on the third day. Now their cities *were* Gibeon, Chephirah, Beeroth, and Kirjath Jearim. But the children of Israel did not attack them, because the rulers of the congregation had sworn to them by the Lord God of Israel. And all the congregation complained against the rulers.**

**Then all the rulers said to all the congregation, "We have sworn to them by the Lord God of Israel; now therefore, we may not touch them. This**

we will do to them: We will let them live, lest wrath be upon us because of the oath which we swore to them."

a. **The children of Israel journeyed and came to their cities on the third day**: This was the proper test of the Gibeonite claims, not merely looking at their bread and sandals. This test came too late, and the Israelites discovered the deception of the Gibeonites.

> i. "Some of the cities mentioned here were afterwards in great repute among the Israelites; and God chose to make one of them, *Kirjath-jearim,* the residence of the ark of the covenant for *twenty years,* in the reigns of *Saul* and *David.*" (Clarke)

b. **All the congregation complained against the rulers**: Even though they **complained** against them, the rulers still knew they had to do what was right and honorable before God: keep their **oath**, even if it was a bad oath.

> i. The rulers of Israel were wise in not allowing a second sin (wiping out the Gibeonites) to follow their previous sin (making the oath without seeking the LORD). This was especially admirable considering the public pressure to do otherwise.

> ii. "Possibly 'the whole assembly grumbled' because they were resentful of the plunder that had been denied them. On the other hand, they may have been fearful of another judgment like that at Ai, because they had failed to keep God's command." (Madvig)

c. **Then all the rulers said to all the congregation, "We have sworn to them by the LORD God of Israel; now therefore, we may not touch them"**: The leaders of Israel would not go back on their oath, even though it caused difficulty to keep it. Keeping one's promises is a mark of godliness: *But he honors those who fear the LORD; he who swears to his own hurt and does not change.* (Psalm 15:4)

> i. Because the oath was made in the name of the Lord, Israel was obliged to keep it. Breaking their promise would be a sin against God more than a sin against the Gibeonites.

d. **Because of the oath which we swore to them**: Later, King Saul broke this promise to the Gibeonites and his sin brought famine upon Israel in the days of David (2 Samuel 21:1-9).

2. (21-27) A glorious punishment for the Gibeonites: Joshua makes them servants to the LORD.

**And the rulers said to them, "Let them live, but let them be woodcutters and water carriers for all the congregation, as the rulers had promised them."**

Then Joshua called for them, and he spoke to them, saying, "Why have you deceived us, saying, 'We *are* very far from you,' when you dwell near us? Now therefore, you *are* cursed, and none of you shall be freed from being slaves; woodcutters and water carriers for the house of my God."

So they answered Joshua and said, "Because your servants were clearly told that the LORD your God commanded His servant Moses to give you all the land, and to destroy all the inhabitants of the land from before you; therefore we were very much afraid for our lives because of you, and have done this thing. And now, here we are, in your hands; do with us as it seems good and right to do to us." So he did to them, and delivered them out of the hand of the children of Israel, so that they did not kill them. And that day Joshua made them woodcutters and water carriers for the congregation and for the altar of the LORD, in the place which He would choose, even to this day.

a. **Let them live, but let them be woodcutters and water carriers for all the congregation**: Joshua could not kill the Gibeonites, but he could control them by making them perpetual workmen for the service of the tabernacle. They would serve in lowly ways such as cutting wood for the sacrificial fires of the tabernacle and carrying water used in its service.

i. Deuteronomy 20:10-11 gives the provision that when Israel fought against a city, they could offer peace, and if it was accepted, the people of the city would be placed under servitude. This was the result of Israel's dealings with the deceptive Gibeonites.

ii. "All these circumstances laid together, prove that the command to destroy the Canaanites was not so *absolute* as is generally supposed: and should be understood as rather referring to the destruction of the *political existence* of the Canaanitish *nations,* than to the destruction of their *lives.*" (Clarke)

b. **Your servants were clearly told that the LORD your God commanded His servant Moses to give you all the land**: The Gibeonites knew what all the Canaanite tribes understood. They knew that the God of Israel sent Israel to take the land from the Canaanites as judgment against them. The Canaanites who willingly remained in the land, knowing the judgment of God was coming, would receive that coming judgment. They could have fled and spared their lives.

c. **So they answered Joshua and said**: Significantly, there seemed to be no complaint from the Gibeonites. They simply said, **here we are, in your hands; do with us as it seems good and right to do to us**. They were happy with being brought into Israel, and being made servants of the LORD, even if it was in lowly service.

i. In this, the Gibeonites expressed the same heart that the Psalmist later did in Psalm 84:10: *For a day in Your courts is better than a thousand. I would rather be a doorkeeper in the house of my God than dwell in the tents of wickedness.*

ii. The Gibeonites did this out of respect and honor to the God of Israel, not out of weakness. It was said of Gibeon that *all its men were mighty* (Joshua 10:2).

iii. "It is interesting to observe that in subsequent history the binding nature of this treaty was recognized and the Gibeonites do not appear anywhere to have made any attempt to corrupt the children of Israel with idolatry." (Morgan)

iv. The Gibeonites found salvation in the God of Israel as Rahab did in Joshua 2. Both Rahab and the Gibeonites:

- Were sinners.
- Heard about the LORD God of Israel.
- Heard about Yahweh's great works.
- Heard that God was with Israel, leading them to great victories.
- Heard that the judgment of Yahweh was coming against the Canaanites.
- Were afraid of the coming judgment of Yahweh.
- Affirmed their faith in the God of Israel.
- Received a promise of protection among God's people.
- Trusted in their alliance with the people of God.
- Left their people to ally themselves with the people of God.
- Found their place among the people of God.
- Gained a privileged standing among the people of God.

v. The story of the Gibeonites after Joshua 9 shows what God can do with sinners who come to Him in humility and honor, seeking mercy.

- The Gibeonites became servants at the tabernacle, just as Joshua had commanded.
- Gibeon became a priestly city. The ark of the covenant stayed at Gibeon often in the days of David and Solomon (1 Chronicles 16:39-40 and 21:29).

- At least one of David's mighty men was a Gibeonite (1 Chronicles 12:4).

- God appeared and spoke to Solomon at Gibeon (1 Kings 3:4-5).

- Gibeonites were among those who rebuilt the walls of Jerusalem with Nehemiah (Nehemiah 3:7 and 7:25).

- Prophets such as Hananiah the son of Azur came from Gibeon (Jeremiah 28:1).

# Joshua 10 – The LORD Fights for Israel, the Southern Kings Conquered

## A. A miraculous victory for Israel.

1. (1-2) Adoni-Zedek and his fear of Israel.

**Now it came to pass when Adoni-Zedek king of Jerusalem heard how Joshua had taken Ai and had utterly destroyed it—as he had done to Jericho and its king, so he had done to Ai and its king—and how the inhabitants of Gibeon had made peace with Israel and were among them, that they feared greatly, because Gibeon *was* a great city, like one of the royal cities, and because it *was* greater than Ai, and all its men *were* mighty.**

a. **Adoni-Zedek king of Jerusalem heard how Joshua had taken Ai**: The king of Jerusalem (**Adoni-Zedek**) was rightly alarmed when he heard of the conquests of Jericho and Ai. He understood that the armies of Israel, supported by their God, would soon come against all the cities of Canaan.

i. Especially troubling was the news that they **had utterly destroyed** both Jericho and Ai – that is, that they had brought the unique judgment of God against the Canaanites. An Israelite army fighting for the glory of God, and as a unique instrument of God's judgment, rightly made them afraid.

ii. Adoni-Zedek also had reason to be concerned from a strategic perspective. The previous victories across the middle of Canaan effectively separated Canaan between north and south. "Israel controlled the Benjaminite plateau, the crossroads between the hill country and the Judean wilderness. It provided access to the coastal plain and lowlands to the west via the Beth Horon pass." (Hess)

iii. "At one time the brilliant British field marshal Edmund H. Allenby must have studied this book too, for Joshua's strategy was the one he adopted in his successful liberation of Palestine in World War I.

Palestine is a hilly country, and the major passage through it is a connecting road that runs from south to north through the highest portions of the land. Joshua's strategy (and Allenby's) was to drive westward from the Jordan Valley to that high road, thus dividing the country. Then, when the enemy forces were divided, they would first destroy the opposition to the south and then the opposition to the north. This is the outline of the campaign described in Joshua 6–11." (Boice)

b. **And how the inhabitants of Gibeon had made peace with Israel**: In addition, the surrender and subordination of the Gibeonites caused Adoni-Zedek to be afraid. Gibeon was a **great city**, and its **men were mighty** – if *they* surrendered to Israel, it was discouraging news for the Canaanites.

i. The Gibeonites did not submit to Israel from a position of weakness; indeed, **all its men were mighty**. In fact, it was because of their respect and honor for the God of Israel that they submitted to perpetual service in His tabernacle.

c. **They feared greatly**: Fear of coming judgment did not make the Canaanites surrender. It made them organize and fight, and **Adoni-Zedek** became the leader of the southern Canaanite kings.

i. The enemies of Israel **feared greatly**; they did not retreat but launched even bolder attacks, as a wild animal might fight when it feels threatened.

2. (3-5) The southern kings of Canaan assemble for an attack on Gibeon.

**Therefore Adoni-Zedek king of Jerusalem sent to Hoham king of Hebron, Piram king of Jarmuth, Japhia king of Lachish, and Debir king of Eglon, saying, "Come up to me and help me, that we may attack Gibeon, for it has made peace with Joshua and with the children of Israel." Therefore the five kings of the Amorites, the king of Jerusalem, the king of Hebron, the king of Jarmuth, the king of Lachish, *and* the king of Eglon, gathered together and went up, they and all their armies, and camped before Gibeon and made war against it.**

a. **Adoni-Zedek king of Jerusalem sent to Hoham king of Hebron**: Acting on his fear, Adoni-Zedek began to organize the kings of southern Canaan. Since Israel occupied the area to their north, he could not get help from the kings of northern Canaan.

i. What Adoni-Zedek did was not unusual. At the same approximate time, "Jerusalem's leader wrote at least five letters to the Pharaoh regarding his town and its security. These letters, part of the collection known as the Armana letters, are longer and more literate than the contemporary missives of other Palestinian town leaders." (Hess)

b. **King of Jerusalem…king of Hebron…king of Jarmuth…king of Lachish…king of Eglon**: This again displays that the Canaanites were organized as city-states instead of one unified nation. It took the leadership of Adoni-Zedek to bring them together.

> i. Each one of these cities – Jerusalem, Jarmuth, Lachish, Eglon, and Hebron – were important cities either for their location or for the trade routes associated with them.

> ii. "Like Adoni-Zedek, the names of the four leaders can be identified with similar names from texts and peoples in and around Palestine during the same period of time that the account in Joshua purports to describe." (Hess)

c. **That we may attack Gibeon**: Though they were afraid, they were still clever. Afraid to attack Israel directly, they attacked their subjects, the Gibeonites. They hoped to make Gibeon a warning to other Canaanite tribes that might consider surrendering to the Israelites.

3. (6) The plea for help from Gibeon.

**And the men of Gibeon sent to Joshua at the camp at Gilgal, saying, "Do not forsake your servants; come up to us quickly, save us and help us, for all the kings of the Amorites who dwell in the mountains have gathered together against us."**

a. **Sent to Joshua at the camp at Gilgal**: Joshua and the armies of Israel were still at **Gilgal**. This was an important place for Israel's conquest of Canaan.

- Gilgal was the place of memorial (Joshua 4:20).
- Gilgal was the place of radical obedience (Joshua 5:2-3).
- Gilgal was the place where reproach was removed (Joshua 5:9).
- Gilgal was the place of obedience and the remembrance of salvation (Joshua 5:10).
- Gilgal was the place where the manna stopped, and they began to live from what the Promised Land provided (Joshua 5:11-12).

b. **Do not forsake your servants; come up to us quickly, save us and help us**: The Gibeonites rightly looked to the people of Israel as their helpers and protectors. They were not too proud to call for help.

i. "If Joshua had been a lesser man, he might have regarded this as a way to escape the consequences of his rash agreement to spare the Gibeonites." (Boice)

ii. Even as the Gibeonites claimed protection based on covenant, so do believers because of their participation in the new covenant. Considering their covenant with God, it is good for believers to also pray, **Do not forsake Your servants…save us and help us**.

## B. The defeat of the southern kings of Canaan.

1. (7) Joshua and the people of Israel are faithful to their vow to the Gibeonites.

**So Joshua ascended from Gilgal, he and all the people of war with him, and all the mighty men of valor.**

a. **So Joshua ascended from Gilgal**: We saw that in Joshua 9, Joshua, the leaders of Israel, and all the people of Israel knew that they had made a bad vow to the Gibeonites, yet they kept faithful to their oath.

i. This is the first example in Joshua of *counterattack*, of the enemy initiating a battle against Israel. "Here for the first time Israel does not initiate the aggression but responds to an ally's appeal." (Hess)

b. **He and all the people of war with him, and all the mighty men of valor**: Joshua not only kept the vow made to the Gibeonites, but he kept it with great energy and dedication. He sent his best men into this battle to defend Gibeon.

i. Allowing these Canaanite kings to wipe out the Gibeonites would have been a convenient way to get out of an oath that should not have been made, but Joshua and the leaders of Israel refused to do that.

ii. God's people should have the same sense of honor. Though Joshua was only bound to not kill the Gibeonites himself (Joshua 9:15), he also felt obliged to fulfill the *spirit* of the oath he made to them.

2. (8) God's command and promise to Joshua.

**And the LORD said to Joshua, "Do not fear them, for I have delivered them into your hand; not a man of them shall stand before you."**

a. **Do not fear them**: This was a *command*. Though Joshua had reason to fear because Israel faced a confederation of **five** kings, God commanded Joshua to not fear his enemies.

b. **I have delivered them into your hand; not a man of them shall stand before you**: The command was joined to a *promise*. Joshua could obey God's command to not fear because he had God's promise of victory.

i. Fear takes away the ability to fight God's battles. Even in the face of strong enemies, Joshua was commanded to not fear. For Joshua, fear was unbelief – being unwilling to believe what God had promised. The same principle is true with believers today.

3. (9) Joshua's response of faith.

**Joshua therefore came upon them suddenly, having marched all night from Gilgal.**

a. **Joshua therefore came upon them suddenly**: With the assurance of God's promise (Joshua 10:8), Joshua did not sit back to passively watch God work without his participation. He went to great effort to participate in the work and will of God.

i. "The battle of Gibeon is the last battle described in any detail in the book (the others are the encounters at Jericho and Ai) since after this the text merely summarizes the campaigns in the south (10:28–43) and in the north (11:1–23)." (Howard)

b. **Having marched all night from Gilgal**: This took initiative and hard work on Joshua's part. The march from Gilgal to Gibeon involved a climb of 3,300 feet (1,000 meters), over about 20 miles (32 kilometers). This was eight to ten hours of hard marching, all through the night.

i. God does His work, but He draws us into working with Him. Often God waits to see our initiative, our willingness to be a partner with Him before He does what only He can do.

ii. This is *not* the idea that "God helps those who help themselves." The idea is, "God wants to draw His people into partnership with Him in seeing His work done."

4. (10-11) God sends large hailstones to defeat the Canaanites.

**So the LORD routed them before Israel, killed them with a great slaughter at Gibeon, chased them along the road that goes to Beth Horon, and struck them down as far as Azekah and Makkedah. And it happened, as they fled before Israel *and* were on the descent of Beth Horon, that the LORD cast down large hailstones from heaven on them as far as Azekah, and they died. *There were* more who died from the hailstones than the children of Israel killed with the sword.**

a. **So the LORD routed them before Israel**: God's work, and the partnership of Joshua's work with the LORD, accomplished something great. The enemies of God were **routed**.

i. "It was Yahweh—and Yahweh alone—who took the decisive actions against the enemies (v. 10). Every verb in this verse is singular,

indicating that he alone *confused, struck, pursued,* and *struck* them."
(Howard)

b. **The LORD cast down large hailstones from heaven**: The **hailstones** that
killed the retreating armies of the Canaanites were obviously miraculous.
The hail itself could have been a phenomenon of nature, but its aim and
timing were evidence of the hand of God.

i. "The Canaanites, who worshiped nature deities, must have thought
that their own gods were aiding the Israelites." (Madvig)

ii. By the hand of God, the large hailstones did not kill the soldiers of
Israel. "Huge hailstones that brained the Canaanites but hurt not the
Israelites, that were at the heels of them." (Trapp)

iii. In his book *Worlds in Collision*, Immanuel Velikovsky suggested
that this rain of hailstones was a sustained meteor show, the train of a
comet. He also theorized that the passing of the comet was related to
the next amazing work of God for Israel and Joshua.

c. **There were more who died from the hailstones than the children of
Israel killed with the sword**: God's miraculous work was much greater
than Israel's work. Yet we notice that Joshua didn't passively wait for the
hail to come. He did what he could do in partnership with God, and God
did what only God could do.

5. (12-15) God extends the day to maximize Israel's victory.

**Then Joshua spoke to the LORD in the day when the LORD delivered up
the Amorites before the children of Israel, and he said in the sight of
Israel:**

**"Sun, stand still over Gibeon;
And Moon, in the Valley of Aijalon."
So the sun stood still,
And the moon stopped,
Till the people had revenge
Upon their enemies.**

*Is* **this not written in the Book of Jasher? So the sun stood still in the
midst of heaven, and did not hasten to go** *down* **for about a whole day.
And there has been no day like that, before it or after it, that the LORD
heeded the voice of a man; for the LORD fought for Israel.**

**Then Joshua returned, and all Israel with him, to the camp at Gilgal.**

a. **"Sun, stand still over Gibeon; and Moon, in the Valley of Aijalon."
So the sun stood still**: Seeing God's miraculous hand in action gave Joshua
the boldness to ask for an even more remarkable miracle – to keep the day

going, to keep the sun from setting so that Israel had time to accomplish a complete victory before darkness fell.

i. This was a bold request but based on the promise God made in Joshua 10:8: *I have delivered them into your hand; not a man of them shall stand before you.* Joshua had reason from God's revealed word to ask for this.

ii. The sun and the moon had long stood as silent witnesses to the sin, wickedness, and demonic religion of these Canaanites. Now, under the command of God, they helped Joshua to complete this victory over the Canaanites.

iii. **He said in the sight of Israel**: "That is, he was open about his expectations. He was not afraid of being humiliated by failure, because he wanted only what God had told him would happen. He laid his belief on the line. If we do as Joshua did, we will find that God honors it." (Boice)

b. **So the sun stood still in the midst of heaven, and did not hasten to go down for about a whole day. And there has been no day like that, before it or after it**: In a completely unique miracle, God answered Joshua's bold prayer and **the LORD fought for Israel** in a unique way during Israel's conquest of Canaan.

i. Some wonder *how* the length of the day was extended. It could have been a slowing of the earth's rotation; it could have been a tilting of the earth's axis; it could have been a miracle of reflection of light; it could have been simply the presence of God manifested in light.

ii. However the miracle happened, the result was clear. The sun seemed to stay still in the sky, and Israel was able to complete the victory.

iii. In his book *Worlds in Collision*, Immanuel Velikovsky suggested that the long day was caused by the near pass of a comet, that was powerful enough to tilt the axis of the earth. "The tilting of the axis could produce the visual effect of a retrogressing or arrested sun; a greater tilting, a multiple day or night" [page 385]. Velikovsky also noted that there are records among the ancient Americans that speak of an extraordinarily long *night* in the same approximate time.

iv. "It is claimed that a Professor Pickering of the Harvard Observatory traced this missing day back to Joshua's time, and that the ten "degrees" in Hezekiah's time were verified by astronomers from Greenwich and Yale. However, such claims have not been verified; they only exist in popular-level works on the Bible and science." (Howard)

v. Some criticize this account, saying that obviously, since the sun *is* still, and the earth rotates around the sun, Joshua was wrong when he wrote, **the sun stood still**. This kind of criticism doesn't account for our normal way of speaking. We use the terms *sunrise* and *sunset* without a second thought. In addition, more modern astronomy tells us that the sun *is* in motion; perhaps in some way the sun did literally stand still.

vi. Hundreds of years later, God used the prophet Isaiah to bring a heavy word of coming judgment to His people. In that word, God remembered Gibeon, where He had won a great victory for Israel in Joshua's day (Isaiah 28:20-22). Isaiah warned the people that this miraculous strength of God would be turned *against* His people if they did not repent. As Isaiah explained, this use of God's strength against His people is surely *His awesome work*, or as the King James Version puts it, *His strange work*.

c. **Till the people had revenge upon their enemies**: Joshua did not ask God to do the fighting for him, even though God did do some of that (Joshua 10:11). Joshua simply asked that God miraculously give him the *opportunity* to fight for Him. Joshua prayed for God's intervention, but he did not neglect his part of the battle. He asked God to work with and for Israel, not instead of Israel.

i. Like Joshua, we often wish that time would stand still. We would do well to imitate Joshua's *reasons* for asking for an extended time. Joshua wanted time to stand still so that:

- God would be glorified.
- God would be obeyed.
- God's work would be continued without hindrance.
- God's people would triumph.

d. **The Book of Jasher**: The phrasing of this reference to the **Book of Jasher** does not require any quotation from the book, merely that these events are also described in that writing.

i. "Rather, he was stating, in effect, 'If you don't believe it, go read about it in the *Book of Jashar.* Even that book has a record of this event.'" (Howard)

6. (16-21) The completion of the battle.

**But these five kings had fled and hidden themselves in a cave at Makkedah. And it was told Joshua, saying, "The five kings have been found hidden in the cave at Makkedah."**

So Joshua said, "Roll large stones against the mouth of the cave, and set men by it to guard them. And do not stay *there* yourselves, *but* pursue your enemies, and attack their rear *guard.* Do not allow them to enter their cities, for the LORD your God has delivered them into your hand." Then it happened, while Joshua and the children of Israel made an end of slaying them with a very great slaughter, till they had finished, that those who escaped entered fortified cities. And all the people returned to the camp, to Joshua at Makkedah, in peace. No one moved his tongue against any of the children of Israel.

a. **Roll large stones against the mouth of the cave.... pursue your enemies, and attack their rear guard**: Joshua would not allow anything – even the personal capture of the kings – to keep him from completing Israel's victory. The kings could be imprisoned and dealt with later.

b. **Made an end of slaying them with a very great slaughter**: This repeats a significant theme throughout the book of Joshua. Israel was to carry out a unique war of judgment against the Canaanites.

c. **No one moved his tongue against any of the children of Israel**: The people of Canaan knew – beyond any doubt – that God was with Joshua and the nation of Israel.

i. "Things had come to such a peaceful, satisfying conclusion that 'no one uttered a word....' The expression is literally 'no one sharpened his tongue,' and, in this context, it refers to opposition against Israel." (Howard)

ii. By analogy and application, the church – just like Israel – should be feared in the sense that it should be a place where people know God will conquer them. They should have the idea "If I keep coming here, God is going to conquer me. I'll have to submit my life to Him." Too many churches present God as a harmless deity who demands no surrender from His people.

7. (22-27) The execution of the Canaanite kings.

Then Joshua said, "Open the mouth of the cave, and bring out those five kings to me from the cave." And they did so, and brought out those five kings to him from the cave: the king of Jerusalem, the king of Hebron, the king of Jarmuth, the king of Lachish, *and* the king of Eglon. So it was, when they brought out those kings to Joshua, that Joshua called for all the men of Israel, and said to the captains of the men of war who went with him, "Come near, put your feet on the necks of these kings." And they drew near and put their feet on their necks. Then Joshua said to them, "Do not be afraid, nor be dismayed; be strong and of good courage, for thus the L ORD will do to all your enemies against whom you fight." And afterward Joshua struck them and killed them, and hanged them on five trees; and they were hanging on the trees until evening. So it was at the time of the going down of the sun *that* Joshua commanded, and they took them down from the trees, cast them into the cave where they had been hidden, and laid large stones against the cave's mouth, *which remain* until this very day.

a. **Open the mouth of the cave, and bring out those five kings**: Joshua *delayed* dealing with the kings so he could finish the battle. Yet in time, he dealt with them. Joshua did not sin in the way Saul later would in failing to carry out God's judgment against Agag (1 Samuel 15).

i. The **king of Jerusalem**, Adoni-Zedek, was among these five kings. This would be the end of his reign and his life. Taken together, he is a fascinating picture or type.

- His name means, "Lord of Righteousness."
- He was the pagan king of Jerusalem.
- He led a confederation of kings.
- He fought against Joshua.
- He resisted God's occupation of the land.
- He was kept with other kings in a cave.

ii. The Bible tells us of a coming false messiah (Revelation 13:3), who will rule over Jerusalem (2 Thessalonians 2:3-4), who will lead a confederation of kings (Revelation 17:12-13), fighting against Yeshua (Revelation 17:14), resisting His occupation of the land (Revelation 19:19), and hiding in caves (Revelation 6:15-17). All in all, Adoni-Zedek is a fascinating picture of the coming Antichrist.

iii. **Bring out those five kings**: "So shall Christ one day say of all, whether kings or caitiffs [cowards], lords or losels [worthless persons], that will not have him to reign over them. Those that will not now obey that sweet voice, 'Come unto me, all ye that are weary and heavy laden,' shall then have no other voice to obey but 'Go, ye cursed.'" (Trapp)

b. **Come near, put your feet on the necks of these kings**: This was dramatic and undeniably brutal. Joshua, directed by God, wanted to give these **captains of the men of war** courage and the sense of victory in obedience to God. This said, "God has allowed you to conquer kings."

i. The idea of partnership with God in the pursuit of victory is again repeated in Joshua 10:25. God promised victory over all **your enemies against whom you fight**.

c. **And afterward Joshua struck them and killed them, and hanged them on five trees**: By this dramatic execution of the kings, Joshua made it clear that there could be absolutely no accommodation with the Canaanites. By performing the executions himself, he accepted a great risk. Often rulers will spare other rulers, thinking they might be on the losing side in the future. In doing this, Joshua knew that if Israel's armies were ever defeated, he would be killed.

i. **Cast them into the cave where they had been hidden**: "In an ironic twist, the kings' bodies were thrown into the cave where they had been hiding earlier: the place they had thought would be their refuge ended up as their tomb." (Howard)

ii. After this pattern, believers can allow no place in their lives to their spiritual enemies. All the ground belongs to Jesus and must be taken for Him.

iii. "Hanging *alive* seems a barbarous custom: among the Hebrews, criminals were first deprived of life; this was the debt required by *justice*: then they were hanged up, perhaps generally by the *hands*, not by the *neck*; this was done by way of *example*, to deter others from committing the crimes for which those had suffered." (Clarke)

iv. This began the third stage of Israel's conquest of Canaan.

- Stage One: Cross the Jordan, push from Jericho westward to Ai to divide Canaan between north and south.
- Stage Two: Conquer the south.
- Stage Three: Conquer the north.

## C. Conquest of the South completed.

*"The annalistic form corresponds as closely as any Ancient Near Eastern conquest account can to the recitation of what we know of as history." (Hess)*

1. (28) The fall of the Canaanite city of Makkedah.

**On that day Joshua took Makkedah, and struck it and its king with the edge of the sword. He utterly destroyed them—all the people who *were* in it. He let none remain. He also did to the king of Makkedah as he had done to the king of Jericho.**

2. (29-30) The fall of the Canaanite city of Libnah.

**Then Joshua passed from Makkedah, and all Israel with him, to Libnah; and they fought against Libnah. And the LORD also delivered it and its king into the hand of Israel; he struck it and all the people who *were* in it with the edge of the sword. He let none remain in it, but did to its king as he had done to the king of Jericho.**

3. (31-32) The fall of the Canaanite city of Lachish.

**Then Joshua passed from Libnah, and all Israel with him, to Lachish; and they encamped against it and fought against it. And the LORD delivered Lachish into the hand of Israel, who took it on the second day, and struck it and all the people who *were* in it with the edge of the sword, according to all that he had done to Libnah.**

4. (33) The fall of the Canaanite city of Gezer.

**Then Horam king of Gezer came up to help Lachish; and Joshua struck him and his people, until he left him none remaining.**

5. (34-35) The fall of the Canaanite city of Eglon.

**From Lachish Joshua passed to Eglon, and all Israel with him; and they encamped against it and fought against it. They took it on that day and struck it with the edge of the sword; all the people who *were* in it he utterly destroyed that day, according to all that he had done to Lachish.**

6. (36-37) The fall of the Canaanite city of Hebron.

**So Joshua went up from Eglon, and all Israel with him, to Hebron; and they fought against it. And they took it and struck it with the edge of the sword—its king, all its cities, and all the people who *were* in it; he left none remaining, according to all that he had done to Eglon, but utterly destroyed it and all the people who *were* in it.**

7. (38-39) The fall of the Canaanite city of Debir.

**Then Joshua returned, and all Israel with him, to Debir; and they fought against it. And he took it and its king and all its cities; they struck them with the edge of the sword and utterly destroyed all the people who *were* in it. He left none remaining; as he had done to Hebron, so he did to Debir and its king, as he had done also to Libnah and its king.**

8. (40-43) Summary of the conquest of the southern Canaanite kingdoms.

**So Joshua conquered all the land: the mountain country and the South and the lowland and the wilderness slopes, and all their kings; he left none remaining, but utterly destroyed all that breathed, as the LORD God of Israel had commanded. And Joshua conquered them from**

**Kadesh Barnea as far as Gaza, and all the country of Goshen, even as far as Gibeon. All these kings and their land Joshua took at one time, because the Lord God of Israel fought for Israel. Then Joshua returned, and all Israel with him, to the camp at Gilgal.**

a. **So Joshua conquered all the land**: In a period of weeks (perhaps months) these six cities were defeated, without a single lost battle for Israel. Each battle was a test. None of them were easy, but under the leadership of Joshua, they all were victorious.

> i. **Conquered all the land**: "Apparently, the campaign against the southern cities did not take much time, as Joshua quickly moved to take advantage of his success at Gibeon." (Boice)

> ii. "Swiftly and surely the divine judgment was falling on the corrupt peoples, and the possibility of a new era in the history of humanity was being created by the coming of the chosen people into possession of the land." (Morgan)

> iii. *This was a lot of war.* "It is eternally true that the land of full blessing is a land of intensive warfare." (Redpath)

> iv. God's desire is that believers should live out the same life of victory. *But we all...are being transformed into the same image from glory to glory, just as by the Spirit of the Lord.* (2 Corinthians 3:18)

> v. "It is significant that Jerusalem is not included in the listing of the cities Joshua is said to have taken, although the king of Jerusalem, Adoni-Zedek, was among those killed. Jerusalem escaped being conquered by the Israelites (Joshua 15:63) and was not taken until the time of David, hundreds of years later (2 Samuel 5:6–7)." (Boice)

b. **The Lord God of Israel fought for Israel**: This was obviously the most important factor. This illustrates the key aspect in the battle against spiritual enemies for believers. They can only win as they see the Lord fighting on their behalf. He provides the victory, and they walk in it.

> i. God's people come to realize that the victory was won at the cross, and now they need to live in consideration of that victory. Colossians 2:15 speaks to this idea: *Having disarmed principalities and powers, He made a public spectacle of them, triumphing over them in it* [the cross]. It is in this sense that God's people are *more than conquerors through Him who loved us.* (Romans 8:37)

> ii. It has been rightly noted, "To be disappointed in yourself is to have trusted in yourself." Such failure reveals that the battle was fought with one's own resources, instead of simple trust in Jesus Christ and His victory.

c. **Then Joshua returned, and all Israel with him, to the camp at Gilgal**: Israel's victories always came from Gilgal. This was the place of surrendered faith, commitment, and fellowship with God.

i. **The mountain country and the South and the lowland and the wilderness slopes**: "Here is an overview of a region that Joshua subdued in Canaan. It included four areas: (1) the hill country and (2) the western foothills, which had been mentioned earlier (cf. 9:1), but it also encompassed (3) the Negev and (4) the mountain slopes." (Howard)

# Joshua 11 – The Northern Canaanite Armies Defeated

## A. The defeat of the northern kings.

### 1. (1-5) The northern kings of Canaan gather against Israel.

**And it came to pass, when Jabin king of Hazor heard *these things*, that he sent to Jobab king of Madon, to the king of Shimron, to the king of Achshaph, and to the kings who *were* from the north, in the mountains, in the plain south of Chinneroth, in the lowland, and in the heights of Dor on the west, to the Canaanites in the east and in the west, the Amorite, the Hittite, the Perizzite, the Jebusite in the mountains, and the Hivite below Hermon in the land of Mizpah. So they went out, they and all their armies with them, *as* many people *as* the sand that *is* on the seashore in multitude, with very many horses and chariots. And when all these kings had met together, they came and camped together at the waters of Merom to fight against Israel.**

a. **And it came to pass, when Jabin king of Hazor heard these things**: After hearing of Israel's total conquest of the south, the northern kings came together to defeat Israel. The huge army reflects an attitude that they believed they must stop Israel at that time or be conquered.

i. All this was prompted by what the northern kings **heard** regarding Israel's success and victory. Israel's success awakened more opposition. The same principle may be the experience of believers today, who find greater spiritual opposition as they dedicate themselves to the LORD and His service.

ii. **Hazor** was north of the Sea of Galilee. Hazor's "archaeological site is not disputed: its remains can be found on a huge mound, more than two hundred acres in area, about eight miles north of the Sea of Galilee. Biblical and extrabiblical evidence alike point to its having been a large and strategic city." (Howard)

110

iii. "'Jabin' appears to have been a dynastic name for kings in Hazor—not a personal name—just as 'Pharaoh' was for kings in Egypt and 'Ben-Hadad' was in Syria." (Howard)

iv. "'Mizpah' means 'watchtower'; consequently there are a number of cities with that name. This one was at the foot of Mount Hermon." (Madvig)

v. "The coalition described in vv. 1–3 is not as neat and tidy as the five-king group in chap. 10. It was a broader coalition…a force much more threatening to the Israelites, gathered as it was from such a widely scattered area." (Howard)

b. **They went out, they and all their armies with them**: Two things indicate that Israel now faced new challenges. First, the size of the enemy army: **as many people as the sand that is on the seashore in multitude**. Second, the technological superiority of the Canaanites: **with very many horses and chariots**.

i. **Horses and chariots**: "This expression occurs in eight other places in the Hebrew text. It describes the most fearful fighting machinery available." (Hess)

ii. The challenges brought to Israel seemed to increase at each step, from Jericho, to Ai, to the battle with the southern kings and now to this battle.

iii. This is the experience of many believers, finding that the challenges facing them in the Christian life increase at each step. God uses each previous victory as a springboard for what His people will face in the future.

2. (6) God's encouragement to Joshua.

**But the Lord said to Joshua, "Do not be afraid because of them, for tomorrow about this time I will deliver all of them slain before Israel. You shall hamstring their horses and burn their chariots with fire."**

a. **Tomorrow about this time I will deliver all of them slain before Israel**: This attack was a new and greater challenge than before. Joshua needed a fresh confirmation of God's promise for Israel, and the Lord was faithful to provide it.

b. **Do not be afraid because of them**: This means that fear was an issue for Joshua and the people of Israel. God has a reason for everything He does, and He would not have assured them **do not be afraid** unless there was a reason for that specific encouragement.

i. "The Bible does not say that Joshua was made fearful by the size and nature of the opposing forces, but it is possible that he was, since God intervened again to promise him success." (Boice)

3. (7-9) Joshua attacks the northern armies, and they are defeated.

**So Joshua and all the people of war with him came against them suddenly by the waters of Merom, and they attacked them. And the LORD delivered them into the hand of Israel, who defeated them and chased them to Greater Sidon, to the Brook Misrephoth, and to the Valley of Mizpah eastward; they attacked them until they left none of them remaining. So Joshua did to them as the LORD had told him: he hamstrung their horses and burned their chariots with fire.**

a. **So Joshua and all the people of war with him came against them suddenly**: Joshua fought with boldness and strategy; he surprised the Canaanite armies with an unexpected ambush.

i. "Joshua, being apprised of this grand confederation, lost no time, but marched to meet them; and before they could have supposed him at hand, fell suddenly upon them, and put them to the rout." (Clarke)

ii. "The 'whole army' came with Joshua; this phrase is literally 'all the people of war,' an expression found only in Joshua, which apparently emphasizes the unity of the nation." (Howard)

b. **The LORD delivered them into the hand of Israel**: Considering the size of the opposing armies (Joshua 11:4, 11:7), the technology used by the Canaanites (Joshua 11:4), and the encouragement needed by Joshua (Joshua 11:6), this was perhaps the largest and most consequential battle Israel fought in the conquest of Canaan. Yet, God sent no obvious miraculous intervention. There were no falling walls or giant hailstones for Israel. God equipped and empowered them in more "normal," familiar ways and Israel won the battle.

i. "This battle was probably the most violent and bloody of the entire conquest, although very few details are given." (Boice)

ii. **Chased them to Greater Sidon**: By some accounts, the Canaanites who came to this port city of Sidon made their way to North Africa. "It is said they founded *Tingris* or *Tangier,* where, according to Procopius [AD 500-565], they erected two white pillars with an inscription in the Phoenician language, of which this is the translation: WE ARE THE PERSONS WHO HAVE FLED FROM THE FACE OF JOSHUA THE PLUNDERER, THE SON OF NAVE or *Nun.*" (Clarke)

c. **So Joshua did to them as the LORD had told him**: Joshua fought with obedience, doing exactly what the LORD told him to do, even destroying the Canaanite weapons (the **horses** and the **chariots**) instead of keeping them for his own army.

i. "Disabling the horses and burning the chariots (v.9) showed disdain for modern weaponry; Israel's confidence was to be in God alone (cf. Psalm 20:7)." (Madvig)

ii. Here is a lesson in the matter of "taking the devil's tools." Many Christians do not hesitate to use the "horses and chariots" of their spiritual enemy. Perhaps they should believe that God wants them to fight the battle on a different level – a level of complete trust in Him.

c. **They attacked them until they left none of them remaining**: Joshua fought with passion and commitment; he did not ease up until he had accomplished as much as possible.

4. (10-15) The defeat of Hazor, the head of the northern Canaanite kingdoms.

**Joshua turned back at that time and took Hazor, and struck its king with the sword; for Hazor was formerly the head of all those kingdoms. And they struck all the people who *were* in it with the edge of the sword, utterly destroying *them*. There was none left breathing. Then he burned Hazor with fire.**

**So all the cities of those kings, and all their kings, Joshua took and struck with the edge of the sword. He utterly destroyed them, as Moses the servant of the Lord had commanded. But *as for* the cities that stood on their mounds, Israel burned none of them, except Hazor only, *which* Joshua burned. And all the spoil of these cities and the livestock, the children of Israel took as booty for themselves; but they struck every man with the edge of the sword until they had destroyed them, and they left none breathing. As the Lord had commanded Moses his servant, so Moses commanded Joshua, and so Joshua did. He left nothing undone of all that the Lord had commanded Moses.**

a. **They struck all the people who were in it with the edge of the sword, utterly destroying them**: The staggering completeness of the destruction (especially in human terms) shows us the *completeness* of God's judgment, of Israel's obedience, and of the depravity of the Canaanites.

i. **Hazor was formerly the head of all those kingdoms**: "The description of Hazor as *the head of all these kingdoms* is attested by its size and also by its prominence in second-millennium BC written records…. The archaeological evidence of a well-fortified city with international contacts confirms its leading status during the second millennium." (Hess)

b. **There was none left breathing**: The Canaanites knew the judgment of God was coming against them and were afraid of it (Joshua 2:9-11, 9:24-25). They could have acted in faith like Rahab, surrendered like the Gibeonites, or left the area. Many did not, and those who remained fell under the judgment of God.

i. In this, God wanted a comprehensive judgment to be carried out not against guilty individuals, but against a guilty society or community.

- God did this with Sodom and Gomorrah in Genesis 19.
- God did this with Midian in Numbers 31.
- God did this with the northern kingdom of Israel in 2 Kings 17.
- God did this with the southern kingdom of Judah in 2 Kings 25.
- God did this with the flood in Genesis 7.

ii. In each of these cases, children and others who were not "individually" responsible for the corruption, rebellion, or degradation of a nation, culture, community, or society perished. It doesn't necessarily mean that their soul went to hell, but their life on this earth was taken. All this is rooted in understanding God's jurisdiction as judge; He is *the Judge of all the earth* (Genesis 18:25).

iii. As such, God has the right to judge not only individuals but also communities of all different sizes. Such judgments go beyond punishing individuals for their personal guilt; judgment comes upon a society as a whole, including those who may not be personally and individually guilty (such as children). Sometimes God sends these judgments directly (as in the Genesis flood or with Sodom and Gomorrah), and sometimes God sends nations as instruments of His judgment (as with the Assyrians against the northern kingdom of Israel and the Babylonians against the southern kingdom of Judah). In the conquest of Canaan, God uniquely used His people (Israel) as that instrument of judgment.

iv. This harsh judgment often makes people uncomfortable but is rooted in both God's fundamental right to judge (Psalm 9:8, 50:6), and in His merciful granting of much time for people to repent (Genesis 15:16). We can rest in the knowledge that God is a righteous judge (Genesis 18:25, Psalm 7:11).

c. **He burned Hazor with fire**: Hazor was one of only three cities burned by the Israelites in the conquest of Canaan, joining Jericho (Joshua 6:24) and Ai (Joshua 8:19, 28). The other Canaanite cities were taken and inhabited by the Israelites.

i. "Archaeological excavations indicate that Hazor was destroyed sometime in the late fourteenth century B.C. and was not rebuilt until the time of Solomon (cf. 1 Kings 9:15)." (Madvig)

**B. Israel's secure place in Canaan.**

1. (16-20) Complete victory over Canaan, over north and south.

**Thus Joshua took all this land: the mountain country, all the South, all the land of Goshen, the lowland, and the Jordan plain—the mountains of Israel and its lowlands, from Mount Halak and the ascent to Seir, even as far as Baal Gad in the Valley of Lebanon below Mount Hermon. He captured all their kings, and struck them down and killed them. Joshua made war a long time with all those kings. There was not a city that made peace with the children of Israel, except the Hivites, the inhabitants of Gibeon. All *the others* they took in battle. For it was of the LORD to harden their hearts, that they should come against Israel in battle, that He might utterly destroy them, *and* that they might receive no mercy, but that He might destroy them, as the LORD had commanded Moses.**

a. **Thus Joshua took all this land**: This was a general description of the land of Canaan.

- The **mountain country** was part of the central highlands running north to south.
- The **South** was the southern desert area.
- **Goshen** was the region between the hill country and the south.
- The **lowland** ran from north to south between the central highlands and the coastal plain.
- The **Jordan plain** is the valley containing the Jordan River and the Dead Sea, continuing to the Gulf of Aqabah.
- The **mountains of Israel** refers to the central highlands that are called the hills of Ephraim.
- The **lowlands** are the coastal plains.

  i. "When the writer says that 'Joshua took this entire land,' he means that he gained control of the whole region even though he did not take every city. The last of the Canaanites were not subjected to Israel's authority until the reign of David." (Madvig)

b. **Joshua made war a long time with all those kings**: It's easy to read the record of Joshua and think it all happened quickly. This was a war that lasted, by many estimates, from five to seven years. God was with Israel, but it was not a quick work.

i. "The whole of these conquests were not effected in one campaign: they probably required *six* or *seven* years." (Clarke)

ii. The extended conquest of the land served God's purpose. He intended Israel to occupy the land little by little (Exodus 23:30, Deuteronomy 7:22). This also gave the Canaanites time to repent, if any of them were inclined to follow the examples of Rahab, the Gibeonites, and possibly the city of Shechem.

iii. "Undoubtedly the Conquest involved many battles that are not mentioned." (Madvig)

c. **For it was of the LORD to harden their hearts, that they should come against Israel in battle, that He might utterly destroy them**: We are told that in part, this judgment on the Canaanites was accomplished when God chose to **harden their hearts** against Israel. This hardening of men's hearts is when God gives man up to the sin that is in his heart (Romans 1:24-28).

i. God accepted truly repentant Canaanites who surrendered and submitted to the God of Israel. Examples of such were rare, but included Rahab and her family, the Gibeonites, and possibly the city of Shechem. What could not be accepted was a grudging surrender, a laying down of arms without true submission to the God of Israel. "God hardened the Canaanites' hearts, not to keep them from repenting, but to prevent them from surrendering to Israel in unrepentance." (Madvig)

ii. "Punishing them with a judiciary hardness, who were before hardened by the deceitfulness of sin and malice of Satan." (Trapp)

d. **As the LORD had commanded Moses**: We need not think that God poured out an absolutely unique judgment on the Canaanites. He dealt with their hearts in the same way He deals with all men's hearts, but God's grace either hardens the heart of man or it softens it.

2. (21-22) The Anakim are defeated.

**And at that time Joshua came and cut off the Anakim from the mountains: from Hebron, from Debir, from Anab, from all the mountains of Judah, and from all the mountains of Israel; Joshua utterly destroyed them with their cities. None of the Anakim were left in the land of the children of Israel; they remained only in Gaza, in Gath, and in Ashdod.**

a. **At that time Joshua came and cut off the Anakim from the mountains**: It was fear of the **Anakim** – a tribe of exceptionally large and strong people

– that had made Israel too afraid to enter the land some forty years before (Numbers 13:27-33).

> i. "The promise of Deuteronomy 9:1–3, which specifically predicts the defeat of the fearsome Anakites, is fulfilled." (Hess)

> ii. **Utterly destroyed them**: "This short account of the elimination of the Anakites is unusual in its harshness and thoroughness, a factor to be attributed, no doubt, to the Anakites' awesome reputation and their intimidating influence on Israel's attitudes heretofore." (Howard)

b. **None of the Anakim were left in the land of the children of Israel**: Here, the foes of 40 years ago fell in defeat. They were no match for an army that was blessed and directed by God.

> i. Significantly, Israel faced the Anakim *last*, only after God had trained them in battle and in working with Him through the months of conquest.

> ii. When Israel refused to enter Canaan out of fear of the Anakim, they did not realize that God would so guide events that they would face this most difficult challenge *last*. God knows how to manage the battles in the lives of His people.

> iii. The believer must submit to God's ordering of such battles. Believers may be convinced that they must go out and fight the difficult enemies first when God would have them face them last.

c. **They remained only in Gaza, in Gath, and in Ashdod**: The Anakim remained only in these coastal cities occupied by the Philistines. The giant Goliath came from the city of Gath some five hundred years later (1 Samuel 17:4).

3. (23) Complete victory, and the land rests from war.

**So Joshua took the whole land, according to all that the LORD had said to Moses; and Joshua gave it as an inheritance to Israel according to their divisions by their tribes. Then the land rested from war.**

a. **So Joshua took the whole land**: This marks another section of the book of Joshua. The power of the Canaanite kings within the land had been crushed, and in this sense, **Joshua took the whole land**. Yet not every small town and village had been conquered and occupied. That was up to each individual tribe to do in the land that was apportioned to them.

> i. "The Germans' 'conquest' of France in World War II involved the defeat of the French army and the occupation of most of France, but it did not thereby mean that all French people became German loyalists or that Germany permanently colonized France or that it killed every

French citizen. So too with many of the cities of Canaan, which were 'conquered' or 'subdued,' but only temporarily or only in part." (Howard)

ii. "Those who finally reign with Christ are they who, through his grace, *conquer* the *world,* the *devil,* and the *flesh;* for it is only of those who thus *overcome* that he says, 'They shall sit with me on my throne, as I have overcome, and am set down with the Father on the Father's throne;' Rev 3:21. Reader, art *thou* a conqueror?" (Clarke)

b. **Gave it as an inheritance to Israel**: This will be the theme of much of the rest of the book of Joshua. The land was conquered in a general sense; now it was up to the individual tribes to possess what God granted them by inheritance.

i. "*Inheritance* is first used here in Joshua, but it will recur forty-two times. It describes that which has been divinely given to the families of Israel for their possession. This could not become an inheritance until God gave it to Israel in the conquest." (Hess)

ii. "Our Joshua, the Lord Jesus, has taken the whole land. All the fruit of Calvary is at the disposal of every one of His children, and He holds out in His arms the whole of it to give it to you as your inheritance." (Redpath)

c. **Then the land rested from war**: The end of this phase of conquest was a greater invitation to the tribes to cooperate with God.

i. "Peace is the daughter of war; a fair and happy daughter of an ugly and direful mother." (Trapp)

ii. "Much territory was yet to be possessed, but it was left to each tribe to possess what potentially it had received through the conquest of the whole people in which it had taken part. Each tribe was to apply individually the lessons it had learned in united war if it was to possess its inheritance. That the tribes failed to do so was not a reflection on the power of God, but on the failure to take for themselves what Joshua had given and allotted to each one of them." (Redpath)

iii. In the same sense, Jesus has already defeated the enemy and conquered the land, but He also calls His people into battle to gain what is theirs.

# *Joshua 12 – List of the Conquered Kings*

**A. Kings defeated by Moses on the east side of the Jordan River.**

1. (1) Introduction: kings conquered by Israel under the leadership of Moses.

**These *are* the kings of the land whom the children of Israel defeated, and whose land they possessed on the other side of the Jordan toward the rising of the sun, from the River Arnon to Mount Hermon, and all the eastern Jordan plain:**

> a. **These are the kings of the land whom the children of Israel defeated**: The land of these kings comprised Israel's land on the eastern side of the Jordan River, **on the other side of the Jordan toward the rising of the sun**.

> b. **These are the kings**: This list only seems tedious to modern readers because they are distant from these great victories. For those who received their inheritance in the land of these kings, these were essential matters that touched everyday life, answering the question: "What land belongs to Israel?"

> > i. "After the narrative conclusion in 11:16–23, it is as though the author were saying, 'Here is the supporting evidence—the raw data—of what I have written about in the previous chapters.'" (Howard)

2. (2-3) The defeat of Sihon, king of the Amorites, and his land that Israel possessed.

***One king was* Sihon king of the Amorites, who dwelt in Heshbon *and* ruled half of Gilead, from Aroer, which is on the bank of the River Arnon, from the middle of that river, even as far as the River Jabbok, *which is* the border of the Ammonites, and the eastern Jordan plain from the Sea of Chinneroth as far as the Sea of the Arabah (the Salt Sea), the road to Beth Jeshimoth, and southward below the slopes of Pisgah.**

119

a. **One king was Sihon**: Numbers 21:21-32 describes the defeat of Sihon. The **Amorites** would not let Israel pass through their land – even though the Israelites promised it would be of no expense or trouble to the Amorites.

b. **King of the Amorites**: This incident is even more interesting considering that God hardened the spirit and made obstinate the heart of Sihon, ensuring his defeat (Deuteronomy 2:30). God hardened the heart of Sihon, so he would provoke the battle and he would lose, and Israel could gain his land.

> i. It was not unrighteous of God to harden Sihon because he was *not* originally favorable towards Israel. God did not *change* Sihon's heart to make him attack Israel. God simply gave Sihon over to what his evil heart desired.

3. (4-5) The defeat of Og, king of Bashan, and his land that Israel possessed.

*The other king was* **Og king of Bashan and his territory,** *who was* **of the remnant of the giants, who dwelt at Ashtaroth and at Edrei, and reigned over Mount Hermon, over Salcah, over all Bashan, as far as the border of the Geshurites and the Maachathites, and over half of Gilead** *to* **the border of Sihon king of Heshbon.**

a. **The other king was Og**: This conquest was recorded in Numbers 21:33-35. This was a battle that Israel did not provoke. Yet, Israel was more than up to the challenge, and through their God they won a glorious victory.

b. **King of Bashan and his territory**: This victory was despite the might of this king. **Og king of Bashan** was noted for his size and strength. Deuteronomy 3:11 says, *only Og king of Bashan remained of the remnant of the giants*. Nevertheless, the land of Bashan became part of Israel's territory on the east side of the Jordan River.

4. (6) The eastern lands are deeded to the tribes of Reuben, Gad, and half the tribe of Manasseh.

**These Moses the servant of the LORD and the children of Israel had conquered; and Moses the servant of the LORD had given it** *as* **a possession to the Reubenites, the Gadites, and half the tribe of Manasseh.**

a. **Moses the servant of the LORD and the children of Israel had conquered**: These conquests were achieved while Israel was still on the eastern side of the Jordan River. Israel's wars of conquest and judgment did not begin with Joshua.

b. **Half the tribe of Manasseh**: Half of the tribe of Manasseh lived east of the Jordan River, and half of the tribe lived west of the Jordan River. This distribution of the land is described in Numbers 32.

**B. Kings defeated by Joshua on the west side of the Jordan River.**

1. (7-8) A broad description of the lands and Canaanite nations conquered by Israel under the leadership of Joshua.

**And these *are* the kings of the country which Joshua and the children of Israel conquered on this side of the Jordan, on the west, from Baal Gad in the Valley of Lebanon as far as Mount Halak and the ascent to Seir, which Joshua gave to the tribes of Israel *as* a possession according to their divisions, in the mountain country, in the lowlands, in the *Jordan* plain, in the slopes, in the wilderness, and in the South; the Hittites, the Amorites, the Canaanites, the Perizzites, the Hivites, and the Jebusites:**

> a. **These are the kings of the country which Joshua and the children of Israel conquered on this side of the Jordan**: The previous section (Joshua 12:1-6) was an overview of Israel's conquests under Moses and on the east side of the Jordan River. Now begins the overview of what was accomplished under Joshua on the west side of the Jordan River.
>
> > i. "East of the Jordan there were only two kings, each of whom ruled a wide area with many cities. The land west of the Jordan was divided into individual city-states. Israel's conquests on both sides of the Jordan are mentioned together here to emphasize the unity of the nation." (Madvig)
>
> b. **These are the kings of the country which Joshua and the children of Israel conquered on this side of the Jordan**: While this list may seem tedious to a modern reader, it was read with great interest by those involved in these conquests, and those who received the land and cities gained by them.
>
> > i. The importance of these lists "lies in confirming the veracity of the claims elsewhere that these lands were indeed conquered, in confirming the tribes' claims to the lands mentioned here, and in confirming that God was faithful to his promises to give these lands to his people." (Howard)

2. (9-24) A specific recounting of the 31 kings conquered by Joshua.

**The king of Jericho, one; the king of Ai, which *is* beside Bethel, one; the king of Jerusalem, one; the king of Hebron, one; the king of Jarmuth, one; the king of Lachish, one; the king of Eglon, one; the king of Gezer, one; the king of Debir, one; the king of Geder, one; the king of Hormah, one; the king of Arad, one; the king of Libnah, one; the king of Adullam, one; the king of Makkedah, one; the king of Bethel, one; the king of Tappuah, one; the king of Hepher, one; the king of Aphek, one; the king of Lasharon, one; the king of Madon, one; the king of Hazor, one; the**

**king of Shimron Meron, one; the king of Achshaph, one; the king of Taanach, one; the king of Megiddo, one; the king of Kedesh, one; the king of Jokneam in Carmel, one; the king of Dor in the heights of Dor, one; the king of the people of Gilgal, one; the king of Tirzah, one; all the kings, thirty-one.**

a. **The king of Jericho**: These descriptions are also important because they make it clear that these things happened at a real time, and in real places. These are not fairy tales that begin with "once upon a time." This history is rooted in specific places, people, and rulers.

i. This type of list also appears in other ancient writings. "Conquest lists of Ancient Near Eastern kings have been compared. Close comparisons exist between this list and those composed for Pharaohs who campaigned in Palestine." (Hess)

ii. **Tirzah** "was the capital of the northern kingdom of Israel until the time of Omri (1 Kings 14:17; 15:21, 33; 16:6–24)." (Madvig)

iii. "Major sites such as Shechem and Dothan are not mentioned. Here is evidence that the conquests of the hill country are not recorded in the narratives of Joshua. The reasons for this remain speculative." (Hess)

b. **All the kings, thirty-one**: As well, this list gave a way for Israel to forever remember the great things God had done for them. In written form, this list served a similar function as the memorial from the crossing of the Jordan (Joshua 4:1-9).

i. "These words refer to the extent of Joshua's victory on the west side of the Jordan, and in their bald simplicity help us to realize at once the difficulty and greatness of what he accomplished." (Morgan)

ii. "Sometimes in the course of human experience it is good to sit down and reflect on what has been conquered by the grace of God. Not boastfully, but with a humble and grateful heart." (Redpath)

iii. These were kings of city-states, not nations as we think of them today. "In ancient times *all* kings had very small territories. Every village or town had its chief; and this chief was independent of his neighbours, and exercised *regal* power in his own district." (Clarke)

c. **All the kings**: With all these kings conquered, with every one of these principalities and powers over the land defeated, there was no doubt that the land belonged to Israel. Nevertheless, the individual tribes still had much to possess for their own.

i. "The chosen people are now seen in actual possession of the land. The destructive part of the divine work was accomplished. The constructive purposes of God might now go forward." (Morgan)

# Joshua 13 – The Remaining Land; Allotments East of the Jordan

**A. God's command to Joshua regarding the land remaining to be conquered.**

1. (1) God speaks to an old Joshua about the land remaining to be possessed.

**Now Joshua was old, advanced in years. And the LORD said to him: "You are old, advanced in years, and there remains very much land yet to be possessed.**

a. **You are old**: Joshua lived to 110 years of age (Joshua 24:29). He was probably somewhere between 90 and 95 at this point. Even while acknowledging Joshua's advanced years, God still told him about work that had to be done. Even in advanced years, God has work for His people to do.

b. **There remains very much land yet to be possessed**: This was true of the land on the west side of the Jordan. The main centers of Canaanite power had been defeated, but Israel had to occupy the land and defeat the smaller groups of Canaanites that might oppose them. On the east side of the Jordan, this complete occupation had already taken place.

c. **Yet to be possessed**: By spiritual analogy, what the land was to Israel, Jesus is to the believer. Christians should press on to continually possess more of Christ, to remain active as they grow in their relationship with, and reliance on, Jesus.

i. "What the land was to Israel, Christ is to us. Mapped out in the pages of God's Word is all the territory which we are to possess.... And it is true for every one of us that there is yet much land to be possessed. Our inheritance in Christ is not part of Christ, but all of Christ." (Redpath)

ii. "In whatever realm we think of the Divine purpose for us, we have to say: 'There remaineth very much land to be possessed.' We have never occupied all the territory provided for us in the Divine intention, and we are ever terribly prone to be satisfied with less than that which is in the will of God for us." (Morgan)

2. (2-6a) Describing the land that remains to be occupied.

**This is the land that yet remains: all the territory of the Philistines and all *that of* the Geshurites, from Sihor, which *is* east of Egypt, as far as the border of Ekron northward *(which* is counted as Canaanite); the five lords of the Philistines—the Gazites, the Ashdodites, the Ashkelonites, the Gittites, and the Ekronites; also the Avites; from the south, all the land of the Canaanites, and Mearah that belongs to the Sidonians as far as Aphek, to the border of the Amorites; the land of the Gebalites, and all Lebanon, toward the sunrise, from Baal Gad below Mount Hermon as far as the entrance to Hamath; all the inhabitants of the mountains from Lebanon as far as the Brook Misrephoth, *and* all the Sidonians—**

a. **This is the land that yet remains**: What follows describes a considerable amount of territory that Israel had yet to possess. The major kings had been defeated (Joshua 12:7-24), but the tribes of Israel had to spread out over Canaan and actually possess the land. This would not be easy; Canaanites remained who would fight Israel for the land.

i. **The territory of the Philistines**: "The Philistines came originally from Caphtor (Crete) as part of the migration of the 'Sea Peoples' who invaded Egypt and Palestine in 1200 B.C.… They continued to oppress and harass the Israelites throughout the period of the Judges and the reign of Saul, until they were subdued by David." (Madvig)

ii. "For the Christian, Israel's failure to conquer the land fully anticipates the inability to enjoy the full favour of God's blessing in this life (1 Cor. 10:1–13). Christians are not perfect, though they are called to perfect holiness. They live in a tension between the rewards of a life lived fully in the Holy Spirit, which are available here and now, and their own failure, which prevents the appropriation of those gifts." (Hess)

3. (6b-7) God's method for possessing the land is described.

**Them I will drive out from before the children of Israel; only divide it by lot to Israel as an inheritance, as I have commanded you. Now therefore, divide this land as an inheritance to the nine tribes and half the tribe of Manasseh."**

a. **Them I will drive out from before the children of Israel**: God promised **I will drive** them **out from before the children of Israel**, but He intended that each tribe trust God for this in the portion of land divided to them by lot. As God was with Joshua in his battles against the major kings of

Canaan, so God would be with the tribes as they fought to possess the portions of land allotted to them.

> i. "The Lord reaffirmed his promise to drive out the inhabitants of the land (cf. 3:10). From this point on, however, further conquests would be the concern of the individual tribes. Moreover, the promise was conditional and was never completely fulfilled due to the incompleteness of Israel's obedience." (Madvig)

b. **Divide this land as an inheritance to the nine tribes and half the tribe of Manasseh**: Each tribe was responsible for completely possessing their own land. God emphasized the idea of personal responsibility and initiative. This is not only because that is how things get done, but also because that is how people are blessed in service. God's people are blessed by personally taking responsibility and initiative in trusting God to do what He has called them to do.

> i. "In order that the chosen people might be able to complete the conquest and perfectly possess the land, it was now to be divided among them, so that the whole area might be covered." (Morgan)

## B. Land allotments east of the Jordan.

1. (8-13) The land to be divided on the east side of the Jordan River.

**With the other half tribe the Reubenites and the Gadites received their inheritance, which Moses had given them, beyond the Jordan eastward, as Moses the servant of the LORD had given them: from Aroer which *is* on the bank of the River Arnon, and the town that *is* in the midst of the ravine, and all the plain of Medeba as far as Dibon; all the cities of Sihon king of the Amorites, who reigned in Heshbon, as far as the border of the children of Ammon; Gilead, and the border of the Geshurites and Maachathites, all Mount Hermon, and all Bashan as far as Salcah; all the kingdom of Og in Bashan, who reigned in Ashtaroth and Edrei, who remained of the remnant of the giants; for Moses had defeated and cast out these.**

**Nevertheless the children of Israel did not drive out the Geshurites or the Maachathites, but the Geshurites and the Maachathites dwell among the Israelites until this day.**

a. **With the other half tribe the Reubenites and the Gadites received their inheritance**: This passage describes the portion of land divided among Reuben, Gad, and half the tribe of Manasseh. It was previously the territory of King Sihon of the Amorites and King Og of Bashan.

i. This was their **inheritance**, granted by the LORD. "God was the ultimate source of the gift of the land to Israel, and in several significant passages, the giving and the inheritance are linked. That which God gave, Israel was to receive by taking possession of it." (Howard)

b. **Nevertheless the children of Israel did not drive out the Geshurites or the Maachathites**: Only two small tribes of peoples were not replaced by the Jewish tribes settling on the east side of the Jordan. These were the **Geshurites** and the **Maachathites**.

i. "The danger was recognized that these people might rest content with victories already gained, and so fail to realize all the purposes of God for them." (Morgan)

ii. Geshur seems to have been absorbed into Israel. David later married a princess from Geshur, and she was the mother of his son Absalom (2 Samuel 3:3). Absalom returned to Geshur and used it as a place to plot against his father David (2 Samuel 13:37-38, 14:23, and 14:32).

iii. The **Maachathites** may have come from the Maachah that is mentioned in Genesis 22:24, who was a nephew of Abraham. Later, when Sheba rebelled against David, he fled and may have taken refuge in one of the cities of the Maachathites (2 Samuel 20:14-15).

2. (14) The unique situation of the tribe of Levi.

**Only to the tribe of Levi he had given no inheritance; the sacrifices of the LORD God of Israel made by fire *are* their inheritance, as He said to them.**

a. **Only to the tribe of Levi he had given no inheritance**: Levi, the priestly tribe, was to receive no allotted land as the other tribes received. Instead, the Levites were given certain cities. This was commanded in Numbers 35:1-8 and fulfilled in Joshua 20-21.

b. **The sacrifices of the LORD God of Israel made by fire are their inheritance**: Instead, the Levites had as their inheritance the offerings that Israel would bring to the LORD. Their provision did not come only from the land, but also from the offerings of Israel.

3. (15-23) The portion of Reuben's land.

**And Moses had given to the tribe of the children of Reuben *an inheritance* according to their families. Their territory was from Aroer, which *is* on the bank of the River Arnon, and the city that *is* in the midst of the ravine, and all the plain by Medeba; Heshbon and all its cities that *are* in the plain: Dibon, Bamoth Baal, Beth Baal Meon, Jahaza, Kedemoth, Mephaath, Kirjathaim, Sibmah, Zereth Shahar on the mountain of**

the valley, Beth Peor, the slopes of Pisgah, and Beth Jeshimoth; all the cities of the plain and all the kingdom of Sihon king of the Amorites, who reigned in Heshbon, whom Moses had struck with the princes of Midian: Evi, Rekem, Zur, Hur, and Reba, who *were* princes of Sihon dwelling in the country. The children of Israel also killed with the sword Balaam the son of Beor, the soothsayer, among those who were killed by them. And the border of the children of Reuben was the bank of the Jordan. This *was* the inheritance of the children of Reuben according to their families, the cities and their villages.

> a. **Inheritance according to their families**: God divided the land to Israel according to their tribes, clans, and **families**. The land was to remain in the family forever.

> b. **Israel also killed with the sword Balaam the son of Beor**: In the conquest of the land later inherited by Reuben, **Balaam** was killed when Moses **struck** the **princes of Midian**.

4. (24-28) The portion of Gad's land.

**Moses also had given** *an inheritance* **to the tribe of Gad, to the children of Gad according to their families. Their territory was Jazer, and all the cities of Gilead, and half the land of the Ammonites as far as Aroer, which** *is* **before Rabbah, and from Heshbon to Ramath Mizpah and Betonim, and from Mahanaim to the border of Debir, and in the valley Beth Haram, Beth Nimrah, Succoth, and Zaphon, the rest of the kingdom of Sihon king of Heshbon, with the Jordan as** *its* **border, as far as the edge of the Sea of Chinnereth, on the other side of the Jordan eastward. This** *is* **the inheritance of the children of Gad according to their families, the cities and their villages.**

> a. **This is the inheritance of the children of Gad**: This area of land marked by names, geography, and rulers was allotted to the tribe of **Gad**. This is a reminder that this was real land, not only a spiritual promise.

5. (29-32) The portion of half the tribe of Manasseh's land.

**Moses also had given** *an inheritance* **to half the tribe of Manasseh; it was for half the tribe of the children of Manasseh according to their families: Their territory was from Mahanaim, all Bashan, all the kingdom of Og king of Bashan, and all the towns of Jair which are in Bashan, sixty cities; half of Gilead, and Ashtaroth and Edrei, cities of the kingdom of Og in Bashan,** *were* **for the children of Machir the son of Manasseh, for half of the children of Machir according to their families.**

**These** *are the areas* **which Moses had distributed as an inheritance in the plains of Moab on the other side of the Jordan, by Jericho eastward.**

a. **An inheritance to half the tribe of Manasseh**: This tribe, descended from one of Joseph's two sons, was unique in its inheritance. Half the tribe of Manasseh possessed land on the eastern side of the Jordan River, and the other half possessed land on the western side.

b. **These are the areas which Moses had distributed**: This distribution of land for Reuben, Gad, and half the tribe of Manasseh happened under Moses, not Joshua (Numbers 32).

6. (33) More on the inheritance of the Levites.

**But to the tribe of Levi Moses had given no inheritance; the LORD God of Israel *was* their inheritance, as He had said to them.**

a. **The LORD God of Israel was their inheritance, as He had said to them**: The tribe of Levi had no land for an inheritance, but instead had the sacrifices Israel brought to God (Joshua 13:14). They also received a greater inheritance than the sacrifices: God Himself was **their inheritance**.

b. **The LORD God of Israel was their inheritance**: In this sense, if there is any tribe that Christians are spiritually connected to, it is the tribe of Levi. Believers are also called priests (1 Peter 2:5) and have a special inheritance in God (Ephesians 1:11, Colossians 1:12, 1 Peter 1:4).

c. **As He had said to them**: This distribution of land to the tribes, and God's special allotment to Levi, was all according to what God **had said**. It was important for each tribe to be content with and find joy in what God had allotted to them. This was especially true for the Levites, who had the LORD for **their inheritance**.

# Joshua 14 – The Division of the Land Begins; Caleb's Inheritance

## A. Preparation for the division of the land.

### 1. (1-2) The distribution of the land on the western side of the Jordan River.

**These *are the areas* which the children of Israel inherited in the land of Canaan, which Eleazar the priest, Joshua the son of Nun, and the heads of the fathers of the tribes of the children of Israel distributed as an inheritance to them. Their inheritance *was* by lot, as the LORD had commanded by the hand of Moses, for the nine tribes and the half-tribe.**

a. **Which the children of Israel inherited in the land of Canaan**: There is a sense in which Israel gained these lands by conquest. Yet in a greater sense they gained them by **inheritance** because God had promised the land by covenant to the descendants of Abraham, Isaac, and Jacob (Genesis 13:15, 17:8).

b. **Eleazar the priest, Joshua the son of Nun, and the heads of the fathers of the tribes**: In this process, Joshua, Eleazar and representatives from each tribe came together to supervise the casting of lots, which was directed by the LORD.

i. "Eleazar was a priest, son of Aaron the high priest; and he had been designated earlier to help Joshua with the distribution, along with representatives from the twelve tribes (Numbers 32:28; 34:18–29)." (Howard)

ii. **The heads of the fathers of the tribes**: "These *heads* or *princes* were twelve, Joshua and Eleazar included; and the reader may find their names in Numbers 34:19–28. It is worthy of remark that no prince was taken from the tribes of *Reuben* and *Gad,* because these had already received their inheritance on the other side of Jordan, and therefore could not be interested in this division." (Clarke)

c. **Their inheritance was by lot**: According to Ginzberg and others, ancient rabbis believed the division by lot happened in this manner: (1) The land west of the Jordan was divided into ten provinces and assigned a number for each province. Numbers one to ten were written on ten pieces of pottery or parchment and put in a container. (2) The names of the ten tribes receiving land on the west side of the Jordan were written on ten pieces of pottery or parchment, and these were put in a second container. (3) Joshua drew a piece from one container, and Eleazar drew a piece from the other container. (4) The tribe drawn received the land of the province drawn.

 i. God had **commanded** that the land be divided by lot (Numbers 26:55-56, 33:54). This was a way to leave the choices up to God (Proverbs 16:33).

2. (3-5) An explanation of the nine and one-half tribes which received their inheritance on the west side of the Jordan.

**For Moses had given the inheritance of the two tribes and the half-tribe on the other side of the Jordan; but to the Levites he had given no inheritance among them. For the children of Joseph were two tribes: Manasseh and Ephraim. And they gave no part to the Levites in the land, except cities to dwell *in*, with their common-lands for their livestock and their property. As the LORD had commanded Moses, so the children of Israel did; and they divided the land.**

a. **For the children of Joseph were two tribes**: We commonly think and speak of the "twelve tribes of Israel" but there were thirteen. Although there were twelve sons of Jacob (Israel), the descendants of one of his sons, Joseph, divided into **two tribes** (**Manasseh** and **Ephraim**).

b. **They divided the land**: This explains why there are two and one-half tribes on the east side of the Jordan, nine and one-half tribes on the west side of the Jordan, and one tribe with no province as their inheritance.

**B. Caleb's inheritance.**

1. (6-9) Caleb remembers Moses' promise.

**Then the children of Judah came to Joshua in Gilgal. And Caleb the son of Jephunneh the Kenizzite said to him: "You know the word which the LORD said to Moses the man of God concerning you and me in Kadesh Barnea. I *was* forty years old when Moses the servant of the LORD sent me from Kadesh Barnea to spy out the land, and I brought back word to him as *it was* in my heart. Nevertheless my brethren who went up with me made the heart of the people melt, but I wholly followed the LORD**

**my God. So Moses swore on that day, saying, 'Surely the land where your foot has trodden shall be your inheritance and your children's forever, because you have wholly followed the LORD my God.'**

a. **Caleb the son of Jephunneh**: Caleb, from the tribe of Judah, was one of the twelve spies who scouted out the land of Canaan some forty-five years before when Israel first was on the threshold of the Promised Land (Numbers 13:1-25). It was appropriate that when it came to the specific allotment of the land, Caleb received his first.

> i. Caleb "appears before Joshua, accompanied by the head men of his tribe, whose presence expresses their official consent to the exceptional treatment of their tribesman, and urges his request in a little speech." (Maclaren)

> ii. Caleb may have come from a Gentile ancestry. He is called **Caleb the son of Jephunneh the Kenizzite**, and may be linked to the Canaanite peoples mentioned in Genesis 15:18-21. Perhaps his father came to Egypt and married a woman from the tribe of Judah, giving Caleb identification with that tribe.

> iii. "Never was he found among the grumblers or among those who were skeptical and unbelieving. Never was he found among the people who hankered again for the leeks and garlic of Egypt. Never was he found among those who disobeyed God or among the people who turned to idolatry." (Redpath)

b. **But I wholly followed the LORD my God**: Caleb was one of only two spies to come back with a good report, a report of faith; believing that God had given Israel the land and would enable them to conquer it (Numbers 13:26-14:9). The other ten spies believed that Israel would be destroyed in the attempt to take Canaan, and the people of Israel believed the ten unbelieving spies.

> i. The other faithful spy was Joshua. The ten faithless spies measured the giants against their own strength, but Joshua and Caleb measured the giants against God's strength.

> ii. Caleb remembered his **brethren who went up with** him were filled with unbelief, and they **made the heart of the people melt**. He recognized the damage that unbelief may do among the people of God, and the negative effect it may have on others.

> iii. This was the cause of Israel's forty years of waiting and wandering in the wilderness. God would not allow the generation of unbelief to enter Canaan, so He waited for them to die in the desert (Numbers 14:26-38). The only ones of age at the time of the rejection who

successfully entered the Promised Land were Joshua and Caleb, the two faithful spies.

iv. So, it was fitting as Judah was the first tribe to receive its allotment on the west side of the Jordan, that Caleb be the first among the people of Judah to receive his inheritance.

c. **So Moses swore on that day, saying, 'Surely the land where your foot has trodden shall be your inheritance and your children's forever'**: Caleb called Joshua back to the promise Moses made in Deuteronomy 1:35-36. When Caleb said, **I wholly followed the LORD my God**, he wasn't being proud. He was simply recalling what Moses had said about him.

i. It is fitting for God's people today to imitate Caleb's boldness in asking for what God promised him. God's people may find this difficult to believe, but God appreciates this kind of boldness (Hebrews 4:16).

d. **Because you have wholly followed the LORD my God**: Caleb recalled what Moses said of him some fifty years before. Because Caleb repeated this phrase twice, it seems to have made a significant impression on him. This was appropriate because it is a great and important thing to **wholly** follow the LORD.

i. It may be observed that most successful people are those who have wholly given themselves over to something. It is appropriate for the people of God to **wholly** give themselves over to following the LORD.

ii. "Caleb was not being self-serving by claiming that he had fully followed the Lord; he was simply stating a fact that Moses also had recognized (see the words at the end of v. 9, which are found in the Lord's mouth almost verbatim in Numbers 14:24 and in Moses' mouth in Deuteronomy 1:36)." (Howard)

iii. "*Wholeheartedly* means with all your heart. It is the idea embodied in what Jesus called the first and greatest of the commandments: 'Love the Lord your God with all your heart and with all your soul and with all your mind' (Matthew 22:37; see Deuteronomy 6:5)." (Boice)

2. (10-12) Caleb's bold request.

**And now, behold, the LORD has kept me alive, as He said, these forty-five years, ever since the LORD spoke this word to Moses while Israel wandered in the wilderness; and now, here I am this day, eighty-five years old. As yet I *am as* strong this day as on the day that Moses sent me; just as my strength *was* then, so now *is* my strength for war, both for going out and for coming in. Now therefore, give me this mountain of which the LORD spoke in that day; for you heard in that day how the Anakim *were* there, and *that* the cities *were* great *and* fortified. It may**

**be that the LORD *will be* with me, and I shall be able to drive them out as the LORD said."**

a. **The LORD has kept me alive**: This was not only of note because of Caleb's many battles and advanced age. It was also of note because only he and Joshua were spared the judgment of death that fell upon all the generation of adults who left Egypt, the generation of unbelief.

> i. "For forty years he had shared the wanderings and discipline of those who had not shared his faith…. He had apparently occupied a comparatively quiet and obscure position among his people, while his friend Joshua had been called into the place of conspicuous and powerful leadership." (Morgan)

b. **Here I am this day, eighty-five years old. As yet I am as strong this day as on the day that Moses sent me**: Though he was advanced in age, Caleb's strength was undiminished. At eighty-five he was out leading the fight, and not against just any foe, but against the mighty **Anakim**. He was willing to take the battle to **great and fortified** cities.

> i. Caleb is a remarkable example of someone who aged in the best way. Spiritually speaking, he grew older but never weaker in his God. He didn't look forward to a life of ease and indulgence in his elderly years.

> ii. "It is the coward and the selfish man who are always looking for an easy place, where somebody else will do the work. This man felt that this miraculously prolonged life of his bound him to special service." (Maclaren)

> iii. **Just as my strength was then, so now is my strength for war**: "Caleb drew on a strength that was irresistible because he had a faith that never wavered." (Redpath)

> iv. "Caleb's words as to his undiminished strength were not meant for a boast. They express thankfulness and praise, and they are put as the ground of the request that he has to make." (Maclaren)

> v. "The drain of the years is amply met by the inflow of his all-sufficient grace. There is no reason why we should decline in usefulness and fruit-bearing with the increase of years; but the reverse." (Meyer)

c. **Now therefore, give me this mountain of which the LORD spoke in that day; for you heard in that day how the Anakim were there**: In fact, Caleb *wanted* the fight, practically demanding the **mountain** where difficult foes lived. He could have asked for an easy place, but he knew these foes must be faced and thought that he may as well be the one to do it. He didn't leave the work to someone else, though he could have, especially at his age.

i. In Caleb's short speech, he referred to what God said at least four times. He was a man who trusted God's word, and who believed in God's promise.

ii. "Old age is generally much more disposed to talk about its past victories than to fight new ones; to rest upon its arms, or upon its laurels, than to undertake fresh conflicts." (Maclaren)

iii. "These factors—'hill country … Anakites … cities … large and fortified'—are the very things that the ten faithless spies used to discourage the Israelites from entering the Promised Land (Numbers 13:28–29). Caleb viewed them as a challenge." (Madvig)

iv. Paul understood that a great and effective door of opportunity had opened to him – probably because there were many adversaries! (1 Corinthians 16:9) Caleb understood there were fearsome adversaries in the area of Hebron, so he said, "That's my door of opportunity."

v. The record of the defeat of the Anakim is given in Joshua 11:21-22. Some of them fled to the cities of Gaza, Gath, and Ashdod. It is likely that some of those Anakim who fled returned and occupied Hebron or some nearby areas.

3. (13-15) Joshua grants Caleb's request.

**And Joshua blessed him, and gave Hebron to Caleb the son of Jephunneh as an inheritance. Hebron therefore became the inheritance of Caleb the son of Jephunneh the Kenizzite to this day, because he wholly followed the Lord God of Israel. And the name of Hebron formerly was Kirjath Arba *(Arba was* the greatest man among the Anakim).**

**Then the land had rest from war.**

a. **Joshua blessed him**: This means that Joshua approved Caleb's request, praised him for the asking, and prayed that God's blessing would be on him in the endeavor to take Hebron and its area.

i. "He approved of his petition: he did not blame him for being too hasty, nor bid him stay till himself were first served; but granted him Hebron." (Trapp)

ii. "His ultimate reward has been long postponed but had never been uncertain." (Morgan)

b. **Because he wholly followed the Lord God of Israel**: If all Israel had the heart and faith of Caleb, their conquest of Canaan would have been much more complete. There was a sense of complete commitment to God in Caleb.

i. Caleb was one of only three people in the Bible of whom it was said, they **wholly followed the LORD**. The others were Joshua (in partnership with Caleb, Numbers 32:11-12) and David (1 Kings 11:6). In the New Testament, the idea of wholly following the LORD is presented in passages such as Romans 12:1-2, which instruct the believer to present themselves to God as living sacrifices.

ii. "In the history of Caleb three things are illustrated concerning faith. Faith sees and dares in the day of overwhelming difficulty. Faith waits patiently through delays caused by failures in others. Faith acts with courage in the day of opportunity." (Morgan)

c. **Then the land had rest from war**: Since Joshua is not necessarily presented in strict chronological order, it is difficult to know if this marked a temporary **rest** or a more permanent end to Israel's wars of judgment and conquest. The statement is made here to connect the idea of Caleb's bold, energetic, and enduring faith with the reward of **rest from war**.

i. "There were no more *general* wars; the inhabitants of Canaan collectively could make no longer any head, and when their confederacy was broken by the conquests of Joshua, he thought proper to divide the land, and let each tribe expel the ancient inhabitants that might still remain in its own territories. Hence the wars after this time were *particular* wars; there were no more general campaigns, as it was no longer necessary for the *whole* Israelitish body to act against an enemy now *disjointed* and *broken*." (Clarke)

# Joshua 15, 16, 17 – The Inheritance of Judah, Ephraim, and Western Manasseh

## A. The inheritance of Judah.

1. (15:1-12) The borders of the province of Judah.

So *this* was the lot of the tribe of the children of Judah according to their families: The border of Edom at the Wilderness of Zin southward *was* the extreme southern boundary. And their southern border began at the shore of the Salt Sea, from the bay that faces southward. Then it went out to the southern side of the Ascent of Akrabbim, passed along to Zin, ascended on the south side of Kadesh Barnea, passed along to Hezron, went up to Adar, and went around to Karkaa. *From there* it passed toward Azmon and went out to the Brook of Egypt; and the border ended at the sea. This shall be your southern border.

The east border *was* the Salt Sea as far as the mouth of the Jordan.

And the border on the northern quarter *began* at the bay of the sea at the mouth of the Jordan. The border went up to Beth Hoglah and passed north of Beth Arabah; and the border went up to the stone of Bohan the son of Reuben. Then the border went up toward Debir from the Valley of Achor, and it turned northward toward Gilgal, which *is* before the Ascent of Adummim, which *is* on the south side of the valley. The border continued toward the waters of En Shemesh and ended at En Rogel. And the border went up by the Valley of the Son of Hinnom to the southern slope of the Jebusite *city* (which *is* Jerusalem). The border went up to the top of the mountain that *lies* before the Valley of Hinnom westward, which *is* at the end of the Valley of Rephaim northward. Then the border went around from the top of the hill to the fountain of the water of Nephtoah, and extended to the cities of Mount Ephron. And the border went around to Baalah (which *is* Kirjath Jearim). Then the border turned westward from Baalah to Mount Seir, passed along to the side of Mount Jearim on the north (which *is* Chesalon), went

**down to Beth Shemesh, and passed on to Timnah. And the border went out to the side of Ekron northward. Then the border went around to Shicron, passed along to Mount Baalah, and extended to Jabneel; and the border ended at the sea.**

**The west border** *was* **the coastline of the Great Sea. This** *is* **the boundary of the children of Judah all around according to their families.**

a. **So this was the lot of the tribe of the children of Judah**: The listing of these specific names, places, and geographic boundaries was of great interest to those who would inherit the land. This collection of places also reminds the reader that these were real places, not the description of a symbolic or spiritual inheritance. When God promised a land to Abraham and his covenant descendants (Genesis 13:15, 17:8), God meant a real land.

i. **To the southern slope of the Jebusite city (which is Jerusalem)**: The description of Judah's border in reference to Jerusalem shows that it was a city right on the border between Judah and Benjamin.

ii. Meyer comments on the land given to Judah: "The position allocated to it was the fighting front. It was touched by enemies on three sides; on the east, Moab; on the west, the Philistines; on the south, Edom.... The tribe whose standard was that of the kingly line, and from which that line presently was to spring, was to have its fiber toughened by the sternest discipline – constant watchfulness against the foe and long-continued fighting."

iii. "The geography of the sacred writings presents many difficulties, occasioned by the changes which the civil state of the promised land has undergone, especially for the last two thousand years. Many of the ancient towns and villages have had their names so totally changed, that their former appellations are no longer discernible; several lie buried under their own ruins, and others have been so long destroyed that not one vestige of them remains. On these accounts it is very difficult to ascertain the situation of many of the places mentioned in this and the following chapters. But however this may embarrass the commentator, it cannot affect the *truth* of the narrative." (Clarke)

b. **According to their families**: God allotted the land to Israel by tribe, clan, and family. The family was the most basic level of organization for the people of God.

i. "A modern reader may question the value of a long list of names of towns like this, but for the Judahite it described the homeland that

God had given to his tribe. It is another evidence of the historical, down-to-earth nature of God's redemptive program." (Madvig)

2. (15:13-19) The land allotted to Caleb and his family.

**Now to Caleb the son of Jephunneh he gave a share among the children of Judah, according to the commandment of the LORD to Joshua, *namely,* Kirjath Arba, which *is* Hebron *(Arba was* the father of Anak). Caleb drove out the three sons of Anak from there: Sheshai, Ahiman, and Talmai, the children of Anak. Then he went up from there to the inhabitants of Debir (formerly the name of Debir *was* Kirjath Sepher).**

**And Caleb said, "He who attacks Kirjath Sepher and takes it, to him I will give Achsah my daughter as wife." So Othniel the son of Kenaz, the brother of Caleb, took it; and he gave him Achsah his daughter as wife. Now it was so, when she came *to him,* that she persuaded him to ask her father for a field. So she dismounted from *her* donkey, and Caleb said to her, "What do you wish?" She answered, "Give me a blessing; since you have given me land in the South, give me also springs of water." So he gave her the upper springs and the lower springs.**

a. **He who attacks Kirjath Sepher and takes it, to him I will give Achsah my daughter as wife**: Caleb was not only a man of great and bold deeds (the driving out of **the children of Anak**) but also a man who encouraged others to great and bold deeds. He did this by offering his daughter in marriage to the man who was bold enough to conquer a city to have her.

i. "Othniel was part of the Kenizzite clan, being Caleb's nephew (v. 17), so the land remained in the family. Othniel later was one of the twelve judges whom God used in delivering the Israelites from foreign oppressions during the turbulent period described in the Book of Judges (3:9–11)." (Howard)

b. **Give me a blessing; since you have given me land in the South, give me also springs of water**: As well, Caleb's daughter imitated her father's boldness in asking for a blessing. She did not hesitate to ask her father for some choice **springs**.

i. "She *hastily, suddenly* alighted, as if she had forgotten something, or was about to return to her father's house. Which being perceived by her father, he said, *What wouldest thou?* What is the matter? What dost thou want?" (Clarke)

ii. "Land in the Negev is of little value without water, but it is very productive when irrigated. Othniel recognized the validity of her request. The word translated 'springs' is the Hebrew *gullot* which may mean 'reservoirs' or 'cisterns.'" (Madvig)

iii. "Caleb had conquered his giants, and so he was able to give his daughter an inheritance of land and springs of water. It was when Jesus had overcome the sharpness of death that He opened the Kingdom of Heaven to all believers; it was as He trampled under his victorious feet the principalities and powers of darkness that He gave to his Church the upper and the nether springs." (Meyer)

iv. With her request from her father, Caleb's daughter **Achsah** serves as a helpful example of effective prayer.

- Achsah was a good example of prayer because *she thought about what she wanted before she went to her father*. She came with a very definite request that had been considered beforehand.

- Achsah was a good example because *she asked for help with her request*, asking her husband – **she persuaded him to ask her father for a field**. It is a good thing to ask for help in prayer.

- Achsah was a good example of prayer because *she went humbly, yet eagerly*.

- Achsah was a good example of prayer because *she asked for what she wanted*. It is a pleasure for God to hear His people ask.

- Achsah was a good example of prayer because of the *simplicity* of her prayer. Her prayer was, **give me a blessing**.

- Achsah was a good example of prayer because *she mingled gratitude with her petition* (**you have given me land in the South**).

- Achsah was a good example of prayer because *she used past blessing as a reason to ask for more*.

- Achsah was a good example of prayer because *her father gave her what she asked*.

- Achsah was a good example of prayer because her prayer was answered; *her father gave to her in large measure*.

- Achsah was a good example of prayer because *her father was not critical of the request in the slightest way*.

v. The favorable answer of Caleb to Achsah's request gives believers confidence in prayer. "What can a kind father deny his child? And shall not God give his dear children 'upper and nether springs,' blessings of both lives? And are they not worthily miserable that will not make themselves happy by asking?" (Trapp)

3. (15:20-62) The cities, villages, and regions occupied by the tribe of Judah.

This *was* the inheritance of the tribe of the children of Judah according to their families:

The cities at the limits of the tribe of the children of Judah, toward the border of Edom in the South, were Kabzeel, Eder, Jagur, Kinah, Dimonah, Adadah, Kedesh, Hazor, Ithnan, Ziph, Telem, Bealoth, Hazor, Hadattah, Kerioth, Hezron (which *is* Hazor), Amam, Shema, Moladah, Hazar Gaddah, Heshmon, Beth Pelet, Hazar Shual, Beersheba, Bizjothjah, Baalah, Ijim, Ezem, Eltolad, Chesil, Hormah, Ziklag, Madmannah, Sansannah, Lebaoth, Shilhim, Ain, and Rimmon: all the cities *are* twenty-nine, with their villages.

In the lowland: Eshtaol, Zorah, Ashnah, Zanoah, En Gannim, Tappuah, Enam, Jarmuth, Adullam, Socoh, Azekah, Sharaim, Adithaim, Gederah, and Gederothaim: fourteen cities with their villages; Zenan, Hadashah, Migdal Gad, Dilean, Mizpah, Joktheel, Lachish, Bozkath, Eglon, Cabbon, Lahmas, Kithlish, Gederoth, Beth Dagon, Naamah, and Makkedah: sixteen cities with their villages; Libnah, Ether, Ashan, Jiphtah, Ashnah, Nezib, Keilah, Achzib, and Mareshah: nine cities with their villages; Ekron, with its towns and villages; from Ekron to the sea, all that *lay* near Ashdod, with their villages; Ashdod with its towns and villages, Gaza with its towns and villages; as far as the Brook of Egypt and the Great Sea with *its* coastline.

And in the mountain country: Shamir, Jattir, Sochoh, Dannah, Kirjath Sannah (which *is* Debir), Anab, Eshtemoh, Anim, Goshen, Holon, and Giloh: eleven cities with their villages; Arab, Dumah, Eshean, Janum, Beth Tappuah, Aphekah, Humtah, Kirjath Arba (which *is* Hebron), and Zior: nine cities with their villages; Maon, Carmel, Ziph, Juttah, Jezreel, Jokdeam, Zanoah, Kain, Gibeah, and Timnah: ten cities with their villages; Halhul, Beth Zur, Gedor, Maarath, Beth Anoth, and Eltekon: six cities with their villages; Kirjath Baal (which *is* Kirjath Jearim) and Rabbah: two cities with their villages.

In the wilderness: Beth Arabah, Middin, Secacah, Nibshan, the City of Salt, and En Gedi: six cities with their villages.

a. **All the cities are twenty-nine**: Many count 38 cities in the previous section, not **twenty-nine**. Clarke explained the difference by noting that nine of the 38 cities were soon given to the tribe of Simeon.

4. (15:63) An incomplete occupation: Jerusalem remains in Canaanite hands.

As for the Jebusites, the inhabitants of Jerusalem, the children of Judah could not drive them out; but the Jebusites dwell with the children of Judah at Jerusalem to this day.

a. **The inhabitants of Jerusalem, the children of Judah could not drive them out:** Jerusalem was understandably a difficult city to conquer. The fact that it was set in hilly terrain made it easy to defend.

b. **The Jebusites dwell with the children of Judah at Jerusalem to this day:** Yet no matter how hard the struggle, with God's promise and God's help, God's people can triumph. There was no good excuse as to why this city had to stay in Canaanite hands until the time of David (2 Samuel 5:6-10).

> i. "The whole history of Jerusalem, previously to the time of David, is encumbered with many difficulties. Sometimes it is attributed to *Judah,* sometimes to *Benjamin;* and it is probable that, being on the frontiers of both those tribes, each possessed a part of it." (Clarke)

## B. The inheritance of the tribes of Joseph.

1. (16:1-4) The borders of the province belonging to the tribes of Joseph, Ephraim and the half-tribe of Manasseh settling on the west side of the Jordan.

**The lot fell to the children of Joseph from the Jordan, by Jericho, to the waters of Jericho on the east, to the wilderness that goes up from Jericho through the mountains to Bethel, then went out from Bethel to Luz, passed along to the border of the Archites at Ataroth, and went down westward to the boundary of the Japhletites, as far as the boundary of Lower Beth Horon to Gezer; and it ended at the sea.**

**So the children of Joseph, Manasseh and Ephraim, took their inheritance.**

2. (16:5-10) The borders of the province of Ephraim.

**The border of the children of Ephraim, according to their families, was *thus:* The border of their inheritance on the east side was Ataroth Addar as far as Upper Beth Horon.**

**And the border went out toward the sea on the north side of Michmethath; then the border went around eastward to Taanath Shiloh, and passed by it on the east of Janohah. Then it went down from Janohah to Ataroth and Naarah, reached to Jericho, and came out at the Jordan.**

**The border went out from Tappuah westward to the Brook Kanah, and it ended at the sea. This *was* the inheritance of the tribe of the children of Ephraim according to their families. The separate cities for the children of Ephraim *were* among the inheritance of the children of Manasseh, all the cities with their villages.**

**And they did not drive out the Canaanites who dwelt in Gezer; but the Canaanites dwell among the Ephraimites to this day and have become forced laborers.**

a. **And they did not drive out the Canaanites who dwelt in Gezer**: Their failure to completely drive out the Canaanites was typical of all the tribes. Even within the Promised Land there remained important work to do and battles to fight.

i. **Gezer**: "It appears that the Canaanites were not expelled from this city till the days of Solomon, when it was taken by the king of Egypt his father-in-law, who made it a present to his daughter, Solomon's queen. See 1 Kings 9:16." (Clarke)

b. **The Canaanites dwell among the Ephraimites to this day and have become forced laborers**: Perhaps the people of Ephraim were guilty of this compromise because they wanted **forced laborers** among them. Having this convenience did not justify their disobedience to God's command. The Canaanites had to either fully surrender to Israel and Israel's God (as did Rahab and the Gibeonites), to leave the area, or suffer the deadly judgment of God.

i. "The use of forced labour among Canaanite towns in the Jezreel Valley was a known practice." (Hess)

ii. If they had the power to make the people of Gezer forced laborers, they certainly had the power to defeat them completely, especially because Gezer was a city that Joshua had already conquered (Joshua 10:33, 12:12).

iii. This sort of compromise seems innocent, but it became the way that idolatry and immoral worship was later adopted by the people of Israel. The later struggles in the days of the judges had some foundation in the incomplete possession of the land in the days of Joshua.

iv. "As a result of this failure, the Israelites were corrupted by intermarrying with these pagans and engaging in their perverse and idolatrous worship (Judges 2:1-3; 3:5-6; 10:6)." (Madvig)

c. **They did not drive out the Canaanites**: The Israelites did not fully conquer for at least two reasons. First, they wanted peace at any cost. Second, they wanted wealth. For *ease* and *money*, they disobeyed God and fell short of what He had for them – as believers may also do today.

i. "They took their inheritance, but they did not take possession of it. In the will of God, and by the consent of Ephraim, it belonged to them; but they failed to appropriate it in all its fullness, because they left these Canaanites in possession." (Morgan)

ii. "The whole history of Ephraim was a sad one for long centuries and their failure began here." (Morgan)

d. Some notable cities in the territory of **Ephraim**: Jericho, Shiloh, Gezer.

3. (17:1-2) Distribution of the land among the remaining families of the tribe of Manasseh.

**There was also a lot for the tribe of Manasseh, for he *was* the firstborn of Joseph: *namely* for Machir the firstborn of Manasseh, the father of Gilead, because he was a man of war; therefore he was given Gilead and Bashan. And there was *a lot* for the rest of the children of Manasseh according to their families: for the children of Abiezer, the children of Helek, the children of Asriel, the children of Shechem, the children of Hepher, and the children of Shemida; these *were* the male children of Manasseh the son of Joseph according to their families.**

4. (17:3-6) The inheritance of Zelophehad's daughters.

**But Zelophehad the son of Hepher, the son of Gilead, the son of Machir, the son of Manasseh, had no sons, but only daughters. And these *are* the names of his daughters: Mahlah, Noah, Hoglah, Milcah, and Tirzah. And they came near before Eleazar the priest, before Joshua the son of Nun, and before the rulers, saying, "The LORD commanded Moses to give us an inheritance among our brothers." Therefore, according to the commandment of the LORD, he gave them an inheritance among their father's brothers. Ten shares fell to Manasseh, besides the land of Gilead and Bashan, which *were* on the other side of the Jordan, because the daughters of Manasseh received an inheritance among his sons; and the rest of Manasseh's sons had the land of Gilead.**

a. **Zelophehad...had no sons, but only daughters**: This is noted in the text because it was unusual for women to receive an inheritance. It was more important that the land remain in the ancestral families than it was to follow the custom that only males should inherit land. Therefore, the daughters of Zelophehad could inherit their father's land.

b. **The LORD commanded Moses to give us an inheritance among our brothers**: This was the implementation of a decision arrived at by Moses in Numbers 27:1-11.

i. It was significant that they carried out what God **commanded Moses**, as recorded in His word. "They regarded the Pentateuch as the Word of God and as something that not only conveyed some sort of religious feeling, but also gave specific commands that were to be obeyed in detail. They were referring to Numbers 27:1–11 and to Numbers 36." (Schaeffer)

5. (17:7-13) The boundaries of the western half-tribe of Manasseh and their incomplete occupation of that land.

**And the territory of Manasseh was from Asher to Michmethath, that *lies* east of Shechem; and the border went along south to the inhabitants of En Tappuah. Manasseh had the land of Tappuah, but Tappuah on the border of Manasseh *belonged* to the children of Ephraim. And the border descended to the Brook Kanah, southward to the brook. These cities of Ephraim *are* among the cities of Manasseh. The border of Manasseh *was* on the north side of the brook; and it ended at the sea.**

**Southward *it was* Ephraim's, northward *it was* Manasseh's, and the sea was its border. Manasseh's territory was adjoining Asher on the north and Issachar on the east. And in Issachar and in Asher, Manasseh had Beth Shean and its towns, Ibleam and its towns, the inhabitants of Dor and its towns, the inhabitants of En Dor and its towns, the inhabitants of Taanach and its towns, and the inhabitants of Megiddo and its towns; three hilly regions. Yet the children of Manasseh could not drive out *the inhabitants of* those cities, but the Canaanites were determined to dwell in that land. And it happened, when the children of Israel grew strong, that they put the Canaanites to forced labor, but did not utterly drive them out.**

a. **Yet the children of Manasseh could not drive out the inhabitants of those cities**: Their failure was after the same pattern as the failure of the tribe of Ephraim in Joshua 16:10.

b. **But the Canaanites were determined to dwell in that land**: It isn't a surprise that the Canaanites would be **determined** to remain in the land. What was lacking was complete determination from the people of Israel. They were satisfied to **put the Canaanites to forced labor** instead of driving them out.

i. "They had the power to remove the Canaanites from the land and so to be God's instruments of judgment to remove wickedness, but they chose to tolerate wickedness and to use for their own purposes that which God had devoted to destruction. And so they sowed the seeds of their own destruction." (Howard)

c. Some notable cities in the territory of Western Manasseh: En Dor, Beth Shean, and Megiddo.

6. (17:14-18) Joshua answers the complaint of the tribes of Joseph.

**Then the children of Joseph spoke to Joshua, saying, "Why have you given us *only* one lot and one share to inherit, since we *are* a great people, inasmuch as the LORD has blessed us until now?"**

So Joshua answered them, "If you *are* a great people, *then* go up to the forest *country* and clear a place for yourself there in the land of the Perizzites and the giants, since the mountains of Ephraim are too confined for you."

But the children of Joseph said, "The mountain country is not enough for us; and all the Canaanites who dwell in the land of the valley have chariots of iron, *both those* who *are* of Beth Shean and its towns and *those* who *are* of the Valley of Jezreel."

And Joshua spoke to the house of Joseph—to Ephraim and Manasseh—saying, "You *are* a great people and have great power; you shall not have *only* one lot, but the mountain country shall be yours. Although it *is* wooded, you shall cut it down, and its farthest extent shall be yours; for you shall drive out the Canaanites, though they have iron chariots *and* are strong."

a. **Why have you given us only one lot and one share to inherit, since we are a great people**: Manasseh and Ephraim were large tribes. Their combined number was greater than any other single tribe. Yet they complained that they were not given adequate land.

i. "In terms of square miles, the Joseph tribes had little reason to complain. Moreover, the land they were given was the most fertile in all Palestine. Joshua was certainly justified in resisting their request." (Madvig)

ii. "They complained, 'We haven't enough room!' The fact was that the enemy was deeply entrenched in the area which they did have." (Redpath)

iii. "The Joseph tribes exhibited a degree of arrogance and greed in their confrontation with Joshua. The tone here sharply contrasts with the far more humble requests presented by Caleb (14:6–12) and the daughters of Zelophehad (17:4), both of whom appealed to the Lord's promises as the basis for their requests." (Howard)

iv. **Only one lot**: "They challenged the outcome of the lot *(goral)*, which was controlled by God. Thus, in their request they were challenging the very workings of God himself." (Howard)

v. "An all-wise God disposes his people according to his sovereign will. Let us not seek to alter our destiny, but let us try to make the best of our circumstances. This is what Joshua exhorted Ephraim and Manasseh to do." (Spurgeon)

b. **If you are a great people**: Joshua's reply was both wise and wonderful. He told them, "**If you are a great people**, then go and take the land for yourself; fully occupy what the LORD has given you." These tribes had not completely taken the mountain country in their allotted territory, because it would be difficult and dangerous work.

i. "Joshua would not reverse the decision of the lot; but as there was much woodland country, he gave them permission to clear away as much of it as they found necessary to extend themselves as far as they pleased." (Clarke)

ii. "If you say you are so great, if you think you are so wonderful, then there is plenty of unoccupied land within the limits of your present lot." (Redpath)

c. **The mountain country is not enough for us**: The tribes of Joseph objected to Joshua's proposal. They complained the wooded areas that could be cleared were **not enough** and the enemies on the plains were too strong with their **chariots of iron**. They felt there were good reasons or excuses why they would not possess what God granted them.

i. "The hill is not enough for us, and the Canaanites are too hard for us." (Trapp)

ii. The tribes of Joseph were afraid of the Canaanite **chariots of iron**. "Iron chariots, understood as chariots reinforced with some iron fittings, are envisaged." (Hess)

iii. This was a different attitude compared to Caleb in Joshua 14:11-12. The men of Manasseh and Ephraim wanted a gift of "easy land." They didn't want to trust God's promises and take what God had given them. The principle applies to believers today. Before expecting more from God, fully live in what He has already granted

iv. "Stop crying for greater opportunities until you have done the work in the place that God has allotted to you." (Redpath)

d. **Although it is wooded, you shall cut it down**: Joshua's reply to their objection was simple. "The work will be difficult, but you are a **great people and have great power**. As God is with you, you can overcome these challenges and fully live in what God has granted you."

i. God had a purpose in allowing these difficult challenges to the tribes of Joseph, even as He has a purpose in allowing such challenges to believers today. "Difficulty is sent to reveal to us what God can do in answer to the faith that prays and works." (Meyer)

# Joshua 18, 19 – Inheritance of the Remaining Tribes

**A. The survey of the land for the seven remaining tribes.**

1. (18:1-3) At Shiloh, Joshua exhorts the remaining tribes to possess their land.

**Now the whole congregation of the children of Israel assembled together at Shiloh, and set up the tabernacle of meeting there. And the land was subdued before them. But there remained among the children of Israel seven tribes which had not yet received their inheritance.**

**Then Joshua said to the children of Israel: "How long will you neglect to go and possess the land which the LORD God of your fathers has given you?**

a. **Israel assembled together at Shiloh**: This would become the new center for Israel, where the **tabernacle of meeting** would stay for a long time. Because the tabernacle was there, so were the important items associated with it, including the ark of the covenant and the sacrificial altar. The tabernacle came from Gilgal to Shiloh, and it remained there until the time of Eli, the high priest (1 Samuel 1-4).

i. **Shiloh** was "a considerable town about fifteen miles from Jerusalem, in the tribe of Ephraim, and nearly in the centre of the whole land." (Clarke)

ii. Writing in the middle of the 1600s, John Trapp considered how the movement of the tabernacle from Gilgal to Shiloh speaks of how the apparent center of God's work may move over time. "All that I fear, saith a reverent divine yet living, is, lest according to Mr. [George] Herbert's prophecy it prove true, viz, that the gospel be, in its solar motion, travelling for the west and American parts, and quitting its present places of residence and unworthy professors and possessors: and then, farewell, England."

b. **Seven tribes which had not yet received their inheritance**: There were several potential reasons why these **seven tribes** had not possessed the land God allotted for them. Perhaps they lacked the faith and courage to drive out the stubborn Canaanites. Perhaps they grew accustomed to a more nomadic life.

i. "That which follows immediately would lead us to believe that after districts had been allotted to Judah, Ephraim, and Manasseh there was some slackness in continuing the work of settlement, for Joshua definitely rebuked the seven tribes for being slow to go up and possess the land." (Morgan)

ii. The **seven tribes** without an inheritance were Benjamin, Simeon, Zebulun, Issachar, Asher, Naphtali, and Dan. Reuben and Gad had received their inheritance (Joshua 13:8), along with half the tribe of Manasseh (Joshua 13:29) on the east side of the Jordan. Judah (Joshua 15:1), Ephraim, and the other half of Manasseh (Joshua 16:4) had received their allotted land on the west side of the Jordan. Levi did not receive an allotment of land as the other tribes did (Joshua 13:33).

c. **How long will you neglect to go and possess the land**: Whatever the exact reason, the bottom line was **neglect**. They did not perform what God had called them to do and did not claim what God had given to them.

i. "Apparently the remaining tribes had grown complacent. They were satisfied with nomadic life in the fertile land of Ephraim and Manasseh and were not eager to be involved in the warfare required to claim their own territory." (Madvig)

ii. "When it was necessary that all the people should go out to battle, they went with a measure of confidence, expecting miraculous help from God, and [trusting] in their numbers; but when each tribe found it necessary to fight for itself, in order to its establishment and the extension of its borders, it was discouraged, and chose rather a life of inglorious ease than the possession of an inheritance which would cost it much labour to conquer." (Clarke)

iii. "The arresting word in this question of Joshua is the word 'slack,' [**neglect**] as it reveals a peril always threatening those who are called to carry out some divine enterprise. How perpetually the work of God suffers because His people become slack!" (Morgan)

2. (18:4-8) Joshua instructs a survey party to go out and assess the land so that it may be divided among the seven remaining tribes.

**Pick out from among you three men for *each* tribe, and I will send them; they shall rise and go through the land, survey it according to**

their inheritance, and come *back* to me. And they shall divide it into seven parts. Judah shall remain in their territory on the south, and the house of Joseph shall remain in their territory on the north. You shall therefore survey the land in seven parts and bring *the survey* here to me, that I may cast lots for you here before the Lord our God. But the Levites have no part among you, for the priesthood of the Lord *is* their inheritance. And Gad, Reuben, and half the tribe of Manasseh have received their inheritance beyond the Jordan on the east, which Moses the servant of the Lord gave them."

Then the men arose to go away; and Joshua charged those who went to survey the land, saying, "Go, walk through the land, survey it, and come back to me, that I may cast lots for you here before the Lord in Shiloh."

a. **They shall divide it into seven parts**: The remaining land would be fairly divided among the seven tribes that had yet to take their inheritance.

i. **Gad, Reuben, and half the tribe of Manasseh have received their inheritance beyond the Jordan on the east**: "The two and one-half tribes from east of the Jordan must have become impatient to have the division of the land completed so that they could return home to their families and possessions." (Madvig)

b. **Survey it and come back to me**: The land would be divided by casting **lots**, a method which relied on God to guide the lot. The survey was man's responsibility, and then they trusted God to guide through the lot.

i. **Bring the survey here to me**: "Writing was so common that the spies were able to write their report and present it to Joshua." (Schaeffer)

ii. "Everything is recorded in a book. Joshua writes the covenant in *the Book of the Law of God* (24:26; see also 8:32, 34). Just as the law guides the people in their life, the map book will guide the people in their possession of God's blessing of the land." (Hess)

iii. There is an analogy connecting these scouts who surveyed the land so the tribes could possess it and some gifted believers God calls to ministry. Their job is to survey, describe, and report what God has appointed for His people, so that they may by faith and patience possess those things. "In every age of the Church's story, God has sent forth men to walk through and describe the land of our spiritual inheritance." (Meyer)

3. (18:9-10) The successful survey party returns and Joshua casts lots to determine which tribes will receive which land.

So the men went, passed through the land, and wrote the survey in a book in seven parts by cities; and they came to Joshua at the camp in Shiloh. Then Joshua cast lots for them in Shiloh before the LORD, and there Joshua divided the land to the children of Israel according to their divisions.

**B. The final division of the land.**

1. (18:11-28) The boundaries and cities for the tribe of Benjamin.

Now the lot of the tribe of the children of Benjamin came up according to their families, and the territory of their lot came out between the children of Judah and the children of Joseph. Their border on the north side began at the Jordan, and the border went up to the side of Jericho on the north, and went up through the mountains westward; it ended at the Wilderness of Beth Aven. The border went over from there toward Luz, to the side of Luz (which *is* Bethel) southward; and the border descended to Ataroth Addar, near the hill that *lies* on the south side of Lower Beth Horon.

Then the border extended around the west side to the south, from the hill that *lies* before Beth Horon southward; and it ended at Kirjath Baal (which *is* Kirjath Jearim), a city of the children of Judah. This *was* the west side.

The south side *began* at the end of Kirjath Jearim, and the border extended on the west and went out to the spring of the waters of Nephtoah. Then the border came down to the end of the mountain that *lies* before the Valley of the Son of Hinnom, which *is* in the Valley of the Rephaim on the north, descended to the Valley of Hinnom, to the side of the Jebusite *city* on the south, and descended to En Rogel. And it went around from the north, went out to En Shemesh, and extended toward Geliloth, which is before the Ascent of Adummim, and descended to the stone of Bohan the son of Reuben. Then it passed along toward the north side of Arabah, and went down to Arabah. And the border passed along to the north side of Beth Hoglah; then the border ended at the north bay at the Salt Sea, at the south end of the Jordan. This *was* the southern boundary.

The Jordan was its border on the east side. This *was* the inheritance of the children of Benjamin, according to its boundaries all around, according to their families.

Now the cities of the tribe of the children of Benjamin, according to their families, were Jericho, Beth Hoglah, Emek Keziz, Beth Arabah, Zemaraim, Bethel, Avim, Parah, Ophrah, Chephar Haammoni, Ophni,

**and Gaba: twelve cities with their villages; Gibeon, Ramah, Beeroth, Mizpah, Chephirah, Mozah, Rekem, Irpeel, Taralah, Zelah, Eleph, Jebus (which *is* Jerusalem), Gibeath, *and* Kirjath: fourteen cities with their villages. This was the inheritance of the children of Benjamin according to their families.**

a. The tribe of **Benjamin** "occupied the space between that of Judah and Ephraim.... In process of time Benjamin drew nearer in sympathy to Judah, and at the great division went with Judah altogether." (Morgan)

b. Some notable cities in the territory of **Benjamin**: Bethel, Kirjath Jearim, Jerusalem (**the Jebusite city**), Gibeon, and Ramah.

i. As with previous lists of cities and locations, this collection of places reminds the reader that these were real places, not describing a symbolic or spiritual inheritance. When God promised a land to Abraham and his covenant descendants (Genesis 13:15, 17:8), God meant a real land.

2. (19:1-9) The boundaries and cities for the tribe of Simeon.

**The second lot came out for Simeon, for the tribe of the children of Simeon according to their families. And their inheritance was within the inheritance of the children of Judah. They had in their inheritance Beersheba (Sheba), Moladah, Hazar Shual, Balah, Ezem, Eltolad, Bethul, Hormah, Ziklag, Beth Marcaboth, Hazar Susah, Beth Lebaoth, and Sharuhen: thirteen cities and their villages; Ain, Rimmon, Ether, and Ashan: four cities and their villages; and all the villages that *were* all around these cities as far as Baalath Beer, Ramah of the South. This *was* the inheritance of the tribe of the children of Simeon according to their families.**

**The inheritance of the children of Simeon *was included* in the share of the children of Judah, for the share of the children of Judah was too much for them. Therefore the children of Simeon had *their* inheritance within the inheritance of that people.**

a. The land of the tribe of **Simeon** was eventually absorbed into or "scattered" into the land of Judah, as Jacob prophesied in Genesis 49:5-7.

i. "The towns of Simeon lie within the southern borders of Judah. The southern (15:26–32) and central Shephelah (15:42) districts of Judah contain these towns." (Hess)

b. A notable city in the territory of **Simeon**: Beer-sheba.

3. (19:10-16) The boundaries and cities for the tribe of Zebulun.

The third lot came out for the children of Zebulun according to their families, and the border of their inheritance was as far as Sarid. Their border went toward the west and to Maralah, went to Dabbasheth, and extended along the brook that is east of Jokneam. Then from Sarid it went eastward toward the sunrise along the border of Chisloth Tabor, and went out toward Daberath, bypassing Japhia. And from there it passed along on the east of Gath Hepher, toward Eth Kazin, and extended to Rimmon, which borders on Neah. Then the border went around it on the north side of Hannathon, and it ended in the Valley of Jiphthah El. Included were Kattath, Nahallal, Shimron, Idalah, and Bethlehem: twelve cities with their villages. This *was* the inheritance of the children of Zebulun according to their families, these cities with their villages.

   a. Some notable cities in the territory of **Zebulun**: Gath Hepher (the city of Jonah, 2 Kings 14:25) and Rimmon.

4. (19:17-23) The boundaries and cities for the tribe of Issachar.

The fourth lot came out to Issachar, for the children of Issachar according to their families. And their territory went to Jezreel, and *included* Chesulloth, Shunem, Haphraim, Shion, Anaharath, Rabbith, Kishion, Abez, Remeth, En Gannim, En Haddah, and Beth Pazzez. And the border reached to Tabor, Shahazimah, and Beth Shemesh; their border ended at the Jordan: sixteen cities with their villages. This *was* the inheritance of the tribe of the children of Issachar according to their families, the cities and their villages.

   a. Some notable cities in the territory of **Issachar**: Jezreel and Shunem.

5. (19:24-31) The boundaries and cities for the tribe of Asher.

The fifth lot came out for the tribe of the children of Asher according to their families. And their territory included Helkath, Hali, Beten, Achshaph, Alammelech, Amad, and Mishal; it reached to Mount Carmel westward, along *the Brook* Shihor Libnath. It turned toward the sunrise to Beth Dagon; and it reached to Zebulun and to the Valley of Jiphthah El, then northward beyond Beth Emek and Neiel, bypassing Cabul *which was* on the left, including Ebron, Rehob, Hammon, and Kanah, as far as Greater Sidon. And the border turned to Ramah and to the fortified city of Tyre; then the border turned to Hosah, and ended at the sea by the region of Achzib. Also Ummah, Aphek, and Rehob *were included*: twenty-two cities with their villages. This *was* the inheritance of the tribe of the children of Asher according to their families, these cities with their villages.

a. A notable place in the territory of **Asher**: Mount Carmel.

6. (19:32-39) The boundaries and cities for the tribe of Naphtali.

**The sixth lot came out to the children of Naphtali, for the children of Naphtali according to their families. And their border began at Heleph, enclosing the territory from the terebinth tree in Zaanannim, Adami Nekeb, and Jabneel, as far as Lakkum; it ended at the Jordan. From Heleph the border extended westward to Aznoth Tabor, and went out from there toward Hukkok; it adjoined Zebulun on the south side and Asher on the west side, and ended at Judah by the Jordan toward the sunrise. And the fortified cities *are* Ziddim, Zer, Hammath, Rakkath, Chinnereth, Adamah, Ramah, Hazor, Kedesh, Edrei, En Hazor, Iron, Migdal El, Horem, Beth Anath, and Beth Shemesh: nineteen cities with their villages. This *was* the inheritance of the tribe of the children of Naphtali according to their families, the cities and their villages.**

a. Some notable cities in the territory of **Naphtali**: Hazor and Beth Shemesh.

7. (19:40-48) The boundaries and cities for the tribe of Dan.

**The seventh lot came out for the tribe of the children of Dan according to their families. And the territory of their inheritance was Zorah, Eshtaol, Ir Shemesh, Shaalabbin, Aijalon, Jethlah, Elon, Timnah, Ekron, Eltekeh, Gibbethon, Baalath, Jehud, Bene Berak, Gath Rimmon, Me Jarkon, and Rakkon, with the region near Joppa. And the border of the children of Dan went beyond these, because the children of Dan went up to fight against Leshem and took it; and they struck it with the edge of the sword, took possession of it, and dwelt in it. They called Leshem, Dan, after the name of Dan their father. This *is* the inheritance of the tribe of the children of Dan according to their families, these cities with their villages.**

a. Some notable cities in the territory of **Dan**: Timnah, Joppa, and Dan (after the northern migration described in Judges 18:29).

8. (19:49-51) Joshua's inheritance.

**When they had made an end of dividing the land as an inheritance according to their borders, the children of Israel gave an inheritance among them to Joshua the son of Nun. According to the word of the LORD they gave him the city which he asked for, Timnath Serah in the mountains of Ephraim; and he built the city and dwelt in it.**

**These *were* the inheritances which Eleazar the priest, Joshua the son of Nun, and the heads of the fathers of the tribes of the children of Israel**

**divided as an inheritance by lot in Shiloh before the LORD, at the door of the tabernacle of meeting. So they made an end of dividing the country.**

a. **When they had made an end of dividing the land**: Joshua received what was promised to him by God, but in remarkable humility, he received his portion last. This kind of humble service and concern for others is part of what makes Joshua such a wonderful picture of Jesus Christ.

i. "Joshua waits until all the other inheritances are assigned before taking any for himself. Thus he preserves his right to a share of the land without any suggestion of an abuse of his leadership responsibilities." (Hess)

ii. Additionally, Joshua did not take an inheritance of land for himself. Israel **gave**; he humbly received. "Joshua, who was usually the agent distributing the land, now received it from the Israelites (v. 49). He could not give himself his own portion." (Howard)

b. **In the mountains of Ephraim**: Being from the tribe of Ephraim, it was appropriate for Joshua to receive his inheritance in the general territory of that tribe. He went to the same difficult, hilly district of Ephraim that the tribes of Joseph had previously complained about (Joshua 17:14-18).

i. "It will be remembered that when Ephraim had complained, Joshua had charged them to go to the mountains and possess their possessions. Now when his opportunity came, he proved that he was prepared to act for himself on the advice he had given. To that very hill country he went, and there is a splendid ring of resoluteness in his character in the statement, 'He built the city, and dwelt therein.'" (Morgan)

c. **So they made an end of dividing the country**: The territory had been allotted to each tribe, but it was up to the tribes to fight and possess what God gave to them.

i. They did this **in Shiloh before the LORD**. "All the inheritances were determined by lot, and this lot was cast *before the Lord*—every thing was done in his immediate presence, as under his eye; hence there was no murmuring, each having received his inheritance as from the hand of God himself, though some of them thought they must have additional territory, because of the great increase of their families." (Clarke)

# Joshua 20 – The Cities of Refuge

**A. God commands the appointment of six cities of refuge.**

1. (1-3) A place of refuge from the avenger of blood.

**The Lord also spoke to Joshua, saying, "Speak to the children of Israel, saying: 'Appoint for yourselves cities of refuge, of which I spoke to you through Moses, that the slayer who kills a person accidentally *or* unintentionally may flee there; and they shall be your refuge from the avenger of blood.**

a. **Appoint for yourselves cities of refuge**: God told Joshua to fulfill the appointment of six cities of refuge, something the Lord commanded through Moses in Exodus 21:12-14, Numbers 35, Deuteronomy 4:41-43 and 19:1-13.

b. **That the slayer who kills a person accidentally or unintentionally may flee there**: The purpose of the cities of refuge was to protect one who killed another, but **accidentally or unintentionally**. They were to protect someone in the case of *manslaughter* as opposed to *murder*.

i. "As a man might *casually* kill another against whom he had no ill-will, and with whom he had no quarrel, and might have his life taken away by him who was called the *avenger of blood*, though he had not forfeited his life to the law; therefore these privileged cities were appointed, where the person might have protection till the cause had been fully heard by the magistrates." (Clarke)

c. **And they shall be your refuge from the avenger of blood**: Such a person needed protection against the **avenger of blood**. The Hebrew word for this phrase is *goel*, and in this context means the representative from the victim's family charged with the responsibility of making sure justice is carried out against the murderer of the family member.

i. God was concerned that murderers were punished in ancient Israel. In that culture, the final responsibility for justice rested with the designated *goel* (**avenger of blood**) in the family.

ii. The principle for capital punishment goes back to Genesis 9:6: *Whoever sheds man's blood, by man his blood shall be shed; for in the image of God He made man.* When murder is unpunished, it defiles a land (Numbers 35:31, 35:33-34). The government's right to use the sword of execution is also stated in the New Testament (Romans 13:3-4). The astounding number of unsolved, unpunished murders in the United States and other nations is a great failing, one that invites God's judgment.

d. **Refuge from the avenger of blood**: The **avenger of blood** tracked down the murderer, and if necessary, delivered him over to the authorities for execution. This provision of the testimony of two or three eyewitnesses could confirm the guilt of the murderer according to Deuteronomy 17:6-7.

i. "Blood vengeance is an ancient custom that can be traced back to the early chapters of Genesis (e.g., Cain expected to be killed in revenge for the murder of his brother Abel [Gen 4:13–14])." (Madvig)

ii. "Numbers 35 states clearly that the avenger of blood was only free to kill someone who had killed another if (1) that person ventured forth from a city of refuge (Num 35:26–28) or (2) that person was guilty of murder, and not manslaughter (Num 35:16–21). The avenger of blood had a legal status in society to carry out society's (i.e., God's) judgments and was by no means one who was to exact private vengeance." (Howard)

e. **Refuge from the avenger of blood**: Since the **avenger of blood** might set himself against a person guilty of manslaughter (accidental or unintentional killing) instead of murder, the cities of refuge were established to protect the person innocent of murder.

i. "If an ancient manslayer did not flee to one of the cities of refuge, there was no hope for him; there was no other provision in the law of Israel by which he might be saved. If he did not flee there, the avenger of blood would overtake him." (Boice)

2. (4) Entrance into the city of refuge.

**And when he flees to one of those cities, and stands at the entrance of the gate of the city, and declares his case in the hearing of the elders of that city, they shall take him into the city as one of them, and give him a place, that he may dwell among them.**

a. **And declares his case in the hearing of the elders of that city**: According to custom, the elders of the city spent much time at the gates of the city. When someone fleeing from an avenger of blood came to a city of refuge, he stated his case to the elders at the city gates.

> i. "It is important to note that this was not an arrangement by which a murderer could avoid justice. The one who murdered another was to be judicially executed. This was a device designed to save someone guilty of manslaughter but innocent of murder." (Boice)

> ii. "A person was to be regarded innocent until proven guilty, and a minimum of two witnesses was required to condemn one accused of murder (Num 35:30)." (Madvig)

b. **They shall take him into the city as one of them**: After explaining the case, the fleeing person could expect to find protection within the walls of the city of refuge, though he would have to stay there, and live in the city to enjoy that protection.

3. (5) Protection against the avenger of blood.

**Then if the avenger of blood pursues him, they shall not deliver the slayer into his hand, because he struck his neighbor unintentionally, but did not hate him beforehand.**

a. **They shall not deliver the slayer into his hand**: The leaders of a city of refuge were obliged to protect the one who had fled to the city. The **avenger of blood** had no legal standing to deliver the slayer over to execution.

b. **Because he struck his neighbor unintentionally, but did not hate him beforehand**: Israel had a sophisticated legal system, with judgments often based on intent and premeditation.

4. (6) Freedom for the slayer.

**And he shall dwell in that city until he stands before the congregation for judgment, *and* until the death of the one who is high priest in those days. Then the slayer may return and come to his own city and his own house, to the city from which he fled.**

a. **He shall dwell in that city**: To be protected against the avenger of blood, the slayer had to stay within the walls of the city of refuge until his case was fully heard by the proper authorities, and until the **death** of the standing **high priest**.

> i. "Since the high priest represented the sacrificial system, his death atoned for the sins of the manslayer.... Only on the occasion of a death—the high priest's—was the manslayer free to leave." (Howard)

b. **Then the slayer may return and come to his own city**: After being declared innocent of murder by the proper authorities, and after the death of the standing high priest, the slayer could go back to his home and be legally protected against the wrath of the avenger of blood.

## B. Six cities selected for cities of refuge.

**1. (7-8) The appointment of six cities.**

**So they appointed Kedesh in Galilee, in the mountains of Naphtali, Shechem in the mountains of Ephraim, and Kirjath Arba (which *is* Hebron) in the mountains of Judah. And on the other side of the Jordan, by Jericho eastward, they assigned Bezer in the wilderness on the plain, from the tribe of Reuben, Ramoth in Gilead, from the tribe of Gad, and Golan in Bashan, from the tribe of Manasseh.**

a. **So they appointed**: The distribution of the cities of refuge across Israel shows they were well spaced throughout the country. No matter where one was in Israel, they were not far from a city of refuge. Under normal circumstances, a city of refuge was within a day's journey from almost anywhere in Israel.

i. "Happily, Christ is nearer than any city of refuge. A runner could fall, but a person who looks to Christ can never fail." (Schaeffer)

b. **They assigned**: Deuteronomy 19:2-3 tells us that proper roads were to be built and maintained to the cities of refuge. The city wasn't very helpful to the slayer if he could not get to it quickly.

i. The cities of refuge were also Levitical cities. "Which were to be cities of Levites, who were presumed to be both wise and merciful men, and such as would not favour wilful offenders." (Trapp)

**2. (9) The purpose for the cities of refuge is again stated.**

**These were the cities appointed for all the children of Israel and for the stranger who dwelt among them, that whoever killed a person accidentally might flee there, and not die by the hand of the avenger of blood until he stood before the congregation.**

a. **For all the children of Israel and for the stranger who dwelt among them**: The cities of refuge were not only for the benefit of the Israelite but also for the **stranger who dwelt among them**. God's justice applied to all without partiality.

i. "As these typified the great provision which God was making for the salvation of both Jews and Gentiles, hence the *stranger* as well as the Israelite had the same right to the benefits of these cities of refuge. Is

HE the God of the *Jews* only? Is HE not also the God of the *Gentiles?*" (Clarke)

b. **And not die by the hand of the avenger**: By providing a place of protection, the cities of refuge serve as an illustration of Jesus Christ and His work.

i. The Bible applies this picture of the city of refuge to the believer finding refuge in God on more than one occasion.

- Psalm 46:1: *God is our refuge and strength, a very present help in trouble.* More than 15 other times, the psalms speak of God as our refuge.

- Hebrews 6:18: *That by two immutable things, in which it is impossible for God to lie, we might have strong consolation, who have fled for refuge to lay hold of the hope set before us.*

ii. There are many points of similarity between the cities of refuge and the believer's refuge in Jesus Christ.

- Both Jesus and the cities of refuge are *within easy reach* of the needy person; they are of no use unless someone can get to the place of refuge.

- Both Jesus and the cities of refuge are *open to all*, not just the Israelite; no one needs to fear that they will be turned away from their place of refuge in their time of need.

- Both Jesus and the cities of refuge become a place where the one in need can *live*; you don't come to a city of refuge in time of need just to look around.

- Both Jesus and the cities of refuge are the *only alternative* for the one in need; without this specific protection, they will be destroyed.

- Both Jesus and the cities of refuge provide protection *only within their boundaries*; to go outside means death.

- With both Jesus and the cities of refuge, full freedom comes upon the *death of the High Priest*.

iii. There is a crucial distinction between the cities of refuge and the believer's refuge in Jesus Christ.

- The cities of refuge only helped the *innocent*, but the *guilty* can come to Jesus and find refuge.

iv. "Our city of refuge is the wounded side of Jesus, our High Priest, who died and rose again.... In our city of refuge we shall always be safe, for our High Priest lives forever." (Redpath)

# Joshua 21 – Cities Appointed for the Levites

**A. The people of the tribe of Levi receive their cities with their common-lands.**

1. (1-3) The leaders of the tribe of Levi ask for what was promised to them.

**Then the heads of the fathers'** *houses* **of the Levites came near to Eleazar the priest, to Joshua the son of Nun, and to the heads of the fathers'** *houses* **of the tribes of the children of Israel. And they spoke to them at Shiloh in the land of Canaan, saying, "The LORD commanded through Moses to give us cities to dwell in, with their common-lands for our livestock." So the children of Israel gave to the Levites from their inheritance, at the commandment of the LORD, these cities and their common-lands:**

> a. **The LORD commanded through Moses to give us cities to dwell in**: The Levites received no region of land as the other tribes did; however, they had to live somewhere. So, each tribe gave certain **cities** and **common-lands** (land immediately surrounding the cities) to the tribe of Levi.
>
>> i. Through Jacob (Genesis 49:5-7) God promised that the tribes of Simeon and Levi would be scattered throughout Israel. Simeon was scattered in somewhat of a negative sense, absorbed into the land given to Judah (Joshua 19:9). Levi was scattered in a blessed sense, distributed all over the land of Israel in 48 Levitical cities, spreading their influence as priests, teachers, and spiritual leaders of the nation.
>>
>> ii. "In the scattering of Levi we see God's righteous judgment on sin. But we also see judgment turned to blessing. If you are suffering from what others have done—perhaps from the sin of a parent, as the descendants of Simeon and Levi suffered for the sin of their parents—do not think you are excluded from God's favor or that it is impossible for you to gain God's favor again by godly living." (Boice)

b. **So the children of Israel gave to the Levites from their inheritance**: The tribe of Levi had no region of land because God had declared that He would be their inheritance (Joshua 13:14, 13:33).

> i. These cities and their common-lands would help ensure that the Levites were supported even if the Israelites failed to tithe as God commanded. "He left not his Levites to the will and devotion of the people: for then they should have had Micah's allowance (Judges 17), prisoners' pittances, such as will neither keep them alive, nor suffer them to die." (Trapp)

2. (4-8) Cities are appointed for the Levites, according to their three family divisions.

**Now the lot came out for the families of the Kohathites. And the children of Aaron the priest,** *who were* **of the Levites, had thirteen cities by lot from the tribe of Judah, from the tribe of Simeon, and from the tribe of Benjamin. The rest of the children of Kohath had ten cities by lot from the families of the tribe of Ephraim, from the tribe of Dan, and from the half-tribe of Manasseh.**

**And the children of Gershon had thirteen cities by lot from the families of the tribe of Issachar, from the tribe of Asher, from the tribe of Naphtali, and from the half-tribe of Manasseh in Bashan.**

**The children of Merari according to their families had twelve cities from the tribe of Reuben, from the tribe of Gad, and from the tribe of Zebulun.**

**And the children of Israel gave these cities with their common-lands by lot to the Levites, as the L**ord **had commanded by the hand of Moses.**

a. **The families of the Kohathites**: The Kohathites were responsible for the sanctuary, including the care of the ark, the table, the lampstand, the altars, the articles of the sanctuary used in ministering, the curtain, and everything related to their use. The priestly family of Aaron came from the family of Kohath. Their allotment of the cities given to the priests is considered here. Their cities came from the central hill country, the regions surrounding Jerusalem.

> i. "It is worthy of remark, that the principal part of this tribe, whose business was to minister at the sanctuary, which sanctuary was afterwards to be established in Jerusalem, had their appointment nearest to that city; so that they were always within reach of the sacred work which God had appointed them." (Clarke)

b. **The children of Gershon**: The Gershonites were responsible for the transport of the tabernacle's coverings and curtains through the wilderness

(Numbers 3:25-26; 4:24-26). Their cities were in the area of Galilee and Bashan.

c. **The children of Merari**: The division of Merari guarded the tabernacle and transported its boards and pillars through the wilderness. Their cities were in the Transjordanian and Zebulun areas.

3. (9-42) The distribution of the cities through the tribes.

**So they gave from the tribe of the children of Judah and from the tribe of the children of Simeon these cities which are designated by name, which were for the children of Aaron, one of the families of the Kohathites, *who were* of the children of Levi; for the lot was theirs first. And they gave them Kirjath Arba *(Arba was* the father of Anak), which *is* Hebron, in the mountains of Judah, with the common-land surrounding it. But the fields of the city and its villages they gave to Caleb the son of Jephunneh as his possession.**

**Thus to the children of Aaron the priest they gave Hebron with its common-land (a city of refuge for the slayer), Libnah with its common-land, Jattir with its common-land, Eshtemoa with its common-land, Holon with its common-land, Debir with its common-land, Ain with its common-land, Juttah with its common-land, and Beth Shemesh with its common-land: nine cities from those two tribes; and from the tribe of Benjamin, Gibeon with its common-land, Geba with its common-land, Anathoth with its common-land, and Almon with its common-land: four cities. All the cities of the children of Aaron, the priests, *were* thirteen cities with their common-lands.**

**And the families of the children of Kohath, the Levites, the rest of the children of Kohath, even they had the cities of their lot from the tribe of Ephraim. For they gave them Shechem with its common-land in the mountains of Ephraim (a city of refuge for the slayer), Gezer with its common-land, Kibzaim with its common-land, and Beth Horon with its common-land: four cities; and from the tribe of Dan, Eltekeh with its common-land, Gibbethon with its common-land, Aijalon with its common-land, *and* Gath Rimmon with its common-land: four cities; and from the half-tribe of Manasseh, Tanach with its common-land and Gath Rimmon with its common-land: two cities. All the ten cities with their common-lands were for the rest of the families of the children of Kohath.**

**Also to the children of Gershon, of the families of the Levites, from the *other* half-tribe of Manasseh, *they gave* Golan in Bashan with its common-land (a city of refuge for the slayer), and Be Eshterah with its common-land: two cities; and from the tribe of Issachar, Kishion**

with its common-land, Daberath with its common-land, Jarmuth with its common-land, *and* En Gannim with its common-land: four cities; and from the tribe of Asher, Mishal with its common-land, Abdon with its common-land, Helkath with its common-land, and Rehob with its common-land: four cities; and from the tribe of Naphtali, Kedesh in Galilee with its common-land (a city of refuge for the slayer), Hammoth Dor with its common-land, and Kartan with its common-land: three cities. All the cities of the Gershonites according to their families *were* thirteen cities with their common-lands.

And to the families of the children of Merari, the rest of the Levites, from the tribe of Zebulun, Jokneam with its common-land, Kartah with its common-land, Dimnah with its common-land, *and* Nahalal with its common-land: four cities; and from the tribe of Reuben, Bezer with its common-land, Jahaz with its common-land, Kedemoth with its common-land, and Mephaath with its common-land: four cities; and from the tribe of Gad, Ramoth in Gilead with its common-land (a city of refuge for the slayer), Mahanaim with its common-land, Heshbon with its common-land, *and* Jazer with its common-land: four cities in all. So all the cities for the children of Merari according to their families, the rest of the families of the Levites, were *by* their lot twelve cities.

All the cities of the Levites within the possession of the children of Israel *were* forty-eight cities with their common-lands. Every one of these cities had its common-land surrounding it; thus *were* all these cities.

a. **They had the cities of their lot**: When these cities are located on a map, it can be seen that God wanted the Levites scattered throughout the land of Israel. He never intended there to be one state or province of Levi, but every tribe was to have the priestly influence and presence among them. Though the Levites were not priests, they were the representatives of the priesthood throughout the land of Israel.

i. 2 Chronicles 17:9 describes the work of the teaching priests, who had the Book of the Law of the LORD, and who went throughout all the cities of Judah and taught the people. The work of these priests and Levites was important. According to Leviticus 10:11, one responsibility of the priests was to teach God's word to the people of Israel. This responsibility on the part of the priests (and their associates, the Levites) is often overlooked. Priests are often seen only as those who offered sacrifices.

ii. Sacrifice was part of a priest's work, but they also were called to be active Bible teachers. The "teaching priest" is seen in many Old Testament passages. Their work was commanded by the Law of Moses

(Deuteronomy 33:10). The prophets reminded Israel of the priest's duty (Malachi 2:7).

iii. The absence of the teaching priest was noted by God and missed by God's people (2 Chronicles 15:3). The prophets criticized the priests who taught God's word prompted by greed (Micah 3:11).

iv. The Levites were assistants to the priests, and God appointed that the Levites be distributed throughout the land of Israel in cities set aside for them. As they were spread evenly through the land, no one in Israel was far from the ministry of God's word. This shows how important it was for God's people to have the ongoing teaching and explanation of God's word.

v. Today, God also wants to distribute His people broadly throughout the world. God does not intend that there be a single Christian nation or state where all the Christians live together in spiritual bliss, and say to the world, "come and join us if you want." Instead, God wants Christians to be as priests (1 Peter 2:5, 2:9) sprinkled throughout the whole world, influencing people for Jesus Christ and being messengers of His word.

b. **All the cities of the Levites**: Perhaps it is also significant that the priests received their cities last of all the tribes. Priests are appointed to serve, not to be served, and there is something priestly about letting others go first.

i. The Levitical cities would not be populated only by Levites, but they were given properties in these cities. "It is therefore very likely that, in the first instance, the Levites had simply the right to choose, in all the cities assigned them, the houses in which they were to dwell, and that those of the tribe to which the city belonged occupied all the other dwellings." (Clarke)

ii. "Copies of this document may have served the purpose of keeping track of the Levites and thus ensuring that their important roles as priests, teachers and spiritual leaders of the people of Israel were fulfilled." (Hess)

iii. "We may also observe that the Levites were not absolutely bound to live in these and no other cities: for when the tabernacle was at *Nob,* priests and Levites dwelt there, see 1 Sam. 21:1, &c.; and when the worship of God was established at Jerusalem, multitudes both of priests and Levites dwelt there, though it was no Levitical city: as did the *courses* of priests afterwards at Jericho." (Clarke)

iv. The list of Levitical cities again reminds the reader that these were real places, not the description of a symbolic or spiritual inheritance.

When God promised a land to Abraham and his covenant descendants (Genesis 13:15, 17:8), God meant a real land.

**B. Israel takes full possession of the land.**

1. (43) The land is Israel's, given to them by God.

**So the LORD gave to Israel all the land of which He had sworn to give to their fathers, and they took possession of it and dwelt in it.**

a. **So the LORD gave to Israel all the land**: All the tribes had their land. They were still required to go into every corner of what God had given, and take full possession, but God had provided everything necessary for them to do so.

i. "The Gibeonite deception and the pockets of resistance still holding out do not contradict the fact that Israel was victorious over every enemy that they faced in battle." (Madvig)

2. (44) The rest in the land is Israel's, given to them by God.

**The LORD gave them rest all around, according to all that He had sworn to their fathers. And not a man of all their enemies stood against them; the LORD delivered all their enemies into their hand.**

a. **The LORD gave them rest all around**: This was the point where Israel stopped commemorating the Passover as if they were equipped to travel (as described in Exodus 12:11). Now they would eat the Passover reclining at rest (as described in John 13:23), because the LORD had given them **rest** in the land.

3. (45) Not one word of God fails.

**Not a word failed of any good thing which the LORD had spoken to the house of Israel. All came to pass.**

a. **Not a word failed of any good thing which the LORD had spoken**: God was completely faithful regarding the land, but Israel was not. Any failure to fully possess was not because God had not made adequate provision, but because Israel had failed to fully follow the LORD.

i. "These three verses (21:43-45) are the trophy reared on the battlefield, like the lion of Marathon, which the Greeks set on its sacred soil. But the only name inscribed on this monument is Jehovah's. Other memorials of victories have borne the pompous titles of commanders who arrogated the glory to themselves; but the Bible knows of only one conqueror, and that is God." (Maclaren)

b. **All came to pass**: God has been completely faithful to each believer and made provision for consistent growth and progress in the Christian life. God has given great things, but not every individual believer possesses what God has given.

i. "Failure to possess what God gives is always due to His people and is never the result of His unwillingness or weakness." (Morgan)

ii. "In the light of the Cross, is it not true that the enemy has no right to dwell in the land? Is it not true that Satan's claim to your life was taken from him at Calvary? Is it not true that sin has no right to a foothold in the life of the child of God? Is it not true that Satan has no power in the presence of Omnipotence? Is it not true that by virtue of His blood and His resurrection, Jesus Christ is pledged to destroy the enemy utterly? Is it not true that in the indwelling power of the Holy Spirit there is strength for every temptation, grace for every trial, power to overcome every difficulty?" (Redpath)

iii. "Heaven will be full of wonder at the way in which God has kept his word, and done all that He had promised, and more." (Meyer)

# Joshua 22 – A Misunderstanding Reconciled

## A. The armies from the tribes east of the Jordan are sent home.

1. (1-4) Joshua thanks the eastern tribes for their help in the conquest of Canaan.

**Then Joshua called the Reubenites, the Gadites, and half the tribe of Manasseh, and said to them: "You have kept all that Moses the servant of the LORD commanded you, and have obeyed my voice in all that I commanded you. You have not left your brethren these many days, up to this day, but have kept the charge of the commandment of the LORD your God. And now the LORD your God has given rest to your brethren, as He promised them; now therefore, return and go to your tents *and* to the land of your possession, which Moses the servant of the LORD gave you on the other side of the Jordan.**

> a. **You have kept all that Moses the servant of the LORD commanded**: In the seven years these eastern tribes had been with Joshua, they had helped the tribes west of the Jordan to conquer their enemies. They had been completely obedient and helpful to Joshua and all the tribes of Israel.

> > i. "Christ, the Captain of our salvation, shall in like sort set forth and celebrate the virtues and praiseworthy practices of his servants and soldiers in that great [festival] at the last day." (Trapp)

> b. **You have not left your brethren these many days**: The eastern tribes had gone out and fought on behalf of their brethren, even though they already had taken possession of their lands (Numbers 32:33). This was what they had promised to do (Numbers 32:16-19, 32:31-32).

> > i. "Their aid had not only been valuable as strengthening Joshua's force, but still more so as a witness of the unbroken oneness of the nation, and of the sympathy which the tribes already settled bore to the others." (Maclaren)

c. **Now therefore, return and go to your tents and to the land of your possession**: Now that the land was conquered and fully distributed to the tribes, the eastern tribes could go back to their families and lands on the other side of the Jordan.

2. (5-6) Before they leave, Joshua gives them an exhortation and a blessing.

**But take careful heed to do the commandment and the law which Moses the servant of the LORD commanded you, to love the LORD your God, to walk in all His ways, to keep His commandments, to hold fast to Him, and to serve Him with all your heart and with all your soul." So Joshua blessed them and sent them away, and they went to their tents.**

a. **But take careful heed to do the commandment**: Joshua told them to **take careful heed** to the word of God, probably here mostly in the sense of diligently hearing it and knowing it.

b. **To love the LORD your God**: Joshua told them to **love** the *LORD*. This was a matter of the heart, but yet it could still be commanded.

c. **To walk in all His ways, to keep His commandments**: Joshua told them to obey God with all they had, to **keep His commandments, to hold fast to Him** in a personal sense, and to **serve Him** with all their heart and soul.

   i. The order of these commands is important. First, God's people should take care to *hear* God. Then they should give Him their *love*. Next comes a walk of *obedience*. To mix this order up is to drift into heresy (loving without hearing) or legalism (obeying before loving).

   ii. "The verbs in v. 5 give a comprehensive picture of what a proper relationship to God was to include: to love God, to walk in all his ways, to obey his commands, to hold fast (or cling) to him, and to serve him. These were to be done not as a matter of external conformity but 'with all your heart and all your soul.'" (Howard)

d. **So Joshua blessed them and sent them away**: Joshua would not send them away without a blessing. Joshua understood that they could not do or be what God wanted them to be without His blessing among them (Numbers 6:23-27).

3. (7-9) The armies of the two and a half tribes depart, with much spoil.

**Now to half the tribe of Manasseh Moses had given a possession in Bashan, but to the *other* half of it Joshua gave *a possession* among their brethren on this side of the Jordan, westward. And indeed, when Joshua sent them away to their tents, he blessed them, and spoke to them, saying, "Return with much riches to your tents, with very much**

livestock, with silver, with gold, with bronze, with iron, and with very much clothing. Divide the spoil of your enemies with your brethren."

So the children of Reuben, the children of Gad, and half the tribe of Manasseh returned, and departed from the children of Israel at Shiloh, which *is* in the land of Canaan, to go to the country of Gilead, to the land of their possession, which they had obtained according to the word of the LORD by the hand of Moses.

> a. **Return with much riches to your tents**: Their obedience to God and faithfulness to their brethren had been rewarded. God had allowed them to gain much **spoil** they could take back with them to the east side of the Jordan. Their obedience was greatly blessed, and in this case, it was blessed materially.
>
> > i. "It was right that those who stayed at home to defend the families of those who had been in the wars, and to cultivate the ground, should have a proper proportion of the spoils taken from the enemy; for had they not acted as they did, the others could not have safely left their families." (Clarke)
>
> b. **So the children of Reuben, the children of Gad, and half the tribe of Manasseh returned, and departed from the children of Israel at Shiloh**: This was probably an emotional departure of brothers who had known the closeness of fighting life-and-death battles and fighting side-by-side. These were true veterans of the army of Israel.

**B. The incident of the altar by the Jordan.**

1. (10) The eastern tribes make an impressive altar.

And when they came to the region of the Jordan which *is* in the land of Canaan, the children of Reuben, the children of Gad, and half the tribe of Manasseh built an altar there by the Jordan—a great, impressive altar.

> a. **When they came to the region of the Jordan**: Before crossing over the Jordan, the soldiers from the two and a half eastern tribes built a large (**great**) and **impressive altar** near the Jordan River.
>
> b. **A great, impressive altar**: This was significant not only because of its size but because of the normal *meaning* of an altar. An altar was a place of sacrifice, and both the Israelites and pagans had altars they used for sacrifice.
>
> > i. "The altar was constructed in the land of Canaan…it was *an imposing altar*. Practically, this would render it visible to the Transjordanians in their homeland. The phrase used to describe the altar…is similar to

that used to describe the burning bush of Exodus 3:3. Thus it would arrest the attention of passers-by." (Hess)

ii, "In Hebrew the phrase 'an imposing altar' literally means 'an altar large in appearance.' It was essential that the altar was large enough to be seen easily, because its function was to be a witness." (Madvig)

2. (11-12) The tribes west of the Jordan River learn of the great altar.

**Now the children of Israel heard *someone* say, "Behold, the children of Reuben, the children of Gad, and half the tribe of Manasseh have built an altar on the frontier of the land of Canaan, in the region of the Jordan—on the children of Israel's side." And when the children of Israel heard *of it,* the whole congregation of the children of Israel gathered together at Shiloh to go to war against them.**

a. **Behold, the children of Reuben, the children of Gad, and half the tribe of Manasseh have built an altar**: When the news came to the rest of Israel, there was no discussion, there was an immediate reaction. They gathered to make war against their own brothers who built this altar. According to God's law, the only authorized altar for sacrifice was at the tabernacle, which was at Shiloh.

i. "Another [altar] besides that in the tabernacle: whereas God will have but one altar, for a figure of Christ's cross, which was the only true altar." (Trapp)

ii. "Nations often lose in peace what they have gained in war. Would Israel abandon its high level of spiritual commitment and integrity and gradually fall into disobedience and paganism? Or would the people remain faithful to God?" (Boice)

b. **The children of Israel gathered together at Shiloh**: The text does not say that Joshua had to gather the tribes. They seemed to gather in spontaneous response. It was an automatic reaction because they feared this was an altar of allegiance to the pagan gods of the region.

c. **To go to war against them**: Their readiness to fight this battle shows the western tribes had great courage to confront their eastern brother tribes on behalf of God's truth and holiness. This was a healthy organism at work, able to purge itself of poisons. Their later actions show that they were not *happy* about taking this action, but they were willing to do it.

i. If there was to be **war**, it would be Israelite soldiers from the west of the Jordan killing Israelite soldiers from the east of the Jordan, soldiers who had fought together against the Canaanites. "We must remember that these men had fought side by side in a conquest that lasted longer than either of our world wars. A special bond would have developed among them in such circumstances." (Boice)

3. (13-15) Personal, direct confrontation is made before military action is taken.

**Then the children of Israel sent Phinehas the son of Eleazar the priest to the children of Reuben, to the children of Gad, and to half the tribe of Manasseh, into the land of Gilead, and with him ten rulers, one ruler each from the chief house of every tribe of Israel; and each one *was* the head of the house of his father among the divisions of Israel. Then they came to the children of Reuben, to the children of Gad, and to half the tribe of Manasseh, to the land of Gilead, and they spoke with them, saying,**

a. **Then the children of Israel sent Phinehas the son of Eleazar the priest**: **Phinehas** led the group because he had the authority. He was high priest over all Israel, including the two and one-half tribes on the east side of the Jordan. He not only had the authority, but he also had the heart of a wise shepherd. He wanted to correct the erring, to protect the people of God, and to drive out the dangerous.

b. **And they spoke with them**: Israel reacted according to God's character. Their assembling for war demonstrated God's holiness, but their personal confrontation of those who were thought to be in error demonstrated God's wisdom and love.

i. "The zeal of the Israelites for the honor of God and the purity of his worship might have ended in terrible disaster had they not obeyed God's command to always investigate carefully before taking action (Deuteronomy 13:14)." (Madvig)

4. (16-18) Phinehas brings the accusation against the eastern tribes.

**"Thus says the whole congregation of the LORD: 'What treachery *is* this that you have committed against the God of Israel, to turn away this day from following the LORD, in that you have built for yourselves an altar, that you might rebel this day against the LORD? *Is* the iniquity of Peor not enough for us, from which we are not cleansed till this day, although there was a plague in the congregation of the LORD, but that you must turn away this day from following the LORD? And it shall be, if you rebel today against the LORD, that tomorrow He will be angry with the whole congregation of Israel.**

a. **What treachery is this**: Clearly, the leadership of Israel thought that the altar at the Jordan represented a *rival* place of sacrifice and worship, to compete with God's tabernacle, which was at Shiloh.

i. God had clearly commanded that there was one place of sacrifice and burnt offerings for Israel (Leviticus 17:8-9). The people of Israel were not permitted to worship God in any way they pleased. They had to worship God in the way God commanded, in a way that pleased Him. The principle remains true for God's people today, who must worship Him in spirit and in truth. (John 4:24)

b. **Is the iniquity of Peor not enough for us**: Phinehas reminded the eastern tribes that Israel had been punished for rebellion against God before, using the rebellion at **Peor** as an example.

i. At Peor, Israel's men had sex with Moabite women, and they gave themselves over to the worship of the Moabite gods. In judgment, God sent a plague that killed 24,000 people (Numbers 25:1-5, 25:9).

ii. This incident would be especially meaningful to Phinehas because he was the one who stopped the plague by making a dramatic stand for righteousness on that occasion of gross sin (Numbers 25:6-9).

c. **He will be angry with the whole congregation**: Phinehas also knew that the sin of these tribes would reflect on the whole nation. If the eastern tribes were in sin, God's corrective judgment might not come against the eastern tribes alone, but on the **whole congregation**.

i. The western tribes were clear about their concerns. They didn't hold back out of a wrong sense of being nice or friendly. They were courageous for truth.

5. (19) A willingness to sacrifice to keep a brother from sin.

**Nevertheless, if the land of your possession *is* unclean, *then* cross over to the land of the possession of the LORD, where the LORD's tabernacle stands, and take possession among us; but do not rebel against the LORD, nor rebel against us, by building yourselves an altar besides the altar of the LORD our God.**

a. **Take possession among us**: To Phinehas, *anything* was better than seeing these tribes drift away in rebellion against God. If there was something **unclean** in their land, he invited them to come and live with the tribes on the western side of the Jordan.

i. The western tribes were willing to sacrifice, to personally pay a price, to bring their brothers back to a right relationship with God and obedience to Him.

b. **Do not rebel against the LORD, nor rebel against us, by building yourselves an altar**: This was a generous invitation; if the eastern tribes agreed to this it would cost the western tribes a lot of territory, meaning a much smaller area of land for the western tribes. Yet Phinehas and the western tribes were willing to *sacrifice* to see their brothers free from this sin.

> i. God's people should do more than simply tell their brethren to stop sinning; they should be willing to pay a price to help their brethren walk rightly before the LORD.

6. (20) A second example of the price of sin: the sin of Achan and its effect on all of Israel is remembered.

**Did not Achan the son of Zerah commit a trespass in the accursed thing, and wrath fell on all the congregation of Israel? And that man did not perish alone in his iniquity.**

> a. **Did not Achan the son of Zerah commit a trespass**: Israel learned by Achan's sin that led to the defeat at Ai (Joshua 7) that the sin of one or of a few can bring God's judgment upon all the community.

> b. **That man did not perish alone**: Achan did not bear the corrective penalty of his sin alone. If the sin of one man resulted in such judgment against Israel, the apostasy of two and one-half tribes might be the end of Israel as a people.

7. (21-23) The eastern tribes respond.

**Then the children of Reuben, the children of Gad, and half the tribe of Manasseh answered and said to the heads of the divisions of Israel: "The LORD God of gods, the LORD God of gods, He knows, and let Israel itself know—if *it is* in rebellion, or if in treachery against the LORD, do not save us this day. If we have built ourselves an altar to turn from following the LORD, or if to offer on it burnt offerings or grain offerings, or if to offer peace offerings on it, let the LORD Himself require *an account.*"**

> a. **The LORD God of gods, the LORD God of gods, He knows**: The eastern tribes first appealed to God, confident in God's knowledge of their heart and intention. They believed that their brothers in the western tribes misunderstood them.

> > i. When believers are misunderstood, their first refuge is God. He knows the heart, and sometimes God's people must be satisfied with being right before God, even if it means others don't understand their actions or intentions.

> > ii. **The LORD God of gods**: "The original words are exceedingly emphatic, and cannot be easily translated.... *El Elohim Yehovah,* are the three principal names by which the supreme God was known

among the Hebrews, and may be thus translated, *the strong God, Elohim, Jehovah.*" (Clarke)

iii. "The repeated confession *The Mighty One, God, the LORD!* can also be translated by the superlative 'The LORD is the greatest God'. With the strongest of oaths, they confirm that they have no intention to worship any other deity at the altar." (Hess)

b. **If it is in rebellion, or if in treachery against the LORD, do not save us this day**: The eastern tribes also recognized the rightness of what the others were doing in challenging their building of a great and impressive altar. If the eastern tribes really were guilty of **treachery** or **rebellion**, they should be called to account.

i. The eastern tribes did what believers should do when they are misunderstood: put themselves in the place of the other person and try to see what they see. The eastern tribes heard the concerns of the western tribes and agreed with them in principle.

ii. "They agreed that if they were worshiping another god or rebelling against God and his commands (including the commands about how to worship), they deserved judgment.... There was no accommodation of relativism, no Hegelian synthesis, no compromise with truth. The reason these people were able to have a real unity and a real peace was that they were locked into the truth and commandments of God." (Schaeffer)

iii. "The defense is passionate, and this is reflected in the syntax. It is choppy in places, and much repetition is found in these verses. It reflects the agitated state of mind in which the Transjordan tribes found themselves, and we can easily imagine them stumbling breathlessly (and perhaps even indignantly) over their words in order to clarify the matter and justify themselves." (Howard)

8. (24-29) The eastern tribes explain the reason for building the altar.

**But in fact we have done it for fear, for a reason, saying, 'In time to come your descendants may speak to our descendants, saying, "What have you to do with the LORD God of Israel? For the LORD has made the Jordan a border between you and us, *you* children of Reuben and children of Gad. You have no part in the LORD." So your descendants would make our descendants cease fearing the LORD.' Therefore we said, 'Let us now prepare to build ourselves an altar, not for burnt offering nor for sacrifice, but *that* it *may be* a witness between you and us and our generations after us, that we may perform the service of the LORD before Him with our burnt offerings, with our sacrifices, and with our**

peace offerings; that your descendants may not say to our descendants in time to come, "You have no part in the LORD."' Therefore we said that it will be, when they say *this* to us or to our generations in time to come, that we may say, 'Here is the replica of the altar of the LORD which our fathers made, though not for burnt offerings nor for sacrifices; but it *is* a witness between you and us.' Far be it from us that we should rebel against the LORD, and turn from following the LORD this day, to build an altar for burnt offerings, for grain offerings, or for sacrifices, besides the altar of the LORD our God which *is* before His tabernacle."

a. **An altar, not for burnt offering nor for sacrifice, but that it may be a witness**: The eastern tribes recognized their distance from the center of worship in Israel, and that there was a natural barrier (the Jordan River) between them and the rest of the nation. So, they built the altar as a memorial to link the two segments of the nation.

b. **That your descendants may not say to our descendants in time to come**: The eastern tribes built a large and impressive altar so that it would last. They wanted it to stand as a witness to future generations that the tribes on both sides of the Jordan worshipped the same God.

c. **Here is the replica of the altar of the LORD which our fathers made, though not for burnt offerings nor for sacrifices**: The eastern tribes understood and agreed with the concern of the western tribes. They explained that the western tribes had misunderstood the meaning of the great, impressive altar. It was **not for burnt offerings** or other sacrifices.

i. "The altar's location should have been a clue from the beginning as to its purpose. Significantly, the Transjordan tribes did not build it on their side of the Jordan, but across the river from where they would live. It served little useful purpose to them there; for it to have been used regularly to offer sacrifices, it would need to have been east of the river." (Howard)

9. (30-31) The explanation of the eastern tribes is accepted by the western tribes.

**Now when Phinehas the priest and the rulers of the congregation, the heads of the divisions of Israel who *were* with him, heard the words that the children of Reuben, the children of Gad, and the children of Manasseh spoke, it pleased them. Then Phinehas the son of Eleazar the priest said to the children of Reuben, the children of Gad, and the children of Manasseh, "This day we perceive that the LORD *is* among us, because you have not committed this treachery against the LORD. Now you have delivered the children of Israel out of the hand of the LORD."**

a. **Now when Phinehas the priest and the rulers...heard the words...it pleased them**: Obviously, Phinehas was pleased by this explanation. Yet he deserves credit for being willing to believe his brothers. Phinehas put himself in the place of the eastern tribes and could see that their explanation made sense.

b. **This day we perceive that the LORD is among us**: Phinehas could see that the LORD **was among** the people of Israel because unity had been restored among them. This fulfilled the idea later expressed in Psalm 133:1: *Behold, how good and how pleasant it is for brethren to dwell together in unity!*

10. (32-34) Epilogue: the matter is resolved.

**And Phinehas the son of Eleazar the priest, and the rulers, returned from the children of Reuben and the children of Gad, from the land of Gilead to the land of Canaan, to the children of Israel, and brought back word to them. So the thing pleased the children of Israel, and the children of Israel blessed God; they spoke no more of going against them in battle, to destroy the land where the children of Reuben and Gad dwelt.**

**The children of Reuben and the children of Gad called the altar, *Witness*, "For *it is* a witness between us that the LORD *is* God."**

a. **So the thing pleased the children of Israel, and the children of Israel blessed God**: Everyone was glad, and everyone enjoyed the blessing of having peace among the people of God.

b. **The children of Reuben and the children of Gad called the altar, Witness**: The altar was given the name **Witness** because it was a witness to the tribes on both sides of the Jordan **that the LORD is God**.

i. God's people should respond to misunderstanding in the same manner, according to these same principles.

- It is right to respond with a concern for God's holiness.
- It is right to respond with directness and clarity.
- It is right to respond with the courage to confront in love.
- It is right to respond with an attempt to reconcile before fighting.
- It is right to be willing to sacrifice to help those believed to be in error; people should not be confronted if there is no willingness to help.
- It is right to see the situation from the perspective of the other person.
- It is right to decide to believe the best of one another.

# Joshua 23 – Joshua's Charge to the Leaders of Israel

## A. The first exhortation: total obedience to the word of God.

1. (1-3) Joshua declares what the LORD has done.

**Now it came to pass, a long time after the LORD had given rest to Israel from all their enemies round about, that Joshua was old, advanced in age. And Joshua called for all Israel, for their elders, for their heads, for their judges, and for their officers, and said to them:**

**"I am old, advanced in age. You have seen all that the LORD your God has done to all these nations because of you, for the LORD your God *is* He who has fought for you.**

> a. **A long time after the LORD had given rest to Israel**: Joshua did not die or step away from leadership as soon as Israel had general **rest** in the wars of judgment and occupation in Canaan. God had a purpose for Joshua beyond his essential role as a military leader for Israel.

>> i. "'Rest' is a common theme in Joshua; it was the goal of the Conquest. This rest was realized when the major battles were ended and Israel was settled in the land (11:23). They were at peace with 'all their enemies' even though all those enemies had not yet been driven out." (Madvig)

> b. **Joshua called for all Israel**: Joshua, in his old age, gathered the leadership of Israel together to give them a farewell address, to communicate to them the things that were, to his heart, the most important for them to hear.

>> i. Joshua could not, as a practical matter, speak to all Israel, so he spoke to the leaders: **elders**, **heads**, **judges**, and **officers**. Joshua could reach all Israel by communicating well to the leaders.

>> ii. This speech to the leaders of Israel, "In its purpose, it resembles the deathbed testaments of other leaders of Israel: Jacob (Genesis 48–49), Joseph (Genesis 50:22–26), Moses and David (1 Kings 2:1–9)." (Hess)

>> iii. "You can picture the scene as the great old warrior addressed his people. Caleb would be among them. Phinehas the high priest would

179

be there. Many who had shared every battle since the day they crossed the Jordan, and had stood with their leader through thick and thin, would be present. Others would be there also: the younger generation aspiring to leadership, eager to press on in life and conquest." (Redpath)

c. **You have seen all that the LORD your God has done to all these nations because of you, for the LORD your God is He who has fought for you**: Joshua began his address by giving glory to God. It would have been easy for Joshua to focus on what *he* had done as a military leader, especially because it was impressive. But he was more interested in glorifying God than talking about himself.

i. Joshua told the leaders of Israel to root their faith and obedience in what God **has done**. His great works for His people proved He was worthy of their trust and loyalty. It wasn't based on philosophies, spiritual experiences, emotions, or feelings. It was based on what God actually had done at a definite time and a definite place.

2. (4-5) Joshua describes the challenges that remain.

**See, I have divided to you by lot these nations that remain, to be an inheritance for your tribes, from the Jordan, with all the nations that I have cut off, as far as the Great Sea westward. And the LORD your God will expel them from before you and drive them out of your sight. So you shall possess their land, as the LORD your God promised you.**

a. **I have divided to you by lot these nations that remain**: Under Joshua's leadership, the army of Israel broke the back of the Canaanite military occupation. It remained for each individual tribe to fully possess what God gave to them.

b. **So you shall possess their land, as the LORD your God promised you**: God promised to **expel** these enemies, to **drive them out**. But God would do this in and through the effort, faith, and courage of Israel.

i. After a similar pattern, God gives every believer an inheritance. In Jesus Christ, His people have been *blessed...with every spiritual blessing* (Ephesians 1:3). God has a definite part for His people to play in coming to possess this inheritance.

3. (6) How Israel will succeed: by total obedience to the word of God.

**Therefore be very courageous to keep and to do all that is written in the Book of the Law of Moses, lest you turn aside from it to the right hand or to the left,**

a. **Therefore be very courageous**: Israel needed to be **courageous**, so they could be obedient. Obedience to God requires courage and sacrifice.

b. **To keep and to do all that is written in the Book of the Law of Moses**: Israel must do **all that is written in the Book**. They could not selectively obey. It was important for them to **keep and do all** of God's law. The emphasis on the authority of God's written revelation is clear.

c. **Lest you turn aside from it**: They must not **turn aside from it to the right hand or to the left**, because there were dangerous extremes on either side. Either legalism or licentiousness among God's people pleases Satan.

## B. The second exhortation: don't make peace with the enemy.

1. (7-8) Hold fast to the LORD.

*And* **lest you go among these nations, these who remain among you. You shall not make mention of the name of their gods, nor cause *anyone* to swear *by them;* you shall not serve them nor bow down to them, but you shall hold fast to the LORD your God, as you have done to this day.**

a. **You shall not make mention of the name of their gods**: Joshua told Israel to not even make mention of the false gods of the Canaanites. Instead of learning about them or promoting them, they should **hold fast to the LORD** their God.

i. "God's people must avoid association with the other nations so that they do not worship their gods. This fundamental command against idolatry (Exodus 20:3–6; Deuteronomy 5:7–10) becomes the chief test of obedience." (Hess)

ii. **These who remain among you**: "Israel's lethargy in driving out the last of their enemies is difficult to understand, but it contributed to the fulfillment of God's promise to drive them out 'little by little' (Exodus 23:30)." (Madvig)

b. **You shall hold fast to the LORD your God, as you have done to this day**: Israel's greatest defense against apostasy would come by holding fast to the LORD, more than by understanding and refuting pagan worship.

i. The normal Christian, by and large, is not called to become an expert in the cults or in heresy, but to become an expert in Jesus Christ – to hold fast to Him.

2. (9-13) Their abiding had been blessed, so if they fail to abide in the LORD, they will also depart from God's blessing.

**For the LORD has driven out from before you great and strong nations; but *as for* you, no one has been able to stand against you to this day. One man of you shall chase a thousand, for the LORD your God *is* He who fights for you, as He promised you. Therefore take careful heed to yourselves, that you love the LORD your God. Or else, if indeed you do**

go back, and cling to the remnant of these nations—these that remain among you—and make marriages with them, and go in to them and they to you, know for certain that the LORD your God will no longer drive out these nations from before you. But they shall be snares and traps to you, and scourges on your sides and thorns in your eyes, until you perish from this good land which the LORD your God has given you.

a. **For the LORD has driven out from before you great and strong nations**: As Israel was faithful and trusted in the LORD, they saw God do great things through them. As they continued to abide in Him, they would continue to see great things as God would fight on their behalf. God's past faithfulness was a reason to trust His continued blessing for His people.

b. **Love the LORD your God**: Israel was called to do more than obey and honor God. They were also called to **love** Him. They must, as Jude would later explain, *keep yourselves in the love of God* (Jude 1:21).

i. Continually loving the LORD takes diligence. There are many things both within and outside of the believer that might draw them from that love.

ii. This call to love God was an appeal to the *will*. Believers must *decide* to love God, even if the feelings of love for Him don't come immediately.

iii. "Everything else is assured if men love Jehovah. Failure to keep the law is always the outcome of failure in love to the Lawgiver. For such failure in love, men are responsible. In order that love may be maintained, they need to take heed to themselves." (Morgan)

c. **If indeed you do go back, and cling to the remnant of these nations**: Continuing in God's love will mean that they keep themselves separate from the ungodly influences around them; they must keep themselves *unspotted from the world* (James 1:27).

i. "The Israelites would demonstrate their lack of faithfulness by intermarrying with the remaining inhabitants of the land. This would be a direct violation of Deuteronomy 7:3." (Hess)

ii. "The problem of mixing with the peoples of the land and adopting their worship loyalties was the most severe problem throughout Israel's history in the land, affecting it in almost every era." (Howard)

d. **They shall be snares and traps to you, and scourges on your sides and thorns in your eyes, until you perish**: If Israel did not separate themselves from the ungodly influences around them, those influences would become instruments of torture, leading to their destruction.

i. "As the fowler catcheth birds, and the hunter wild beasts in their snares and traps; so shall these Canaanites catch you by their familiarity and commerce, and draw you to participate in their sins and plagues." (Trapp)

ii. What today seems like an "innocent Canaanite" in the life of a believer may become a torture and a snare tomorrow. Such ungodly influences never advertise themselves as instruments of torture; they present themselves as wonderful additions. Such deceptions need to be discerned and rejected.

iii. "How often we see that the temptation we have pampered and encouraged and indulged in has become a scourge and a thorn in our side. The compromising Christian is not a happy man. Let the enemy remain in a Christian life, let him have one foothold, and he soon becomes a scourge." (Redpath)

## C. The warning: God's faithfulness works both ways.

1. (14) Joshua asks each man to prove God's faithfulness in his own heart.

**"Behold, this day I *am* going the way of all the earth. And you know in all your hearts and in all your souls that not one thing has failed of all the good things which the LORD your God spoke concerning you. All have come to pass for you; not one word of them has failed.**

a. **You know in all your hearts and in all your souls that not one thing has failed**: Joshua required that every man search his heart and see if there was ever a time when he could rightly accuse God of unfaithfulness.

i. "Joshua may die but God will not change.... Joshua repeats the fact that every word has come true. However, his purpose is not to praise God for his faithfulness but to warn Israel that God will apply this same faithfulness to his judgments upon the sinful nation: he will destroy it." (Hess)

b. **All have come to pass for you; not one word of them has failed**: Joshua could speak on behalf of all Israel and say that God had remained completely faithful to every promise to His people.

i. "God had so remarkably and literally fulfilled his promises, that not one of his enemies could state that even the smallest of them had not had its most literal accomplishment: this all Israel could testify." (Clarke)

2. (15-16) As surely as God has been faithful to bless their obedience under Joshua, He will be faithful to curse their later disobedience.

**Therefore it shall come to pass, that as all the good things have come upon you which the LORD your God promised you, so the LORD will bring upon you all harmful things, until He has destroyed you from this good land which the LORD your God has given you. When you have transgressed the covenant of the LORD your God, which He commanded you, and have gone and served other gods, and bowed down to them, then the anger of the LORD will burn against you, and you shall perish quickly from the good land which He has given you."**

a. **As all the good things have come upon you which the LORD your God promised you, so the LORD will bring upon you all harmful things**: Joshua emphasized that God would be just as faithful to judge His disobedient people as He had been to bless His obedient people, according to the terms of Israel's covenant with God.

i. "God's faithfulness to his promises is proof positive that he will keep his threats as well. Israel should not suppose that being the recipients of God's blessings made them immune to his judgment." (Madvig)

ii. **You shall perish quickly from the good land which He has given you**: "The loss of their land would mean that God took back what was his all along. Although the entire book of Joshua describes the occupation and allocation of the land, it will be lost if Israel does not remain faithful to God and worship him alone." (Hess)

b. **So the LORD will bring upon you all harmful things**: Joshua repeated the principle of blessing for obedience and cursing for disobedience that was a specific part of Israel's covenant with God (Leviticus 26, Deuteronomy 28).

i. "To the sweetness of the promises he fitly adjoineth the tartness of the menaces. Sour and sweet make the best sauce: promises and threatenings mingled serve to keep the heart in the best temper." (Trapp)

ii. God's people today relate to Him under a different covenant, a new and better covenant (Hebrews 8:6-7), by which Jesus Christ has *redeemed us from the curse of the law* (Galatians 3:10-14).

iii. Therefore, in Jesus Christ, believers no longer experience God's faithfulness to curse as Israel knew it. Yet they do experience God's faithfulness to correct as a loving Father (Hebrews 12:7), and they will experience a lack of appropriated blessing if they do not abide in Jesus.

# Joshua 24 – The Covenant Renewed

**A. Joshua remembers God's great works on Israel's behalf.**

1. (1) Joshua speaks to the nation again, through its leaders.

**Then Joshua gathered all the tribes of Israel to Shechem and called for the elders of Israel, for their heads, for their judges, and for their officers; and they presented themselves before God.**

    a. **Then Joshua gathered all the tribes of Israel to Shechem**: This was a dramatic last gathering of Israel before the passing of Joshua. The address to the leaders of Israel in Joshua 23 was a separate event.

        i. **Shechem** is modern Tel Balata. "This ancient city was situated on the floor of a valley near its entrance, Mount Gerizim and Mount Ebal forming the respective walls. The contour of the land resulted in a natural amphitheater, the acoustics of which were so good that the human voice carried to exceptional distances." (Pink)

        ii. So near to Ebal and Gerizim, Israel was reminded of the reading of God's word and the blessing and curses performed there years before (Joshua 8:30-35).

    b. **To Shechem**: Shechem was a place of rich history for Israel. There were at least four notable events there in the lives of the patriarchs. In the first two instances, *Shechem was a place of calling and commitment.* In the second two, *Shechem was a place of shame.*

        i. Abraham came into the Promised Land and first camped at Shechem. There God appeared to Abraham and confirmed His promise; Abraham built an altar to the LORD there (Genesis 12:6-7).

        ii. When Jacob came back into the Promised Land, he first camped at Shechem. He purchased land at Shechem and built an altar there, calling the place, *El Elohe Israel* (God, the God of Israel, Genesis 33:18-20).

185

iii. Jacob's sons Simeon and Levi deceptively lured the men of Shechem into a massacre, murdering all the men of the city (Genesis 34).

iv. In a season of recommitment to God in Jacob's life, God told him to go to Bethel. Jacob did so and commanded all in his household to put away their idols. Jacob took those idols and buried them at the terebinth tree near Shechem (Genesis 35:1-5).

c. **Called for the elders of Israel...their heads...their judges... their officers; and they presented themselves before God**: This was an impressive gathering. The leaders of the nation met together at this significant place; meeting in the conscious presence of **God**.

i. There are some people who believe that **they presented themselves before God** means that they did this before the tabernacle, which seems at this time to have been at Shiloh (Joshua 18:1). Either they **presented themselves before God** without the tabernacle, or the tabernacle was moved to Shechem for this occasion.

ii. The people also presented themselves to God for the making of the covenant in Exodus 19:17.

2. (2-4) God's faithfulness to the patriarchs.

**And Joshua said to all the people, "Thus says the Lord God of Israel: 'Your fathers, *including* Terah, the father of Abraham and the father of Nahor, dwelt on the other side of the River in old times; and they served other gods. Then I took your father Abraham from the other side of the River, led him throughout all the land of Canaan, and multiplied his descendants and gave him Isaac. To Isaac I gave Jacob and Esau. To Esau I gave the mountains of Seir to possess, but Jacob and his children went down to Egypt.**

a. **Thus says the Lord God of Israel**: We don't often think of Joshua as a prophet, but here he spoke as an inspired messenger of God. Prophecy is not necessarily a prediction of the future. It can simply be a uniquely direct and spontaneous word from God.

b. **Your fathers... dwelt on the other side of the River in old times; and they served other gods**: Through Joshua, the Lord reminded Israel that their forefathers came from the other side of the Euphrates (the **River**) and worshipped pagan gods there.

i. There are ancient legends (*only* legends) that say Abraham [Abram] served the Lord God among the idol worshippers that he was raised among. One legend says that Abraham's father Terah was an idol maker and seller with his own shop. One day Terah had some business to do, so he left Abram in charge of the idol shop. While his father was gone,

Abram took the biggest idol and set him in the middle of the shop floor. Then he put all the other idols in a circle around the biggest idol. Then Abram took a hammer, smashed all the smaller idols and put the hammer in front of the one big idol that was still standing. When his father came home, Terah was angry and asked Abram why he smashed all his idols. Abram explained that it wasn't he who did it; it was the one large idol with the hammer in front of it. Terah became even more angry and said, "Abram you know that that idol is nothing but a statue and can't do anything like that." Abram answered, "Yes father, that is true. If they cannot do anything, why do we make and sell them for people to worship as gods?"

ii. It's worth noting the truth – that Abraham, the father of the Jewish people and the first Jew, *was not born a Jew.* He grew up in a pagan, idolatrous home.

iii. "We know that Ur and Haran were centers of moon worship. Joshua was telling the people, 'Your past heritage is a people that were not God's people.'" (Schaeffer)

iv. *Thus says the Lord GOD to Jerusalem: "Your birth and your nativity are from the land of Canaan; your father was an Amorite and your mother a Hittite."* (Ezekiel 16:3)

c. **Then I took your father Abraham from the other side of the River**: Before God challenged Israel, He reminded them of His previous faithfulness. His goodness was shown at the very beginning of His dealings with Abraham and Abraham's descendants.

i. "Abraham is not mentioned to remind the people of their supposed illustrious ancestry but rather to remind them of their humble and utterly pagan beginnings." (Boice)

ii. The message was not, "We are all really amazing, so now we must live for God." Instead, it was "We were all a real mess, but God did many amazing things for us and in us. Now, we must live for the God who did such amazing things." The same principle should motivate Christians today.

3. (5-7a) God's faithfulness in the escape from Egypt.

**Also I sent Moses and Aaron, and I plagued Egypt, according to what I did among them. Afterward I brought you out.**

**"Then I brought your fathers out of Egypt, and you came to the sea; and the Egyptians pursued your fathers with chariots and horsemen to the Red Sea. So they cried out to the LORD; and He put darkness between**

you and the Egyptians, brought the sea upon them, and covered them. And your eyes saw what I did in Egypt.

a. **Also I sent Moses and Aaron, and I plagued Egypt**: God did not leave Israel in slavery in Egypt forever. When the time was right, He **sent** a deliverer to His people.

b. **Your eyes saw what I did in Egypt**: There were still many among the leaders and elders of Israel who were children when Israel came out of Egypt, and who saw God destroy the Egyptian army at the Red Sea.

4. (7b-10) God's faithfulness in the wilderness.

**Then you dwelt in the wilderness a long time. And I brought you into the land of the Amorites, who dwelt on the other side of the Jordan, and they fought with you. But I gave them into your hand, that you might possess their land, and I destroyed them from before you. Then Balak the son of Zippor, king of Moab, arose to make war against Israel, and sent and called Balaam the son of Beor to curse you. But I would not listen to Balaam; therefore he continued to bless you. So I delivered you out of his hand.**

a. **Then you dwelt in the wilderness a long time**: Through Joshua, the LORD summarized most of the Exodus journey with this one sentence.

i. Notably missing from this review of Israel's history was any mention of Israel's sin, rebellion, and failure. Though God recorded those things at the time (in Exodus, Numbers, and Deuteronomy), when He reviewed their history through Joshua, He made no mention of them. Later, God said *their sin I will remember no more* (Jeremiah 31:34). Here, it was as if He had "forgotten" Israel's past sin.

b. **Arose to make war against Israel**: Numbers 22-25 explains that the war Balak made against Israel was *spiritual* in nature. He wanted to destroy them either through Balaam's curse (which did not work) or through the seduction and idolatry of the Moabite women (which worked to some degree). Though it wasn't a **war** fought with swords and spears, it was a **war**, nonetheless.

5. (11-13) God's faithfulness in the land of Canaan.

**Then you went over the Jordan and came to Jericho. And the men of Jericho fought against you; *also* the Amorites, the Perizzites, the Canaanites, the Hittites, the Girgashites, the Hivites, and the Jebusites. But I delivered them into your hand. I sent the hornet before you which drove them out from before you, *also* the two kings of the Amorites, *but* not with your sword or with your bow. I have given you a land for which you did not labor, and cities which you did not build, and you**

dwell in them; you eat of the vineyards and olive groves which you did not plant.'

a. **You went over the Jordan and came to Jericho.... But I delivered them into your hand**: Speaking through Joshua, God linked the *ancient* history of Israel (all the way back to Abraham) to their *recent* history. This was what God had done among them in their own lifetime.

b. **Not with your sword or with your bow. I have given you a land for which you did not labor...vineyards and olive groves which you did not plant**: There is a sense in which every blessing is undeserved, but some are more obviously so. When Israel enjoyed vineyards and olive orchards in Canaan, it should have made them *especially* grateful for those undeserved blessings.

i. They should also have remembered that those who planted the vineyards and orchards were removed by God's righteous judgment, and if they disobeyed and rejected God, they might also be so judged.

## B. Choosing to covenant with the LORD.

1. (14) The challenge: serve God exclusively.

**"Now therefore, fear the LORD, serve Him in sincerity and in truth, and put away the gods which your fathers served on the other side of the River and in Egypt. Serve the LORD!**

a. **Now therefore, fear the LORD, serve Him in sincerity and in truth**: Joshua did not call Israel to a blind leap of faith. They saw God's works and experienced His blessings, so it made *sense* for them to exclusively serve a God who had done so much for them.

i. "Joshua gave a promise for the future which was rooted in a space-time past. He did not ask the people to make a Kierkegaardian leap of faith. This stress on God's action in history recurs throughout his farewell." (Schaeffer)

b. **Serve the LORD**: In this review of Israel's history, Schaeffer noted that Joshua contrasted God's great work for Israel with three sets of gods, associated with three bodies of water.

- Joshua 24:2-4 shows that on the other side of the Euphrates were the gods of Sumerian and Babylonian culture – *gods of heritage.*
- Joshua 24:5-7a shows that on the other side of the Red Sea were the gods of ancient Egypt – *gods of upbringing.*
- Joshua 24:7b-13 and 24:15 shows that as they crossed the Jordan there were the gods of the Amorites – *gods of the culture.*

i. Joshua applied the principle. The LORD God of Israel is greater than all these idols; therefore, **serve the LORD!**

c. **Serve Him in sincerity and truth**: Joshua boldly called for a *deep* commitment and a *true* commitment.

> i. "The best test of sincerity is not always the open hostility of foes, for this often braces up the energies of combat, while at the same time it makes the path of duty clear. Still less is it at the hour of triumph over our foes, then there is no temptation to rebel. The real test of our faithfulness to God is in most cases our power to continue steadfastly in one course of conduct when the excitement of conflict is removed, and the enemies with which we have to contend are the insidious allurements of ease or custom amid the common place duties of life." (Lias)

2. (15) The challenge to choose God or to choose an alternative.

**And if it seems evil to you to serve the LORD, choose for yourselves this day whom you will serve, whether the gods which your fathers served that *were* on the other side of the River, or the gods of the Amorites, in whose land you dwell. But as for me and my house, we will serve the LORD."**

a. **If it seems evil to you to serve the LORD**: Joshua had just given a strong exhortation to *serve the LORD* (Joshua 24:14). Yet perhaps some among them did not want to serve the LORD. What of them?

b. **Choose for yourselves this day whom you will serve**: If they chose *not* to serve the LORD, they were then responsible for choosing which deity they **will serve**. They might choose to serve the gods of their heritage (**the gods which your fathers served that were on the other side of the River**) or they might choose to serve the gods of Canaan (**the gods of the Amorites, in whose land you dwell**). Yet they had to make a choice. Everyone serves some kind of deity.

> i. "Joshua was no abstract, unconcerned homilist. He preached for decisions. He was earnest. He preached, as one of the great Puritan preachers once described himself, 'as a dying man to dying men.'" (Boice)

> ii. A choice for God should be made with a clear view of the *alternatives*. Some feel a life lived for God is a bad choice, but to what do they compare it? The other choices are *far worse*. As Peter said, *Lord, to whom shall we go? You have the words of eternal life.* (John 6:68)

c. **But as for me and my house, we will serve the LORD**: Joshua offered an alternative for those who did not want to **serve the LORD** as he encouraged in Joshua 24:14. Yet his course was clear and sensible – he chose to **serve the Lord**.

> i. "The English uses a future tense here, but the Hebrew tense has a fuller meaning. It expresses continuous action. It involves the future, but it can also point to the past. Joshua was undoubtedly affirming, 'I have chosen, and I will choose.'" (Schaeffer)

> ii. Joshua could make this statement because he had lived a life in which he continuously chose to **serve the Lord**.

> * Joshua chose to fight against the Amalekites – choosing when it might have cost everything.
> * Joshua chose to reject the golden calf – choosing when the flesh might have been satisfied.
> * Joshua chose to serve the Lord by serving Moses – choosing a humble place.
> * Joshua chose to believe God's promise about the Promised Land – choosing against the majority.
> * Joshua chose to recognize the leadership of the Captain of the Lord's army – choosing surrender to God.
> * Joshua chose to take leadership of Israel and lead them into the land – choosing faith instead of unbelief.

> iii. *God gives humanity choices.* God is a choosing God; we are made in His image. He wants us to also choose.

d. **But as for me and my house**: This shows that Joshua also understood that he, as the priest of his family, was charged with the responsibility to see that his whole **house** served **the Lord**. He had the job of representing his whole house before God.

> i. The sense is that Joshua would do whatever was right and godly to make sure that his household did **serve the Lord**. They would serve Him together; it was **we will serve the Lord**.

e. **But as for me and my house**: The contrasting word **but** gives the sense that Joshua was determined on this course no matter what anyone else thought. His relationship with God was not based on any man, but on the Lord alone, and he would serve God no matter what anyone else did.

* Joshua's decision meant *hesitation was gone.*
* Joshua's decision meant *he lived above the evil influence of others.*
* Joshua's decision was *deep, calm, clear, fixed, well-grounded, and solemnly made.*

- Joshua's decision was *openly made.*
- Joshua's decision was *earnestly carried out.*
- Joshua's decision was *kept throughout his whole life.*

f. **We will serve the LORD**: Inherent in Joshua's declaration is that he would **serve the LORD** *only*; he would not **serve the LORD** *and* someone or something else. There was one God in his life, and that God was the LORD.

3. (16-18) Israel responds: they also will serve the LORD.

**So the people answered and said: "Far be it from us that we should forsake the LORD to serve other gods; for the LORD our God *is* He who brought us and our fathers up out of the land of Egypt, from the house of bondage, who did those great signs in our sight, and preserved us in all the way that we went and among all the people through whom we passed. And the LORD drove out from before us all the people, including the Amorites who dwelt in the land. We also will serve the LORD, for He *is* our God."**

a. **For the LORD our God is He who brought us and our fathers up out of the land of Egypt**: Significantly, their declaration was based on God's past dealings with them. How could they *not* serve such a great God?

b. **We also will serve the LORD, for He is our God**: This was essentially the same attitude reflected by Jesus' disciples in John 6:66-69: *Lord, to whom shall we go? You have the words of eternal life.* If serving God sometimes seems hard to believers, they should think of the alternatives.

4. (19-21) Joshua cautions against a lightly made commitment.

**But Joshua said to the people, "You cannot serve the LORD, for He *is* a holy God. He *is* a jealous God; He will not forgive your transgressions nor your sins. If you forsake the LORD and serve foreign gods, then He will turn and do you harm and consume you, after He has done you good."**

**And the people said to Joshua, "No, but we will serve the LORD!"**

a. **You cannot serve the LORD, for He is a holy God**: Joshua was not trying to discourage their faith but hoped to discourage a superficial commitment to following the LORD. They needed to be reminded that they served God under a covenant that *promised* they would be cursed for disobedience.

i. "Joshua seemed to detect a note of insincerity, or at least glibness, in this predictable and ready response. Did he suspect they were taking the whole thing too lightly? Were they supposing they had the power in themselves to serve God, instead of acknowledging that only God himself could keep them faithful?" (Boice)

ii. Jesus later expressed the same kind of warning, explaining that following Him took total commitment (Luke 14:25-33). It wasn't that Jesus didn't want followers, but He did not want lightly made and easily broken commitments.

iii. "So it becomes us to speak very reverently and leniently of our ability to obey. We are probably overestimating our powers." (Meyer)

b. **No, but we will serve the LORD**: This was the response Joshua wanted. It was a commitment made with full understanding of the consequences.

5. (22-28) A covenant renewed.

**So Joshua said to the people, "You *are* witnesses against yourselves that you have chosen the LORD for yourselves, to serve Him."**

**And they said, *"We are* witnesses!"**

**"Now therefore," *he said*, "put away the foreign gods which *are* among you, and incline your heart to the LORD God of Israel."**

**And the people said to Joshua, "The LORD our God we will serve, and His voice we will obey!"**

**So Joshua made a covenant with the people that day, and made for them a statute and an ordinance in Shechem.**

**Then Joshua wrote these words in the Book of the Law of God. And he took a large stone, and set it up there under the oak that *was* by the sanctuary of the LORD. And Joshua said to all the people, "Behold, this stone shall be a witness to us, for it has heard all the words of the LORD which He spoke to us. It shall therefore be a witness to you, lest you deny your God." So Joshua let the people depart, each to his own inheritance.**

a. **You are witnesses.... this stone shall be a witness**: Joshua required that the covenant be confirmed by the testimony of two witnesses. Here, the first witness was the people and the second witness was the stone. Therefore, this was a binding covenant before God (Deuteronomy 19:15).

i. As Hess notes, there are some points of similarity between this covenant and the normal practice of making covenants in the ancient world between a king or ruler and his people, especially among the Hittites.

b. **Now therefore...put away the foreign gods which are among you, and incline your heart to the LORD God of Israel**: Israel just *said* they were willing to enter into and obey God's covenant. Joshua immediately called them to act on their words.

i. "As you have promised to reform, begin instantly the work of reformation. A man's promise to serve God soon loses its moral hold of his conscience if he do not instantaneously begin to put it in practice. The grace that enables him to promise is that by the strength of which he is to begin the performance." (Clarke)

ii. "They bind themselves again to keep touch with God by an unalterable resolution. Vows rightly made and renewed are of singular use to keep the heart within the bounds of obedience, and to make men constant, firm, and peremptory in well-doing." (Trapp)

iii. **So Joshua made a covenant with the people that day**: "Literally, *Joshua cut the covenant*, alluding to the *sacrifice* offered on the occasion." (Clarke)

iv. **Joshua wrote these words in the Book of the Law of God**: "Moses' books were accepted as normative at the time of his death; and by the time Joshua died, he had written another book and added it to the canon, which was the authority for God's people." (Schaeffer)

## C. The death of Joshua and Eleazar.

1. (29-31) A beautiful epitaph for Joshua.

**Now it came to pass after these things that Joshua the son of Nun, the servant of the LORD, died, *being* one hundred and ten years old. And they buried him within the border of his inheritance at Timnath Serah, which *is* in the mountains of Ephraim, on the north side of Mount Gaash.**

**Israel served the LORD all the days of Joshua, and all the days of the elders who outlived Joshua, who had known all the works of the LORD which He had done for Israel.**

a. **Being one hundred and ten years old**: Joshua died at an old age and was buried in the land of his inheritance. There seemed to have been no great funeral or mourning for him, as was surely his wish – to simply be known as **the servant of the LORD**.

b. **Israel served the LORD all the days of Joshua**: This was the greatest tribute to Joshua. His godly influence was effectively communicated to and through the whole people of Israel.

2. (32) The burial of Joseph's bones.

**The bones of Joseph, which the children of Israel had brought up out of Egypt, they buried at Shechem, in the plot of ground which Jacob had bought from the sons of Hamor the father of Shechem for one hundred**

**pieces of silver, and which had become an inheritance of the children of Joseph.**

a. **The bones of Joseph**: This may seem like an inconsequential point, but it fulfilled the oath recorded in Genesis 50:25. God likes to complete what is started. This is also mentioned in Hebrews 11:22 as an example of Joseph's faith.

3. (33) The death and burial of Eleazar.

**And Eleazar the son of Aaron died. They buried him in a hill *belonging to* Phinehas his son, which was given to him in the mountains of Ephraim.**

a. **And Eleazar the son of Aaron died**: Eleazar's death meant that another link with the wilderness generation had passed. Now **Phinehas** was high priest.

b. **They buried him**: As the generations pass, they are each challenged to conquer the land of blessing and promise that God has for them. God's people will continue to do this as they pay close heed to their Joshua, Jesus Christ.

i. "Where his monument was to be seen in Jerome's time, as he testifieth in his questions upon Genesis." (Trapp)

# Bibliography - Joshua

Boice, James Montgomery *Joshua, an Expositional Commentary* (Grand Rapids, Michigan: Baker Books, 1989)

Clarke, Adam *The Holy Bible, Containing the Old and New Testaments, with A Commentary and Critical Notes, Volume II – Joshua to Esther* (New York: Eaton and Mains, 1827?)

Ginzberg, Louis *The Legends of the Jews, Volumes 1-7* (Philadelphia: The Jewish Publication Society of America, 1968)

Hess, Richard S. Joshua – *An Introduction and Commentary* (Nottingham, England: Intervarsity Press, 1996)

Howard, David M. Jr. *Joshua* (Nashville, Tennessee: Broadman & Holman, 1998)

Lias, J.J. *"Joshua" The Pulpit Commentary, Volume 3 – Deuteronomy, Joshua, Judges* (McLean, Virginia: MacDonald Publishing, ?)

Maclaren, Alexander *Expositions of Holy Scripture, Volume 2* (Grand Rapids, Michigan: Baker Book House, 1984)

Madvig, Donald H. *"Joshua" The Expositor's Bible Commentary, Volume 3* (Grand Rapids, Michigan: Zondervan, 1992)

Meyer, F.B. *Joshua and the Land of Promise* (Fort Washington, Pennsylvania: Christian Literature Crusade, 1977)

Meyer, F.B. *Our Daily Homily* (Westwood, New Jersey: Revell, 1966)

Morgan, G. Campbell *Searchlights from the Word* (New York: Revell, 1926)

Morgan, G. Campbell *An Exposition of the Whole Bible* (Old Tappan, New Jersey: Revell, 1959)

Orr, J. Edwin *Full Surrender* (London: Marshall, Morgan & Scott, 1951)

Pink, Arthur W. *Gleanings in Joshua* (Chicago: Moody Press, 1964)

Redpath, Alan *Victorious Christian Living – Studies in the Book of Joshua* (Westwood, New Jersey: Revell, 1965)

Schaeffer, Francis A. *Joshua and the Flow of Biblical History* (Downer's Grove, Illinois: Intervarsity Press, 1975)

Spurgeon, Charles Haddon *The New Park Street Pulpit, Volumes 1-6 and The Metropolitan Tabernacle Pulpit, Volumes 7-63* (Pasadena, Texas: Pilgrim Publications, 1990)

Trapp, John *A Commentary on the Old and New Testaments, Volume 1 – Genesis to Second Chronicles* (Eureka, California: Tanski Publications, 1997)

Velikovsky, Immanuel *Worlds in Collision* (Garden City, New York: Doubleday & Company, 1950)

As the years pass I love the work of studying, learning, and teaching the Bible more than ever. I'm so grateful that God is faithful to meet me in His Word.

For the second time I am tremendously grateful to Alison Turner for her proofreading and editorial suggestions, especially with a challenging manuscript. Alison, thank you so much!

Thanks to Brian Procedo for the cover design and the graphics work.

Most especially, thanks to my wife Inga-Lill. She is my loved and valued partner in life and in service to God and His people.

***David Guzik***

David Guzik's Bible commentary is regularly used and trusted by many thousands who want to know the Bible better. Pastors, teachers, class leaders, and everyday Christians find his commentary helpful for their own understanding and explanation of the Bible. David and his wife Inga-Lill live in Santa Barbara, California.

You can email David at
david@enduringword.com

For more resources by David Guzik,
go to www.enduringword.com